Educating for Advanced
Foreign Language Capacities

EDUCATING FOR ADVANCED FOREIGN LANGUAGE CAPACITIES
Constructs, Curriculum, Instruction, Assessment

Heidi Byrnes, Heather Weger-Guntharp, and Katherine A. Sprang, *Editors*

GEORGETOWN UNIVERSITY PRESS
Washington, D.C.

As of January 1, 2007, 13-digit ISBN numbers will replace the current 10-digit system.
Paperback: 978-1-58901-118-2

Georgetown University Press, Washington, D.C.

Library of Congress Cataloging-in-Publication Data

Georgetown University Round Table on Languages and Linguistics (2005).
Educating for advanced foreign language capacities : constructs, curriculum, instruction, assessment / Heidi Byrnes, Heather Weger-Guntharp, and Katherine A. Sprang, editors.
    p. cm. — (Georgetown university round table on languages and linguistics series)
    ISBN 1-58901-118-X (pbk. : alk. paper)
    1. Language and languages—Study and teaching (Higher)—Congresses. I. Byrnes, Heidi. II. Weger-Guntharp, Heather. III. Sprang, Katherine A. IV. Title.
P53G39a 2005
418′.0071′1—dc22   2006003221

This book is printed on acid-free paper meeting the requirements of the American National Standard for Permanence in Paper for Printed Library Materials.

13 12 11 10 09 08 07 06   9 8 7 6 5 4 3 2
First printing

Printed in the United States of America

Contents

Figures and Tables

Preface

This volume comprises a small subset of the presentations that made up the 2005 Georgetown University Round Table on Languages and Linguistics (GURT). From among the rich palette of plenary addresses, individual papers, invited symposia, extended colloquia, and workshops, we—the editors of this volume as well as the organizers of the conference—present a set of papers that constitutes one way of addressing the four challenges expressed in the conference theme: "Educating for Advanced Foreign Language Capacities: Constructs, Curriculum, Instruction, Assessment."

We are grateful to all of the participants who shared their theoretical insights, research, and educational expertise and experience at the event—to our knowledge one of the first professional conferences expressly devoted to advanced instructed foreign language learning. Because advanced language learning only recently has begun to capture the interest and attention of applied linguists and professionals in language education in the United States, we note with particular pleasure the breadth of positions participants took in addressing the topic and express our thanks for their interest in submitting their scholarship for publication consideration. To us, part of the excitement of the conference was that its theme offered many participants the opportunity to consider their particular research foci in light of a still-unexplored advanced language learning perspective. We thank participants for enabling new linkages as well as asserting existing connections among various subspecialties in theoretical linguistics, second-language acquisition (SLA) research, and educational practice in the interest of advancing the cause of the advanced learner. The possibility that their insights might influence future discussion about advanced learning is all the greater because the conference enabled conversations among attendees from the United States as well as those who hailed from other countries, where discussions about the nature of and development toward advanced language abilities have had a long presence.

Within that professional context, the presentations at GURT 2005 and the papers assembled in this volume are primarily about expanding horizons and laying the groundwork for fruitful ways of imagining advanced language learning—which is both an opportunity and a challenge at a time when the advanced learner has become an increasingly prominent topic, not only in professional discussion but also in larger societal considerations regarding multilingual societies, globalization, and even security. Such a generative role is in line with the best traditions of Round Table conferences for more than half a century!

Finally, it is our pleasure to acknowledge with gratitude the generous support and personal dedication that Georgetown University faculty, graduate students, and staff contributed to ensure the success of this conference. That, too, is a treasured institutional tradition.

Heidi Byrnes, Chair, GURT 2005
Heather Weger-Guntharp, GURT Coordinator
Katherine A. Sprang, GURT Webmistress

1

Locating the Advanced Learner in Theory, Research, and Educational Practice:
An Introduction

HEIDI BYRNES
Georgetown University

THE ABILITY—or, as the case may be, inability—to use a second or foreign language (L2) at advanced levels of performance has a long and well-established history in lay references to language learning as well as in theorizing about the human languaging capacity.[1] In the former case, we speak with admiration about someone who knows an L2 "fluently," "without a trace of an accent," or "like a native." In the second case, language theorizing attempts to account for the rarity of this feat by postulating "a critical period" in the maturation of human beings beyond which, for diverse reasons, they are unable to respond to language stimuli in their environment in a fashion that facilitates movement toward "target language" norms (Birdsong 1999). Even highly competent learners appear to stop short of native-like ultimate attainment, seemingly stabilizing at a certain point—perhaps even fossilizing in nontarget-like norms (Long 2003).

Given that general and, at the same time, quite specific theoretical interest in the phenomenon, the dearth of a kind of scholarship on L2 "advancedness" that might locate central features of that level of ability within an encompassing framework is surprising. Just what we mean by "advanced L2 abilities," how they are acquired either naturalistically or in tutored settings, and what environmental influences might hinder or help their development at different ages and in different settings, is remarkably constricted in its scope and vision, remarkably neglected in second language acquisition (SLA) research, and treated at a remarkably experiential level in educational practice. As a result, whatever insights might have been gained in specific contexts tend to apply primarily to their immediate setting (see, for example, the contributions in Byrnes and Maxim 2004; Leaver and Shekhtman 2002a).

Although such a restricted level of generalizability—akin to a case study approach—should be expected and may be a necessary stage at this point of the profession's engagement with the phenomenon of advancedness, more principled and fundamental considerations need to be framed to understand it in an expansive and coherent fashion. In the United States in particular, where collegiate language teaching—with its academic and, frequently, text-oriented demands—performs a crucial role for enabling societal multilingual competence, evolving findings probably would amount to a challenge directed at the SLA field itself, not least for its seeming inability or, at the least, reluctance to tackle the issue of advancedness in the first place. An oft-repeated, partly humorous and partly exasperated L2 learner comment has been this: "I was lost in X (choose your country) because they did not speak Intermediate Y (choose your language)." Most likely, the necessary broader framework also will require an opening toward the humanities and cultural studies, which are quintessentially textual, interpretive, and historical forms of knowing and inquiry; such a framework could lead to what Becker (1995) has called a new philology. The extent to which SLA research and educational practice can take that interpretive and textual turn would seem to be closely related to the extent to which the field can develop new ways of being scientific in the human sciences (as the German term *Geisteswissenschaften* suggests), as contrasted with the approach taken in the natural sciences. A thorough engagement with advanced learning might force both long-standing issues.

Context for Inquiry into Advanced Foreign Language Learning

The GURT 2005 theme of "Educating for Advanced Foreign Language Capacities: Constructs, Curriculum, Instruction, Assessment" arose from that context of still diffuse, tentative, and separate pockets of knowledge about advancedness in the language field. When the conference was being planned, not only had advanced language learning suddenly become a prominent scholarly concern; it also had gained much societal interest because of migration, the greater visibility of heritage learners in diverse public and professional settings, and various globalizing forces (for discussion, see Byrnes 2004). More fortuitously, the time seemed right for an exchange of ideas across theoretical, research, and educational foci that were showing potential for convergences. In particular, the desire and ability to foreground language use and acquisition in a social and cultural context, the preference for cognitive approaches to theories of language and language learning, adoption of a textual orientation that would emphasize meaning-making over sentence-level structural properties, and— last but certainly not least—considerable rethinking of assessment practices seemed sufficiently well developed to serve as a conference focus and a basis of an exchange of insights on advanced L2 learning.

The goal of the conference reflected that judgment and that promise. The conference was intended to present the opportunity for broad consideration of advancedness and to lay the groundwork for a kind of encompassing framework that we often characterize with the term "interdisciplinarity" but that may be no more and no less than taking a broader view of one's engagement with the study of language than is otherwise favored because of the entrenched opposition between theoretical and applied linguistics, not to mention research and teaching, along with the increasing specialization of our field and its particular notions of scientific rigor. Martin (2000) notes that we are far from breaking out of disciplinary constraints in a way that understands our engagement with linguistics as a form of social engagement; by extension, as Ortega (2005) states, we also are far from seeing our disciplinary work in terms of ethical commitments to a range of constituents.

These three aspects—a newfound interest in advanced L2 learning and teaching, research, and assessment at the advanced level, at least in the United States; its considerable challenge to and promise for our own disciplinary practices; and its undeniable social component—guided conference planning. In my own thinking, the event was the culmination of many years of fascination with advanced learners and advanced learning through teaching at the advanced levels in the German Department at Georgetown University. The conference theme and approach also were shaped by my extended search for a theoretical and SLA research literature that would substantively contribute to my daily and reflected experiences with advanced learning—a desire (and frustration) that colleagues who were similarly engaged seemed to share. After years of exploration I recently had been much encouraged by insights that were available for the project of advanced learning in three areas: semantically oriented cognitive linguistics (e.g., Fauconnier 1997; Fauconnier and Turner 2002; Langacker 1990; Tomasello 1998), systemic-functional linguistics in the Hallidayan tradition (e.g., Halliday 1994), and sociocultural theory, particularly as influenced by Vygotsky (1986) and the textual orientation of Bakhtin (e.g., 1981, 1986); I believed that these diverse strands should be brought into conversation with one another in a single time and place to consider their synergistic possibilities. That time and place was to be GURT 2005.

Issues in Advanced Acquisition as Catalysts for Change

Accordingly, the conference was intended to consider fundamental issues rather than merely expedient or ad hoc recommendations for advanced L2 learning. First and foremost, it was designed to provide a venue for beginning to specify the construct of advancedness in theory and research and for laying out broad parameters for curriculum, instruction, and assessment in support of the acquisition of advanced levels of L2 ability. In contrast to other recent and concurrent projects that have seized on newfound interest in the advanced learner, GURT 2005 attempted to approach the topic in an expansive yet focused way. It was to be expansive in the theoretical frameworks that were regarded as potential contributors to an emerging understanding of the nature of advancedness, and it was to be focused in that it would devote special attention to adult foreign language (FL) learning, primarily at the college level.

That focus was regarded as contrasting, on one hand, with instructional settings— in the academy, the for-profit sector, or government—that are highly instrumentalized and, on the other hand, with second-language learning that can draw on naturalistic or immersion learning opportunities. Of course, both distinctions are fluid in a global environment of migration and multilingualism as well as ever-changing reasons and opportunities for learning languages and sojourns in other linguistic environments. They also are fluid with regard to the distinction of second and foreign languages, as the diverse roles of English around the globe readily show. Nevertheless, exploring advancedness in the delimited setting of instruction seemed profitable precisely because it would force careful consideration of the contributions formal L2 education can and does make to the acquisition of advanced levels of language ability.

Second, because instructed foreign language learning in the United States has been constricted by considerations that were derived primarily from introductory and intermediate levels of ability, to the point that advanced instructed FL learning has been interpreted through those constructs or otherwise relegated to the realm of the impossible (i.e., necessitating extended stays abroad), the conference was intended to be open to shifts in theoretical, research-methodological, and educational assumptions and practices. To put matters simplistically, yet aptly: It was to imagine advancedness in terms other than "more and more accurate" realizations of what was considered "intermediate" or "high intermediate" performance according to criteria that essentially adhered to the same paradigm.[2]

An indication of that broader orientation for the conference was given with the use of the word "capacity" in its theme. For SLA researchers and language practitioners, the prevailing terms "competence" and "performance" long ago had become both theoretically burdened and needlessly dichotomous. Their more recent and revamped appearance as "communicative competence," along with "input" and "interaction" the primary paradigm for research and practice over roughly the past three decades, had developed its own kind of burden. As professional discussion—particularly among faculty members who are engaged in shaping collegiate language learning—shows, when communicative competence is essentially restricted to mostly oral and mostly transactional performance, it is poorly suited to framing and fostering the kind of academic work in foreign language study that the field owes itself and owes the remainder of the academy to be intellectually viable and, even more, to take on a leadership role in crosscultural and crosslinguistic work in the age of globalization and multiculturalism. Among many sources one could cite for this increasingly more prominent position are the contributions in Byrnes (2006b); the papers in Byrnes and Maxim (2004), particularly Maxim's concluding observations; Kern (2000); and Swaffar and Arens (2005).

Finally, and more subtly, although communicative competence is well intentioned in its focus on "natural" performance, it runs the risk of downplaying or even excluding several interrelated features of advancedness. The first such feature has been particularly well considered in L1 educational circles under the notion of literacy: Literacy scholars such as Cope and Kalantzis or Gee distinguish between primary discourses, which are part of socialization into a cultural and linguistic community, and secondary discourses, which we acquire for use in a more public sphere where institutions play a central role. Education is indispensable for the latter, inasmuch as it expects and, ideally, enables students to "learn a specific 'social language' (variety or register of English) fit to certain social purposes and not to others" and to come to appreciate and apply an awareness that "to know any specific social language is to know *how its characteristic design resources are combined to enact specific socially-situated identities and social activities*" (Gee 2002, 162; emphasis in original).

In other words, literacy is not a natural outgrowth of orality (Cope and Kalantzis 1993), and instruction and education in general are not merely a matter of polishing up, as it were, existing language abilities but of enabling learners to gain access to new ways of being, even new identities, through language-based social action and interaction (see also the seminal statement by the New London Group 1996). Language—and, by extension, language teaching and learning—is a means to a social end; from the perspective of the speaker/user, "Discourse models are narratives, schemas, images, or (partial) theories that explain why and how certain things are connected or pattern together. Discourse models are simplified pictures of the world (they deal with what is taken as typical) as seen from the perspective of a particular Discourse" (Gee 2002, 166).

If that is so, language and learning the secondary discourses of public life, in particular, are about the ability to make choices with and in language—an insight that requires a grammatical theory that is quite different from the structuralist and generativist theories that have been so prominent in SLA research as in language pedagogy. As Halliday (1994) states, the fundamental opposition in theories of language is

> between those that are primarily syntagmatic in orientation (by and large the formal grammars, with their roots in logic and philosophy) and those that are primarily paradigmatic (by and large the functional ones, with their roots in rhetoric and ethnography). The former interpret a language as a list of structures, among which, as a distinct second step, regular relationships may be established (hence the introduction of transformations); they tend to emphasize universal features of language, to take grammar (which they call 'syntax') as the foundation of language (hence the grammar is arbitrary), and so to be organized around the sentence. The latter interpret a language as a network of relations, with structures coming in as the realization of these relationships; they tend to emphasize variables among different languages, to take semantics as the foundation (hence the grammar is natural), and so to be organized around the text, or discourse (Halliday 1994, xxviii).

Halliday's statement that such a theory is essentially about "meaning as choice" (Halliday 1994, xiv) appears to capture well both the challenges and the opportunities that learning and teaching toward advanced levels of ability presents. Professionals who have dealt with advanced learners reiterate that the issue is not primarily one of adherence or nonadherence to grammatical rules. The issue, instead, is making choices and the capacity to make those choices in a meaningful—that is, culturally and situationally conscious—fashion, including deliberate and now meaningful violations of "rules" and "fixed norms" (see also the theoretical and empirical discussion in Pawley and Syder 1983). For both considerations, the educational setting—with its need for a language of schooling to conduct its "business" of schooling and its considerable struggle to teach just that kind of schooled language (see particularly Schleppegrell 2004)—becomes central.

The fundamental notions I have described about advancedness in L1 appear to apply equally to advancedness in L2—except at much higher levels of complexification and, I would say, much higher levels of intellectual excitement and potential for insightfulness regarding human knowing through language. First, recognizing the importance of language education for the development of advanced forms of literacy would free all instructed language learning from the onerous judgment of being a deficitary, unsatisfactory, even "nonreal" (as contrasted with the "real world") or inauthentic enterprise. Along with that reorientation, a focus on contextual choices by variously bilingual speakers would move the discussion from dwelling on profiles of errorful interference from L1 to L2 and a focus on the language *learner* to complex portraits of the advanced language *user* (Cook 2002). The discussion would shift as well from "competence" in one language or perennially *near*-native, or *ersatz* native, speakers to consideration of the multicompetent speaker—a situation characterized by systematic knowledge of an L2 that is not assimilated to the L1 (Cook 1992). We would advance from justified concerns about assuring acquisition of native-language literacy—even though that might run the risk of reiterating, even solidifying, power relationships that are expressed in and through language—to issues associated with *multiple* literacies, with their potential for hybridization and border crossings. We would move from an interest in choices within a single cultural and linguistic framework to an exponential increase in choices in multiple cultural and linguistic frameworks and, thereby, to opportunities for the kind of broadening and deepening of frames of reference that is at the heart of creativity.

In sum, in taking such a stance GURT 2005 was intended to facilitate not only better understanding of the notion of advancedness but, more expansively, reconsideration of well-established theoretical and methodological approaches and, therefore, well-established findings in the SLA research literature and received wisdoms regarding pedagogies, curricula, and assessment practices. In that context, this publication, as well as others arising from the conference (e.g., Byrnes 2006a and Ortega and Byrnes 2007) ultimately would be about the possibility of an exciting intellectual renewal of the language field by a convergence of resources that have taken note of one another through a shared focus on advanced learning and the advanced learner.

Exploring Advancedness: Constructs, Research Evidence, Practices

The essays assembled in this volume speak to these issues from three broad perspectives: the construct of advancedness, descriptive and instructional considerations in advanced learning, and the role of assessment. They present general insights as well as language-specific considerations that span a range of languages, from commonly taught languages such as English, French, and German to less commonly taught languages such as Farsi, Korean, Norwegian, and Russian.

With regard to theoretical bases for advancedness, this volume assembles papers from the conference that take a cognitive-semantic approach and the issues it raises regarding the relation of embodied knowing in a cultural context in more than one language. In this context, it is worth recalling that the term "cognitive," as used in contemporary SLA discussions, has at least two dramatically different meanings: the semantic orientation intended here and the psycholinguistically driven processing orientation that, most recently, has been well presented by Doughty and Long (2003). Because of the breadth of offerings at the conference, contributions that built on two other prominent bases for construing advancedness—namely, systemic-functional linguistics and a sociocultural orientation—have been gathered in a separate edited volume (Byrnes 2006a). Accordingly, readers who wish to obtain a more complete sense of how the conference framed a good part of its conversations should consult that publication and another volume that considers strengthening a longitudinal research paradigm to develop a more robust understanding of advancedness (Ortega and Byrnes 2007).

Cognitive Approaches to Advanced Language Learning

Part I of this volume begins with an extensive theoretical treatment of the conceptual basis of grammatical structure by Ronald W. Langacker. Although Langacker's treatment of the topic does not explicitly target L2 acquisitional issues, its broad parameters for the study of any language readily direct inquiry toward important characteristics of advanced learning. First and foremost is Langacker's insistence on language being all about meaning—with meaning residing in conceptualization and mental construction, as contrasted with an objectively given reality. Furthermore, as an embodied phenomenon, cognition and language are contextually embedded—an embedding that, critically, involves social and cultural realities outside the individual knower. Indeed, Langacker notes, "language use is replete with subtle interactive fictions, so frequently and easily used that we are hardly aware of them." Finally, language use and conceptualization are about construal—"our manifest capacity to conceive and portray the same objective situation in alternate ways." That focus on construal has numerous consequences, including the need to think of conceptualization as dynamic and imaginative and language as presenting suggestive prompts more than containers for fixed meanings, as well as affording us various ways, through blending of various conceptual domains, to vastly expand our expressive capacities. As Langacker asserts, construal, dynamicity, and imaginative capacities (such as blending and fictivity in imagined scenarios that reveal a certain perspective or give prominence to certain features) are of central importance in semantics and grammar. If that is so, divisions of language theories into syntax, semantics, and pragmatics or—more pointedly for SLA work—divisions of language competence into grammatical competence, discourse competence, sociocultural or pragmatic competence, and strategic competence (cf. Canale and Swain 1980) are not merely inadequate for describing language use and cognition; indeed, they run a serious risk of creating false certainties and misrepresentations of the phenomena in question. At the advanced level, the latest additive and fixed ways of describing language—not to mention additive ways of imagining its teaching and learning—are unable to reveal the intricate and dynamic relation between "the nature of linguistic structure, linguistic meaning, and the conceptualization they embody and reflect."

The central question uniting the succeeding three essays in part I of this volume is the extent to which the conceptual factors of blending, scanning, fictivity, and imagined scenarios, as universal cognitive abilities, nonetheless are shaped by language. These three essays, which are part of a larger integrated project, attempt to answer that question through coordinated cross-linguistic studies of text production in L1 and L2 performance in several European countries. Christiane von Stutterheim and Mary Carroll probe whether and how in the process of the creation of coherent text (e.g., narratives, descriptions, and directives) language users draw on language-specific features in selecting, organizing, and expressing relevant information. Using Levelt's magisterial study on speaking as their theoretical ground, von Stutterheim and Carroll conclude that "information organization in language production follows distinct patterns that correlate with typological differences" and that "principles of information organization are shown to be perspective driven and linked to patterns of grammaticization in the respective language." More to the point with respect to advanced learning is their finding that even very advanced learners find it extraordinarily difficult to discover the implications of specific grammatical features in the L2 for event construal. With regard to reasons, von Stutterheim and Carroll suggest that "evidence needed to construct this conceptual network [for the interpretation and conceptualization of reality] comes from many domains . . . [therefore] it presents a degree of complexity that second language learners will find difficult to process." They conclude that "the central factor impeding the acquisitional process at advanced stages ultimately is grammatical in nature in that learners have to uncover the role accorded to grammaticized meanings and what their presence, or absence, entails in information organization."

Carroll and Monique Lambert's contribution explores this finding—that grammaticized concepts play a determining role in the organization of information for expression in a given language—in the specific case of narratives to specify more closely whether the differences in L1 and L2 production can be located at the point of selecting and organizing information or at the point of selecting linguistic forms for its expression. Corroborating the complex nature of information selection, they conclude that differences among L1 and L2 speakers (here English, French, and German) "cannot be explained by a single feature but are determined by a coalition of grammaticized features—particularly temporal concepts, the role of the syntactic subject, and word order constraints. Structural features—which affect the domains of time, events, and entities—interact in different ways in information organization and information structure in the languages studied." Once more, grammatical features seem heavily implicated, but, as Carroll and Lambert rightly note, these are hardly the kinds of decontextualized sentence-level grammatical features that have been the mainstay of language instruction; instead, they are dynamic instantiations of particular narrative functions that reveal "an interconnected set of *choices* [emphasis added] with a deeply rooted logic" that resides across the entire language system, from morphology, to syntax, to discourse features.

The third essay in this section from that European project, by Bergljot Behrens, explores the intriguing possibility that "particular features of language use in advanced L2 production and translation into L1 may reside in the same or similar underlying constraints." By examining what she calls "marked" phenomena (i.e., odd choices in wordings) in these two contexts of language use, Behrens pushes further the possibility of pinpointing the nature and location of language-specific or language-independent aspects of knowledge conceptualization. Although at this point her study is exploratory, language planning appears to be a textually complex phenomenon, particularly when two language systems are simultaneously actively held in memory—a situation that appears to describe aspects of advanced language use and the process of translation.

The concluding essay in the first part of this volume, by Susan Strauss, takes insights from cognitive approaches to the Korean language classroom, focusing on two auxiliary constructions that express similar yet distinct aspectual meanings. Her study is located at the intersection of cognitive linguistics, discourse analysis, and corpus linguistics. The intent is to draw learners' attention to apprehending a situation and then construing it linguistically in ways that otherwise might not be apparent to them and therefore would be particularly difficult to use productively and correctly. In line with a highly contextual understanding of meaning-making, such a pedagogy relies on extensive oral and written corpora to facilitate a multi-step approach of detection and discernment of macro- and microtextual components, at the end of which learners should be able to make their own meaning-driven choices.

However one wishes to interpret the theoretical as well as data-based findings of these contributions, they make eminently clear that devising an approach that can overcome a variety of standard separations in our field to be able to put into focus central phenomena of language is more than a matter of explanatory elegance. It is a matter of being able to take note of critical phenomena of any language use, where that demand is made particularly insistently in the case of advanced learning.

Descriptive and Instructional Considerations in Advanced Learning

Essays in part II of this volume explore curricular and instructional approaches in terms of four broad areas. These areas offer more descriptive and instructional treatments: the centrality of narrativity (Pavlenko); vocabulary expansion as a particular challenge in advanced learning (Paribakht and Wesche); the demands for efficiency and effectiveness that instructed programs must meet, resulting in the challenge to devise principled approaches to constructing curricula that are horizontally and vertically articulated (Rinner and Weigert); and the link between language use and identity that commands careful attention in language use in the professions, here the legal profession (Abbuhl).

A textual orientation may be the most obvious way in which the difference between "intermediate" and "advanced" levels of ability has been characterized. Instead of regarding the development of textual coherence as an additive process, however, Aneta Pavlenko reminds readers that what is at issue is an L2 narrative competence that cannot be captured by the traditional hierarchy of core grammar, lexicon, rhetorical expressiveness, and register appropriateness. Instead, using a process of triangulation that involves cross-linguistic evidence, findings from narrative development in monolingual and bilingual children, and research on narrativity in SLA, Pavlenko looks at the nature of narrative structure in both personal and fictional narratives, the degree and type of evaluation and elaboration being deployed, and forms of cohesion that are manifested, with particular emphasis on reference, temporality, and conjunctive cohesion. In all areas she takes note of cross-linguistic and cross-cultural differences that pose particular challenges for the L2 classroom and therefore need explicit and long-term attention.

The second customary distinguisher for advanced over intermediate learners is in terms of vocabulary. The essay by T. Sima Paribakht and Marjorie Wesche seeks to determine what makes learners succeed or fail at lexical inferencing—the most important strategy for tackling the enormous task of vocabulary expansion, particularly for highly specialized content areas. Specifically, Paribakht and Wesche explore how a given L1—in this case, Farsi for learners of English—might influence how learners go about inferring the meaning of unfamiliar L2 vocabulary. Documenting again the strikingly low success rate that even advanced learners have with lexical inferencing, Paribakht and Wesche point to numerous knowledge sources—linguistic and nonlinguistic, L1- and L2-based—that instruction might bring to learners' conscious awareness. The critical insight is that simultaneously high levels of difficulty in terms of both content and language can drastically undermine learners' successful deployment of inferencing strategies. On the positive side, inferencing strategies do seem to be learnable, particularly if they are taught gradually over extended periods of time and include cross-linguistic information. Not surprisingly, multiple and meaningful encounters also are key for moving from recognition to production in ways that are most appropriate for individual learners.

The succeeding essay in this section, by Susanne Rinner and Astrid Weigert, tackles a particularly vexing issue: locating advanced instruction in a curricular context. As scholars have noted with much consternation, few language programs are conceptualized in terms of the undisputed long-term nature of language learning—that is, in terms of an extended curricular progression (for an early statement, see Byrnes 1998). Yet, as the essays in this volume reiterate, precisely such a trajectory is indispensable if advanced levels of acquisition are to be realized.

Even if that first step is accomplished, major hurdles remain. Among them is the considerable range of performance characteristics bundled together under the term "advanced." Curriculum development requires disentanglement of this bundling into curricular levels and even individual courses that can foster continued L2 development. Rinner and Weigert report on a program that has chosen the dual notions of literacy and genre to overcome the division between content and language and, by extension, the dichotomy between language courses and content courses that is characteristic of most college programs. More important, they suggest how the construct of genre can provide a conceptual foundation for articulating courses that focus on different content areas—for example, sports and economic issues in the European Union—both horizontally and vertically at advanced levels of the curriculum. Horizontal articulation is critical for enabling a program to calibrate comparable acquisitional goals and outcomes for different courses at a particular curricular level; vertical articulation enables them to determine subsequent content and pedagogical emphases to specify future learning goals and ensure their attainment. For collegiate programs, particularly in upper-level offerings, few considerations are more central.

Rebekha Abbuhl's essay addresses yet another feature that is readily identified with advanced L2 performance—namely, the ability to function in a professional context. Presenting data from a program that trains international lawyers, Abbuhl focuses on how these professionals can acquire competent use of epistemic modality as one aspect of lawyerly discourse in the legal memorandum genre within the common law legal system of the United States—which, in contrast with code law, relies heavily on interpretation of precedent. Like Strauss, Abbuhl also argues that raising learners' ability to notice the subtle linguistic and pragmalinguistic features associated with hedging and boosting is critical if they are to incorporate such features into their productive L2 repertoire. Not only does Abbuhl's study show particularly well the intimate link between (professional) identity construction and language use; it also provides further evidence for the need to rethink a deeply rooted prohibition against explicit teaching that has characterized much of communicative language teaching (see also the discussion in Byrnes and Sprang 2004), presumably because explicitness was regularly associated with a decontextualized focus on formal features. Finally, it also reorients an often ambiguous stance vis-à-vis the efficacy of feedback: Abbuhl concludes that, "without explicit instruction and feedback, advanced L2 learners in the disciplines may not notice or have the full ability to bridge this gap" and thereby gain access to a particular discourse community.

The Role of Assessment in Determining the Nature of Advancedness

Part III of this volume explores the role of assessment in advanced language learning. The premise is that assessment is central to the field's evolving understanding of advancedness and that much of the potential benefit of rethinking language learning and teaching as well as assessment in the context of advancedness depends on proper understanding of that connection in terms of the construct, in terms of assessment methods, and in terms of shaping programs in ways that aid learners toward attainment of advanced levels of ability.

John M. Norris makes that point particularly insistently. Although the claimed link, of course, applies at all levels of learning, getting it right in this instance becomes critical because assessment traditionally has defined the scope of language education in classrooms and programs. In this era of accountability, assessment takes on potentially far-reaching, even punitive dimensions. To Norris, the key is to worry less about the *how* of assessment and to focus more on the *why*. He highlights two areas: assessment as a measurement tool in research on language learning and assessment of learners as an essential educative component in language programs. For both areas he outlines potential contributions and major challenges by focusing on a model that specifies intended uses that "consider the underlying social and educational value of assessments as part of our practice" as a critical way to enable education toward advanced capacities.

The second essay that explores how assessment must be reconsidered when advanced levels of competence are at issue comes from Elana Shohamy. She, too, sounds cautionary notes with regard to simply expanding the *how*, or the methods of testing, to accommodate advanced abilities. Instead, Shohamy points to the intricate relation between the construct that is being assessed (i.e., advancedness) and testing practices; she counsels caution precisely because of the well-established power of tests to shape definitions of language, often in restrictive ways. Of particular concern are additive, guidelines-based forms of assessment, such as the highly influential Interagency Language Roundtable rating scales for proficiency assessment that were popularized through U.S. government–related language agencies, and, more recently, the Common European Framework project. In their place, Shohamy presents a comprehensive set of characteristics for advancedness as a crucial first step and then offers proposals for assessing advanced abilities.

Concluding Thoughts

As I state at the beginning of this chapter, an interest in advanced levels of foreign language acquisition is relatively new for the U.S. context. In that assessment, of course, I am aware that SLA research, like other forms of academic inquiry, is not geographically isolated. Indeed, as GURT 2005 amply demonstrated, the influence of European research foci and traditions—typically with a strong textual, functional, and cross-linguistic orientation (e.g., Dimroth and Starren 2003; Hyltenstam and Obler 1989; Ventola 1991; Ventola and Mauranen 1996)—and, recently, Australian systemic-functional linguistics, with its elaborated theoretical apparatus for the understanding and interpretation of texts and particularly its strong focus on genre-based approaches to teaching and learning (e.g., Christie and Martin 1997), is beginning to be felt in the United States (see particularly Johns 2002; Schleppegrell 2004; Schleppegrell and Colombi 2002; Swales 1990, 2000). Closer to home, a cognitivist-semantic orientation—though generally not yet applied to adult L2 learning (but see some of the contributions in the GURT 2003 volume edited by Tyler, Takada, Kim, and Marinova 2005), much less to advanced L2 learning—also seems to open conceptual and practice-oriented possibilities that give much hope for advancing the cause of advanced learning in this country. GURT 2005 endeavored to provide a first forum for such exchanges; the essays assembled in this volume are intended as one tangible way of continuing that important conversation. ▓

NOTES

1. I use the term *L2 learning* to refer to both second language learning and foreign language learning. Where the distinction between the two is relevant, I refer to foreign language learning as FL learning.
2. For an example of the persistence of such an approach even in the face of a strong desire to understand the unique characteristics of advanced learning, see Leaver and Shektman's (2002b) introductory chapter to their volume on the advanced learner. For its insufficiency in capturing central qualities of advanced abilities, see Byrnes (2002) and Elana Shohamy's essay in this volume.

REFERENCES

Bakhtin, M. M. 1981. Discourse in the novel. In *The dialogic imagination*, ed. Caryl Emerson and Michael Holquist. Austin: University of Texas Press, 259–422.

———. 1986. *Speech genres and other late essays*. Edited by Caryl Emerson and Michael Holquist. Austin: University of Texas Press.

Becker, Alton L. 1995. *Beyond translation: Essays toward a modern philology*. Ann Arbor: University of Michigan Press.

Birdsong, David, ed. 1999. *Second language acquisition and the critical period hypothesis*. Mahwah, N.J.: Erlbaum.

Byrnes, Heidi. 1998. Constructing curricula in collegiate foreign language departments. In *Learning foreign and second languages: Perspectives in research and scholarship*, ed. Heidi Byrnes. New York: MLA, 262–95.

————. 2002. Toward academic-level foreign language abilities: Reconsidering foundational assumptions, expanding pedagogical options. In *Developing professional-level language proficiency*, ed. Betty Lou Leaver and Boris Shekhtman. Cambridge: Cambridge University Press, 34–58.

————. 2004. Advanced L2 literacy: Beyond option or privilege. *ADFL Bulletin* 36, no. 1:52–60.

————, ed. 2006a. *Advanced language learning: The contribution of Halliday and Vygotsky*. London: Continuum.

————. 2006b. Perspectives: Interrogating communicative competence as a framework for collegiate foreign language study. *Modern Language Journal* 90:244–66.

Byrnes, Heidi, and Hiram H. Maxim, eds. 2004. *Advanced foreign language learning: A challenge to college programs*. Boston: Heinle Thomson.

Byrnes, Heidi, and Katherine A. Sprang. 2004. Fostering advanced L2 literacy: A genre-based, cognitive approach. In *Advanced foreign language learning: A challenge to college programs*, ed. Heidi Byrnes and Hiram H. Maxim. Boston: Heinle Thomson, 47–85.

Canale, Michael, and Merrill Swain. 1980. Theoretical bases of communicative approaches to second language teaching and testing. *Applied Linguistics* 1:1–47.

Christie, Frances, and James R. Martin, eds. 1997. *Genre and institutions: Social processes in the workplace and school*. London: Continuum.

Cook, Vivian. 1992. Evidence for multicompetence. *Language Learning* 42:557–91.

————, ed. 2002. *Portraits of the L2 user*. Clevedon, England: Multilingual Matters.

Cope, Bill, and Mary Kalantzis. 1993. The power of literacy and the literacy of power. In *The powers of literacy: A genre approach to teaching writing*, ed. Bill Cope and Mary Kalantzis. Pittsburgh: University of Pittsburgh Press, 63–89.

Dimroth, Christine, and Marianne Starren, eds. 2003. *Information structure and the dynamics of language acquisition*. Amsterdam/Philadelphia: John Benjamins.

Doughty, Catherine J., and Michael H. Long. 2003. The scope of inquiry and goals of SLA. In *The handbook of second language acquisition*, ed. Catherine J. Doughty and Michael H. Long. Malden, Mass.: Blackwell, 3–16.

Fauconnier, Gilles. 1997. *Mappings in thought and language*. New York: Cambridge University Press.

Fauconnier, Gilles, and Mark Turner. 2002. *The way we think: Conceptual blending and the mind's hidden complexities*. New York: Basic Books.

Gee, James Paul. 2002. Literacies, identities, and discourses. In *Developing advanced literacy in first and second languages: Meaning with power*, ed. Mary J. Schleppegrell and M. Cecilia Colombi. Mahwah, N.J.: Lawrence Erlbaum, 159–75.

Halliday, M. A. K. 1994. *An introduction to functional grammar*, 2nd ed. London: Edward Arnold.

Hyltenstam, Kenneth, and Loraine K. Obler, eds. 1989. *Bilingualism across the lifespan*. Cambridge: Cambridge University Press.

Johns, Ann M. ed. 2002. *Genre in the classroom: Multiple perspectives*. Mahwah, N.J.: Lawrence Erlbaum.

Kern, Richard. 2000. *Literacy and language teaching*. Oxford: Oxford University Press.

Langacker, Ronald W. 1990. *Concept, image and symbol: The cognitive basis of grammar*. Berlin: Mouton de Gruyter.

Leaver, Betty Lou, and Boris Shekhtman, eds. 2002a. *Developing profession-level language proficiency*. Cambridge: Cambridge University Press.

————. 2002b. Principles and practices in teaching superior-level language skills: Not just more of the same. In *Developing profession-level language proficiency*, ed. Betty Lou Leaver and Boris Shekhtman. Cambridge: Cambridge University Press, 3–33.

Long, Michael H. 2003. Stabilization and fossilization in interlanguage development. In *The handbook of second language acquisition*, ed. Catherine J. Doughty and Michael H. Long. Malden, Mass.: Blackwell, 487–535.

Martin, James R. 2000. Design and practice: Enacting functional linguistics. *Annual Review of Applied Linguistics* 20:116–26.

Maxim, Hiram H. 2004. Expanding visions for collegiate advanced foreign language learning. In *Advanced foreign language learning: A challenge to college programs*, ed. Heidi Byrnes and Hiram H. Maxim. Boston: Heinle Thomson, 180–93.

New London Group. 1996. A pedagogy of multiliteracies: Designing social futures. *Harvard Educational Review* 66:60–92.

Ortega, Lourdes. 2005. For what and for whom is our research? The ethical as transformative lens in instructed SLA. *Modern Language Journal* 89:427–43.

Ortega, Lourdes, and Heidi Byrnes, eds. 2007. *The longitudinal study of advanced L2 capacities.* Mahwah, N.J.: Erlbaum.

Pawley, Andrew, and Frances Syder. 1983. Two puzzles for linguistic theory: Nativelike selection and nativelike fluency. In *Language and communication,* ed. Jack Richards and Richard Schmidt. London: Longman, 191–226.

Schleppegrell, Mary J. 2004. *The language of schooling: A functional linguistics perspective.* Mahwah, N.J.: Erlbaum.

Schleppegrell, Mary J., and M. Cecilia Colombi, eds. 2002. *Developing advanced literacy in first and second languages: Meaning with power.* Mahwah, N.J.: Erlbaum.

Swaffar, Janet, and Katherine Arens. 2005. *Remapping the foreign language curriculum: An approach through multiple literacies.* New York: MLA.

Swales, John M. 1990. *Genre analysis: English in academic and research settings.* Cambridge: Cambridge University Press.

———. 2000. Languages for specific purposes. *Annual Review of Applied Linguistics* 20:59–76.

Tomasello, Michael, ed. 1998. *The new psychology of language: Cognitive and functional approaches to language structure.* Mahwah, N.J.: Erlbaum.

Tyler, Andrea, Mari Takada, Yiyoung Marinova, and Diana Kim, eds. 2005. *Language in use: Cognitive and discourse perspectives on language and language learning.* Washington, D.C.: Georgetown University Press.

Ventola, Eija, ed. 1991. *Functional and systemic linguistics: Approaches and uses.* Berlin: Mouton de Gruyter.

Ventola, Eija, and Anna Mauranen, eds. 1996. *Academic writing: Intercultural and textual issues.* Amsterdam/Philadelphia: John Benjamins.

Vygotsky, Lev. 1986. *Thought and language.* Cambridge, Mass.: MIT Press.

I

Cognitive Approaches to Advanced Language Learning

2

▨ The Conceptual Basis of Grammatical Structure

RONALD W. LANGACKER
University of California, San Diego

▨ **THE IDEAS AND DISCOVERIES** of cognitive linguistics have fundamentally altered our view of language structure, linguistic meaning, and their relation to cognition. This new linguistic worldview has major implications for language teaching, which scholars are starting to explore seriously (Achard and Niemeier 2004; Pütz, Niemeier, and Dirven 2001a, 2001b). I consider the pedagogical application of cognitive linguistic notions to be an important empirical test for their validity.

In this new worldview, language is all about meaning. Crucially, meaning resides in conceptualization. It does not just mirror objective reality; it is a matter of how we apprehend, conceive, and portray the real world and the myriad worlds we mentally construct. My emphasis here is on the elaborate **mental constructions** that intervene between the situations we describe and the form and meaning of the expressions employed (*cf.* Fauconnier 1985).

This meaning construction, however, is not the product of disembodied minds working individually in solipsistic isolation—quite the contrary. For one thing, cognition is **embodied** (Johnson 1987; Lakoff 1987; Lakoff and Núñez 2000). It consists in processing activity of the brain, which is part of the body, which is part of the physical world. Cognition also is **contextually embedded**. It is prompted, guided, and constrained by interactions at numerous levels: with the physical, psychological, social, cultural, and discourse contexts. Cognitive linguists, therefore, understand conceptualization in the broadest sense. It subsumes any kind of mental experience (sensory, motor, emotive, intellectual), as well as apprehension of the context in all its dimensions. Moreover, it is regarded as a primary means of engaging both the real and constructed worlds.

Given a properly formulated conceptualist semantics, for which there is strong independent motivation, grammar can be regarded as meaningful. The central claim of cognitive grammar (Langacker 1987, 1990, 1991, 1999a) is that lexicon, morphology, and syntax form a continuum consisting solely of **assemblies of symbolic structures**—that is, constructions (Croft 2001; Fillmore, Kay, and O'Connor 1988; Goldberg 1995; Langacker 2005). A symbolic structure is simply the pairing of a semantic structure and a phonological structure. It follows that all grammatical elements and structures have meanings, though these meanings often are quite schematic.

Crucial for linguistic semantics is our manifest capacity to conceive and portray the same objective situation in alternate ways. I refer to this process as **construal**. Obvious dimensions of construal include perspective and prominence, each of which is multifaceted.

One facet of perspective, for example, is the presumed vantage point from which a scene is apprehended. Thus, in sentence (1)(a) Jack's location depends on whether the description presupposes the speaker's own vantage point or that of Jill (assuming that the speaker is facing both Jack and Jill). Another facet is whether a description takes a local perspective on the scene or a global one. In sentence (1)(b) the progressive form *is rising* imposes a local view: It is what one would say while actually moving along the trail. On the other hand, the simple verb *rises* imposes a global view: It is what one would say while looking at the trail from a distance, where its full contour is visible at once.

(1) (a) *Jack was sitting to the left of Jill.*

(b) *The trail {is rising/rises} very quickly.*

Among the many kinds of prominence that have to be distinguished, two prove especially important for grammar. The first is **profiling**: Within the conceptual content it evokes as the basis for its meaning (its conceptual **base**), an expression profiles some substructure. Its profile is that portion of its base that the expression designates (or refers to) and as such is a focus of attention with respect to the symbolizing relationship.

A simple lexical example is the contrast among *hub*, *spoke*, and *rim*, all used in reference to a wheel, as shown in figure 2.1. The configuration of a wheel provides the conceptual content for all three expressions; because they all share this content, the difference in their meanings has to be attributed to their choice of profile within this common base. Note that heavy lines indicate profiling.

An expression can profile either a **thing** or a **relationship** (under highly abstract definitions of those terms). An expression's profile determines its grammatical category. In particular, a noun profiles a thing, a verb profiles a **process** (a relationship scanned sequentially in its evolution through time), and adjectives, adverbs, and prepositions profile nonprocessual relationships.

The verbs *like* and *please*, sketched in figure 2.2, illustrate profiled relationships. Like *hub*, *spoke*, and *rim*, they are distinguished semantically by the imposition of different profiles on the same conceptual base. Elements of this base include two things: one functioning as stimulus and the other as experiencer. The stimulus somehow impinges on the experiencer (solid arrow), and the experiencer somehow apprehends the stimulus (dashed arrow), resulting in a positive experience (dashed

(a) Base	(b) *hub*	(c) *spoke*	(d) *rim*

Figure 2.1 Base and Profile

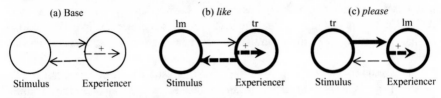

Figure 2.2 Profiling and Trajector/Landmark Alignment

arrow labeled "+"). Both verbs profile the induced experience. They contrast with regard to which additional facet of this complex relationship they profile. *Like* also profiles the experiencer's apprehension of the stimulus, whereas *please* emphasizes the latter impinging on the former.

These examples illustrate that meaning and meaning contrasts do not reside in conceptual content alone. The overall content is essentially the same in figure 2.1 and in figure 2.2. The crucial semantic differences instead reside in construal (e.g., in perspective or prominence), which is equally important to linguistic meaning. Besides profiling, the examples in figure 2.2 illustrate another kind of prominence—namely, trajector/landmark alignment. Expressions that profile relationships accord different degrees of prominence to the relational participants. Usually there is a primary focal participant, referred to as the **trajector** (tr). The trajector can be described as the participant the expression serves to locate or characterize in some fashion. Often there is a secondary focal participant evoked for this purpose. The latter is referred to as a **landmark** (lm). Because *like* puts primary focus on the experiencer, in relative terms it highlights the experiencer's apprehension of the stimulus. Conversely, because *please* puts primary focus on the stimulus, it highlights the relationship of the stimulus impinging on the experiencer. I take the semantic notions *trajector* and *landmark* to be the conceptual basis for the grammatical notions *subject* and *object*.

Importantly, conceptualization is **dynamic** rather than static (Barsalou 1999; Langacker 2001a). It has a time course, unfolding through processing time, and how it develops through processing time is one dimension of construal and linguistic meaning.

An initial example is the well-known contrast in (2). The difference is not just a matter of alternate word orders, freely chosen; it has conceptual import. Whereas sentence (2)(a) represents the neutral order in English, sentence (2)(b) instantiates a special construction that is based on a particular way of mentally accessing the situation described: It first invokes an accessible location as a spatial point of reference, thereby inducing the expectation that a less accessible participant will be presented as occupying that location. This conceptual flow from location to participant makes the construction suitable for introducing new discourse participants.

(2) (a) *Some expensive-looking suits were in the closet.*

    (b) *In the closet were some expensive-looking suits.*

Fundamental to conceptualization and linguistic semantics are various capacities that are reasonably described as **imaginative**. Among these capacities are metonymy, metaphor, blending, mental spaces, and fictivity. Like construal and dynamicity, these imaginative phenomena have at best a minor role in traditional and formal semantics. They are essential, however, and are a prime concern in what follows.

The basis for **metonymy** is the fact that linguistic expressions are not (metaphorically speaking) containers for meaning; they serve as prompts for the construction of meaning (Reddy 1979). They provide flexible, open-ended access to established domains of knowledge and trigger whatever mental constructions are necessary to achieve conceptual coherence. An expression can then be interpreted as referring to any facet of the elaborate conceptual structure it evokes. Hence, the specific mention of one entity provides a way of mentally accessing any number of associated entities, some of which may be more directly relevant for the purpose at hand. This definition constitutes metonymy in the broadest sense (Barcelona 2004; Kövecses and Radden 1998; Langacker 1984, 2004a; Panther and Radden 2004). More narrowly, metonymy can be defined as a shift in profile: An expression that normally designates one entity instead is construed as designating some other entity within the same conceptual complex. An attested example is sentence (3), which makes no sense on a strictly literal interpretation. The context was that of looking at a Mormon temple illuminated at night by spotlights. In this context, the word *temple* evokes this entire conceptual complex, including the lights—thus affording mental access to the entity that directly participates in the *turn off* relationship. The thing profiled by the object nominal is not the one most directly involved in the process profiled by the clause, but it does serve as a reference point for accessing it.

(3) *They just turned off the temple.*

When we talk about linguistic expressions being *containers* for meaning, or prompting the *construction* of meaning, we are resorting, of course, to **metaphor**. In cognitive linguistics, metaphor is regarded as a basic and pervasive aspect of cognition (Lakoff 1987, 1990; Lakoff and Johnson 1980; Lakoff and Núñez 2000; Turner 1987). It is primarily a conceptual phenomenon, which is manifested linguistically but usually is independent of any particular expression. A conceptual metaphor consists of a set of mappings (or correspondences) between a **source domain** and a **target domain** partially understood in terms of it.

In recent years, linguists have come to accept that metaphor is a special case of **blending** (or **conceptual integration**) (Fauconnier and Turner 1998, 2002). A **blend** emerges when selected elements from two **input spaces** are projected into a third space, where they are integrated to form a structure that is distinct from both inputs. Usually a blend is something that does not exist in actuality—an imaginative creation that is inconsistent with the constraints imposed by objective reality. Nonetheless, it is real as an object of thought and a basis for linguistic meaning. A simple example of a blend is a cartoon character—for example, a dog that thinks in English and fancies itself to be a World War I flying ace. In the case of metaphor, the source domain and the target domain function as the two input spaces. The result of apprehending the target in terms of the source produces a blend: the target as metaphorically understood. Figure 2.3 shows this blend for the metaphorical conception of

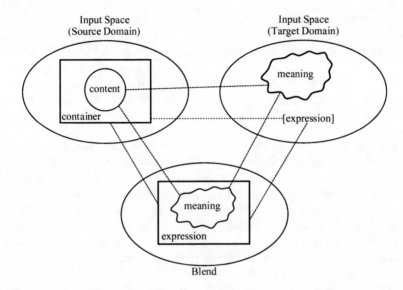

Figure 2.3 Blending

expressions (e.g., lexical items) as containers for a "substance" called meaning. Although it has a powerful impact on how we think and theorize about language, this particular metaphor actually is quite misleading. It is not the case that meanings are "in" the words we use. This should become abundantly clear in what follows.

If metaphor is a special case of blending, blending in turn is a special case of **mental space configurations** (Fauconnier 1985, 1997; Fauconnier and Sweetser 1996). As exemplified in figure 2.3, mental spaces are like separate working areas, each the locus for a conceptual structure representing some facet of a more elaborate conception. Although each has a certain measure of autonomy, the crucial factor is how the structures in the various spaces are related to one another (the space configuration). One aspect of their relationship is the correspondences between their elements (as shown by the dotted correspondence lines). Another is their relative status and how they derive from one another. For instance, each structure in figure 2.3 has a different functional role. The source domain is used to apprehend the target domain (rather than conversely). Likewise, the blend derives from the input spaces (rather than conversely). Although the inputs are more closely tied to reality than the blend, which is imaginative, the latter functions directly as the conceptual base for metaphorical expressions. When we talk about *empty words*, for example, we are invoking the blend and describing a situation in which the amount of meaning contained in the expression happens to be zero.

Metaphor is just one source of conceptual structures representing entities that are **fictive** (or **virtual**) in nature. Fictivity has been extensively studied in cognitive linguistics (e.g., Langacker 1986, 1999b, 2003; Matlock 2001; Matlock, Ramscar, and Boroditsky 2004; Matlock and Richardson 2004; Matsumoto 1996, 1997; Sweetser 1997; Talmy 1996). It is so pervasive, in fact, that I am led to wonder whether we ever engage in direct description of **actuality** (the term I use in opposition to fictivity or virtuality). Even when we are talking about actual entities, we commonly do so only indirectly, by means of expressions that pertain directly to virtual entities. When we talk about *empty words*, for instance, our intent is to describe an actual situation. What this expression describes directly, however, is a virtual entity, created by blending. Only indirectly—by projecting back from the blend to the input space pertaining to expressions and their import—do we understand what the phrase actually means.

The various phenomena I have briefly introduced—construal, dynamicity, and imaginative capacities such as blending and fictivity—are far removed from the concerns that have dominated linguistic semantics for many decades. Yet they are readily apparent when one examines linguistic meanings in their own terms, without theoretical preconception and with full awareness of the conceptual abilities we clearly manifest. I now discuss numerous examples of these phenomena to demonstrate their prevalence and central importance in semantics and grammar. I focus in particular on the role of **covert imagined scenarios** in structuring the meanings of expressions and determining their form.

I start with sentence (4) (cited from Talmy 1988, 189), which I have used often because it so neatly illustrates some basic points. The sentence in (4) is the sort of thing one might actually say, and it seems unremarkable until we try to analyze it. It is readily understood and structurally fairly simple, consisting of just a single, existential clause (*there's a house*) expanded by two adverbial phrases (*every now and then* and *through the valley*). The sentence poses a basic analytical problem, however: What do the adverbs modify? *Every now and then* describes the frequency of events, but the clause it appears to modify—*there's a house*—designates a stable situation. A house endures continuously, rather than flashing in and out of existence. Moreover, *through the valley* describes a spatial path and normally would modify a motion verb, such as *hike* or *travel*, but the sentence contains no such verb or any other explicit indication of motion.

(4) *There's a house every now and then through the valley.*

We understand this sentence through a mental construction that is merely prompted by the words it contains (as opposed to being compositionally derived from them). It evokes the scenario of a person traveling through the valley and observing the scenery—for example, by looking out the window while riding in a train. The adverb *through the valley* describes this covert path of motion. As the imagined viewer moves through the valley, the field of view moves along with the viewer, subtending a different portion of the valley at each moment. At certain moments, the field of view reveals a situation of the sort describable by the expression *there's a house*. The adverbial phrase *every now and then* pertains to the frequency of these viewing experiences, not the existence of any actual house. The house explicitly mentioned in the sentence is a virtual house, conjured up just to characterize a type of situation various instances of which are viewed at different times. Hence, the covert scenario of a viewer traveling through the valley provides the basis for both the semantic and the grammatical integration of the clause and the modifying adverbs.

The scenario providing this conceptual and grammatical coherence is not only covert but generally also fictive. It may well have been inspired by an actual journey (which could be reported using the past tense: *There was a house every now and then through the valley*). Nonetheless, sentence (4) describes the valley in generalized fashion, indicating what anyone might see while traveling through it. Understanding the sentence does not require that there ever was or ever will be an actual journey. For instance, I could utter sentence (4) while looking at an areal photograph of a valley that I have never traveled through and nobody can travel through because it is too dangerous (e.g., a valley in Iraq); nevertheless, we still understand the sentence in terms of the imagined travel scenario.

Consider next the examples in (5). Sentence (5)(a) describes an actual motion event. By contrast, sentence (5)(b) exemplifies **fictive motion** because in actuality the trail does not move. As in sentence (4), this expression makes sense when it is construed in terms of a covert scenario—that of someone moving along the trail toward the summit. Also as in sentence (4), a central factor is the mover's field of view—what he or she perceives at any one moment while moving along the trail. The key to this construction is this local, moving field of view. What counts as *the trail* in sentence (5)(b) is not the trail in its entirety. Instead, the subject is construed metonymically as designating the portion of the trail that falls within the field of view at any given moment. Objectively, this portion—the metonymic referent of *the trail*—is different from one moment to the next. In this construction, however, these distinct trail segments are fictively identified as being the same entity from moment to moment. Construed in this fashion, *the trail* does indeed change position through time, rising as the viewer moves along it. This fictive identification of the trail segments as being a single entity, tracked through time, provides the basis for conceptualizing *the trail* as moving through space. The term **perfective** indicates that the sentence profiles a relationship conceived as changing through time (albeit fictively).

    (5) (a) *The balloon rose quickly.*   [actual motion (perfective)]

       (b) *The trail rose quickly near the summit.* [virtual motion (perfective)]

       (c) *The trail rises quickly near the summit.* [virtual motion (imperfective)]

By contrast, sentence (5)(c) is **imperfective**—that is, it profiles a situation that is stable through time. This correlates with taking a global view of the scene, where the entire contour of the trail is apprehended simultaneously. Sentence (5)(c) might be uttered while looking at a map prior to any actual hike. Once more, the motion coded by *rise* is fictive because the trail does not move in actuality. Here, however, the sense of motion arises in a different manner. Instead of being generated by the perceptual experience of someone physically moving along the trail, it resides in the conceptual experience of mentally scanning along the trail: The conceptualizer scans mentally along the trail's expanse in building up to a full conception of its configuration. Only this full configuration, representing a global view of its contour, is profiled by the clause, and because that contour is stable through time, the clause is imperfective.

As evidence for this difference, observe that only imperfective virtual motion is possible for situations in which it is hard to imagine anybody physically moving along the path in question. Thus, sentence (6)(a) is well-formed, but sentence (6)(b) is not because we can hardly hike along someone's forehead. The analysis predicts, however—correctly, I believe—that sentence (6)(b) is quite acceptable if it is uttered while hiking on Mt. Rushmore.

(6) (a) *His forehead rises steeply near*
     the hairline.   [imperfective virtual motion]
(b) **His forehead is rising steeply near*
     the hairline.   [perfective virtual motion]

In these examples, there is a close relationship between the scenario invoked by perfective virtual motion and the mental scanning that is characteristic of imperfective virtual motion. The scenario responsible for sentence (5)(b)—that of a viewer moving along a spatial path—engenders the perceptual experience of the viewer apprehending the constitutive segments of the path in a particular sequence. This sequenced perceptual access by the mover is precisely analogous to the sequenced mental access carried out by the conceptualizer in the scanning responsible for the directionality in sentence (5)(c). This mental scanning is the abstracted, purely mental counterpart of the physically grounded perceptual experience. Their relationship illustrates embodiment, as well as **subjectification**, in either Traugott's sense or mine (Langacker 1999c, 2004b; Traugott 1989). As one goes from sentence (5)(a) to sentence (5)(c)—from actual motion, to perfective virtual motion, to imperfective virtual motion—the locus of the motion coded by *rise* goes from being external and objectively observable, to being experiential (though still engendered by physical motion), to being purely mental.

Mental scanning and invoked scenarios are not always so closely associated. Each can occur independently of the other. Moreover, when scanning does relate to a scenario, the extent to which it invokes it is a matter of degree. In a case such as sentence (7)(a), the scenario of physically moving along a spatial path is fairly salient—if only because the description pertains to a road, which inherently evokes this notion. It is less salient in sentence (7)(b) because a fence does not usually function as a path of motion. Nevertheless, we certainly can imagine walking along the fence. With a scar, as in sentence (7)(c), the physical motion scenario lies even farther in the background. Yet even if it fades away altogether, a vestige remains in the expression's dynamicity, wherein the conceptualizer evokes the scar sequentially in building up to the full conception of its configuration. This sequenced mental access provides the directionality that is reflected linguistically in the prepositions *from* and *to*, respectively indicating a source and a goal. Owing to this subjective directionality, sentences (7)(c) and (7)(d) are semantically distinct even though they describe precisely the same objective situation. Although the situation itself is static (and the sentences imperfective), it is accessed dynamically, through processing time, and in a particular direction. The appearance in these expressions of *go*, *from*, and *to* makes sense only in terms of this dynamic process of mentally constructing the profiled configuration.

(7) (a) *This road goes along the coast for a while and then turns inland.*

　(b) *The fence goes all around the estate.*

　(c) *The scar goes all the way from his knee to his ankle.*

　(d) *The scar goes all the way from his ankle to his knee.*

Understood as sequential mental access, whereby entities are evoked or attended to in a certain natural order, scanning is not inherently tied to space or physical motion. It figures in a wide spectrum of expressions that are structurally quite diverse and open-ended with regard to their subject matter. Most obviously, we can mentally scan through time, as in (8). A special case of temporal scanning is the kind of **fictive change** exemplified in sentences (8)(c) and (8)(d) (Sweetser 1997). On one interpretation of sentence (8)(d), for instance, the president has a series of different planes, each more luxurious than the last. Each actual plane is a different instantiation (or "value") of the general "role" described by the nominal *the president's plane* (Fauconnier 1985). Presumably, each is constant in the degree of luxury it affords. Only by fictively identifying these different instantiations of the abstract role do we obtain the notion of change expressed by the predicate.

(8) (a) *From time to time, she has brilliant insights.*

　(b) *Through the centuries, we have had many great leaders.*

　(c) *Every year my Christmas letter is longer.*

　(d) *The president's plane keeps getting more luxurious.*

We can mentally scan through any sequence of options, not just space or time. The expressions in (9) illustrate scanning in other domains. In sentence (9)(a) we evoke a series of stores and compare their prices. In sentences (9)(b) and (9)(c) we scan upward along a scale (price or size) and track what happens to an associated property (quality or average length of gestation). In sentence (9)(d) the *from* and *to* phrases induce us to scan downward along the cline of intelligence, as the basis for a generalization pertaining to all positions on the scale. The language of change and motion—expressions such as *from*, *to*, *improve*, *increase*, and *get longer*—reflects this dynamic constructive process of building up a full conception of the situation described.

(9) (a) *From one store to the next, prices vary greatly.*

　(b) *Quality improves with the more expensive brands.*

　(c) *As body size increases, the average gestation period gets longer.*

　(d) *From the brightest student in the class to the dumbest, they all work hard.*

In figure 2.4 I sketch the scanning prompted by *from* and *to* in sentence (9)(d). The circles represent students, each located at a certain position along the intelligence scale. The boxes represent mental spaces. One space corresponds to what is

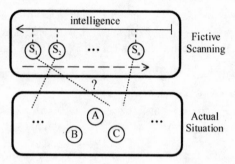

Figure 2.4 Fictive Mental Scanning

known about the actual situation. The listener, for example, might know only that the class consists of students—three of whom are Alice, Bill, and Cindy—and have no specific knowledge about either their total number or their relative intelligence. The other mental space is evoked by the *from* and *to* phrases, which invite us to perform the scanning indicated by the dashed arrow. The property of working hard is then ascribed to every student who is mentally accessed in this manner.

A key point is that this scanning is fictive in nature: We do not actually perform it. In particular, the listener understands the sentence perfectly well without knowing the identity of all the students, their total number, or how intelligent any particular student might be. Instead of mentally accessing all the actual students one by one in the proper sequence, interlocutors apprehend this expression by constructing a **mental model** (Johnson-Laird 1983) consisting of a small number of imagined students and using these surrogates to **simulate** the scanning experience (Barsalou 1999). (This mental simulation is comparable to what we do in understanding the statement that 3 million people visited the San Diego Zoo last year—it invokes the image of people passing through turnstiles, but only a handful of people actually figure in this dynamic image, not all 3 million.) This **fictive scanning** is projected onto the actual situation and serves to partially structure it, but without providing any specific information about particular students and their ranking.

Lurking in the background is the familiar scenario of actually examining a list where entities are ranked with respect to a scale, directing our attention successively to each entry in the proper sequence. Our real-life experience with actual scenarios of this sort underlies the simulated scanning implicated in the form and meaning of this expression. Another generalized scenario pertains to our cumulative experience, in the course of our lives, with multiple instances of a given type. As we travel through the world and metaphorically travel through life, we successively encounter many different people, cats, houses, breakfasts, and so forth. In some cases we encounter enough instances of a category that we can reasonably take the sample as being representative, so that we can make an informed judgment about its overall membership. This scenario, I suggest, motivates the phenomenon illustrated in (10).

(10) (a) *A linguistic theorist is always*
        arrogant.   [= All linguistic theorists are arrogant.]

(b) *A basketball player is usually tall.* [= Most basketball players are tall.]

(c) *A calico cat is often unfriendly.* [= Many calico cats are unfriendly.]

(d) *A politician is seldom honest.* [= Few politicians are honest.]

These sentences are initially striking and analytically problematic because temporal adverbs such as *always, usually, often*, and *seldom*, which normally express the temporal frequency of events, apparently are being used instead as nominal quantifiers. I suggest that the adverbs in (10) still specify the frequency of events, even on the relevant interpretation, where the property ascribed to the subject is stable through time. The only thing special about their use is that the events in question are not actual occurrences but virtual events in the kind of covert fictive scenario I have just described. For example, sentence (10)(a) invokes the imagined scenario of traveling through the world or through life, encountering various linguistic theorists along the way, and ascertaining in each case that the individual examined is arrogant. This frequency of examining events, where the examined individual has the property in question, is coded by the adverb *always*. Of course, the scenario does not imply that we actually encounter every linguistic theorist—or any at all, for that matter. The scenario simply is conjured up as a way of making a generalization about the members of a category, however we might arrive at the judgment. It is a fictive means of accessing category members for this purpose. Nevertheless, it is central to the expression's meaning and responsible for an important aspect of its form—namely, the frequency adverb *always*.

A partial sketch appears in figure 2.5, where the circles represent members of a category, P is the property in question (e.g., being arrogant), and boxes are imagined events of examining a category member to ascertain whether it exhibits the property. Again the dashed arrow indicates the path of mental scanning. Given the virtual scenario, it follows directly that the frequency of events where the property is found correlates with the proportion of members exhibiting the property. This correlation is inherent in the mental construction underlying the expression and does not have to be

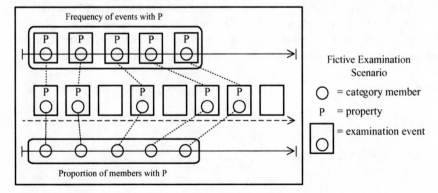

Figure 2.5 Fictive Examination Scenario

separately computed or accounted for by positing distinct meanings for frequency adverbs. Of course, everything shown in the diagram is fictive, even though the expression is offered as a characterization of what the world actually is like.

The examples in (10) do not reflect an idiosyncrasy or extended meaning of any single adverb. They represent an established conventional pattern of English that is based on a mental construction incorporating a covert imagined scenario. Adverbs commonly serve as a window on covert scenarios and/or mental scanning. In sentence (7)(a), for instance, the adverbs *for a while* and *then* pertain to the imagined scenario of traveling along the road. In sentence (8)(c), *every year* specifies the temporal path of mental scanning. Another well-known case is the use of *then* in conditionals (Fauconnier 1985; Sweetser 1996), as in sentence (11).

(11) *If he's a linguistic theorist, then he must be arrogant.*

In sentence (11), *then* does not index the temporal sequence of occurrences; indeed, the clauses describe stable situations. Instead, it indicates the temporal course of conditional reasoning. The word *if* invokes a **hypothetical** mental space containing the situation described in the clause it heads—in this case, his being a linguistic theorist. The conditional construction carries the import that further examination of this mental space will reveal the circumstance described in the second clause. In expressions of the form *if P then Q*, the adverb *then* reflects the temporal sequence of this fictive process of constructing and searching the hypothetical mental space—of first arriving at P, and *then* encountering Q, as shown in figure 2.6. It obtains at the level of mental construction, not the level of the objective situations described in the clauses.

Adverbs such as *still* and *already* also have well-established uses in which their temporal import applies to a fictive scanning process. Canonically, as illustrated in sentence (12), they apply to the situation being described, indicating either that it has continued longer than expected or has started sooner than expected:

(12) *Jack is still working on his paper, but Jill has already finished hers.*

In (13), however, the objective situation—the one profiled by the clause containing the adverb—is stable through time, and its duration is not at issue. Instead, the adverbs pertain to imagined scanning along a scale. In sentence (13)(a), we scan through a list of sports ranked in decreasing order of violence. The import of *still* is that, in the process of this mental scanning, the situation of the sport considered being too violent for her continues longer than one might expect. In sentence (13)(b), we scan through a list of beverages ranked in increasing order of alcoholic content. Here the import is that the situation of a beverage being more than he can handle is

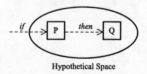

Hypothetical Space

Figure 2.6 Conditional Construction

encountered sooner than expected. Of course, in each case the scanning is only partial and basically fictive. In sentence (13)(b), for example, we do not actually have to direct our attention successively to every alcoholic beverage in the ranking; we merely simulate this process with respect to a limited mental model.

(13) (a) *She can't stand boxing, football, or hockey, and golf is still too violent for her.*

(b) *Forget about whiskey—beer is already more than he can handle.*

I have discussed scanning through space, through time, and through various kinds of scales or rankings. Another domain through which we scan, actually or virtually, is the ongoing discourse. As discourse proceeds, we retain at least a partial record of what was said and in what sequence. The apprehended discourse is itself a kind of mental construction, to be distinguished from the events and situations being talked about. Once again, adverbs canonically used with respect to profiled, onstage occurrences come to be used instead for an aspect of the offstage conceptualization involved in their apprehension. One example is the preceding sentence: *Once again* indicates that the statement it introduces constitutes the second discourse occurrence of a proposition. It does not indicate the repeated use of adverbs but the repeated occurrence in the discourse of a proposition concerning their use.

Of course, this is just one minor example of the bits of language devoted to tracking and managing the flow of discourse as well as the social interaction comprising it. Like the bits of language devoted to objective circumstances, these draw upon elaborate conceptual structures including both real and imagined scenarios as well as other mental constructions. Let us briefly examine a few such phenomena, starting with the English present tense (Langacker 2001b).

The theory of cognitive grammar claims that a verb profiles a process, defined as a relationship scanned sequentially in its evolution through time. Perhaps by now this characterization seems less ad hoc and less fanciful than it might have at the outset. It can be regarded as a special case of mental scanning—namely, simulation of a temporally extended experience. A full, finite clause profiles a process, and tense specifies how that process relates to the **ground**—that is, the speaker-hearer interaction. My central claim about the English present tense is simple and straightforward: It specifies that the profiled clausal process precisely coincides with the time of speaking.

If the claim itself is simple and straightforward, its explication and justification are much less so. Indeed, linguists—in a rare consensus—agree that the English "present tense" is anything but an indication of present time. For one thing, the simple present generally is not permitted with perfective verbs—that is, those designating bounded occurrences. For present-time perfectives, we have to use the imperfectivizing progressive construction, as in (14). Imperfectives, which profile stable situations not inherently bounded, do occur in the simple present.

(14) (a) **He paints the fence.*   [*paint* = perfective (bounded)]

(b) *He is painting the fence.*   [*be painting* = progressive (imperfective)]

(c) *He likes the fence.*   [*like* = imperfective]

The apparent problem is even worse, however. Not only do most present-time occurrences resist the present tense, but the present tense also is used for nonpresent occurrences, as in (15):

(15) (a) *They leave for Europe tomorrow.*   [scheduled future]

  (b) *I'm sitting in the study last night*   [historical present]
  and the phone rings.

  (c) *A kitten is born with blue eyes.*   [generic/timeless]

The first difficulty, that perfectives resist the true present tense, actually can be turned into an argument supporting the analysis. If the profiled event has to be temporally coincident with the speech event, the analysis predicts that most perfectives will be excluded. The reason, quite simply, is that most events have the wrong inherent duration. For instance, uttering the clause *He paints the fence* takes only a second, but actually painting a fence takes much longer. If this is the source of the problem, bounded events of the right duration should indeed be expressable in the simple present (provided that the speaker does not have to observe the event to begin describing it).

In fact, they can. The clearest examples are **performatives**, in which the profiled event is a **speech act**, and uttering the sentence under the proper conditions constitutes a **performance** of that speech act (Austin 1962; Searle 1969). For instance, by uttering the sentence *I promise to quit smoking* (under the proper circumstances), I perform the act of promising. Performatives are perfective and always in the simple present tense. This is possible because of their special property: The profiled event and the speech event are one and the same. Hence, they are necessarily temporally coincident. This special property is shown diagrammatically by the contrast between figure 2.7(a), representing present-tense perfectives in general, and 2.7(b), representing performatives.

With regard to imperfectives, occurrence in the simple present is possible because of their special property (which they share with mass nouns) that any subpart of an instance is itself an instance of the same type. Consider sentence (14)(c). If he likes the fence over a long span of time (e.g., a year), then during any limited sample from that time frame—a month, a day, or even just a moment—it also is the case that he likes the fence. Any temporal portion of the overall steady-state process itself qualifies as a valid instance of the process. Thus, if a stable situation of indefinite duration extends through the time of speaking, the portion that coincides with the time of speaking is an instance of the process type in question. As shown in figure 2.7(c),

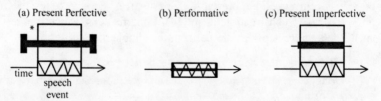

(a) Present Perfective   (b) Performative   (c) Present Imperfective

Figure 2.7 Present Tense

that portion is segmented out of the continuing situation as the portion being attended to—that is, as the relationship profiled by the clause. The semantic value of the present tense resides in its imposition of this restricted scope of attention, to which the profiled process (a focus of attention) is necessarily confined. It implies that the profiled relationship is immediate to the ground, being fully instantiated during the time of speaking. With imperfectives, the profiled segment is taken as a representative sample revealing a situation with indefinite temporal extension.

Our real interest, however, lies with nonpresent uses of the present, like those in (15). The key to their analysis, I suggest, is that such expressions do not constitute direct descriptions of actual events. Instead, a covert mental construction intervenes between the expression and the actual event at issue. In sentence (15)(a), the intervening construct is some kind of schedule, plan, or projected course of events. Of course, there may be an actual schedule, physically instantiated; sentence (15)(a) is the sort of thing one might say in reading an itinerary. In general, however, there need only be a tacit plan analogous to one. What I therefore am calling the "scheduled future" is a conventional pattern of English that invokes as its basis a virtual schedule that the speaker consults in forming the expression. Producing such a sentence amounts to the fictive act of reading off an entry on this imagined document. Thus, sentence (15)(a) does not constitute a direct description of the projected actual event of their leaving for Europe; the profiled event is a virtual event that merely represents the actual event, one of the event representations that collectively constitute the schedule.

This scheduled future is sketched in figure 2.8. Each event inscribed on the schedule **corresponds** to a projected actual event but is not to be **identified** with it. Nevertheless, the nature of this mental construction is such that by **directly** describing a virtual event we **indirectly** describe the actual event to which it corresponds. Indeed, we are hardly aware of the distinction. They are distinct, however, in that the schedule—even though it represents the **future**—is available for consultation in the **present**. This availability provides the **immediacy** conveyed by the present tense. In a sentence such as (15)(a), the profiled event coincides with the time of speaking in the sense that producing or understanding the expression amounts to "reading off" this entry in the virtual schedule. Because the profiled event is only virtual, it "occurs" in the only way it can—by being apprehended in a reading of the document, which makes it temporally coincident with the time of speaking (regardless of the duration or temporal location of the actual event it represents).

A virtual schedule is only one kind of virtual document. I would posit a mental construction of this sort for each distinct pattern of using present-tense forms for

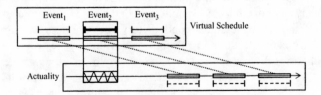

Figure 2.8 Scheduled Future Use of Present Tense

nonpresent events and situations. For example, the historical present, as in sentence (15)(b), invokes the implicit scenario of viewing a mental "replay" of past occurrences. The document in this case is like a videotape that is played at the speed determined by its narration. For generic statements, such as sentence (15)(c), the virtual document might be likened to a set of blueprints describing the world's "essential" structure (Goldsmith and Woisetschlaeger 1982; Lakoff and Johnson 1999; Langacker 1997). Each entry is a fictive event or situation, involving fictive participants, that is conjured up to represent a facet of what the world is like by its very nature (as opposed to an "accidental" occurrence taking place within this framework). As such, it projects to an open-ended set of actual occurrences that instantiate it.

As a kind of grounding, tense invokes the speaker-hearer interaction. I argue, in fact, that every expression invokes this interaction to some degree as one aspect of its semantic value. Like its onstage content, this offstage portion of an expression's meaning often is apprehended via mental constructions involving fictivity and covert scenarios. Consider sentence (16), for example:

(16) *I'm not here right now.*

If we interpret this sentence with respect to the default arrangement of a face-to-face interaction, it is rather puzzling. Interpreted literally—not as a metaphorical description of mental state—it is contradictory: *Here* is where I am, as a matter of definition. Yet sentence (16) seems quite straightforward when it is heard as the message on an answering machine. Conceptually, however, it is quite elaborate, invoking multiple scenarios as well as both real and imagined situations.

First there is the default scenario of a face-to-face interaction. Another scenario, derivative of the first, is the basic scenario of a phone call, wherein technology allows the interlocutors to be in different places. The answering machine gives rise to a further scenario that is based on the others: It allows an exchange in which the interlocutors are separated in both space and time, as part of a more elaborate script in which the caller leaves another message for later review. In sentence (16), *here* refers to the location where the speaker records the original message and where the caller is expected to try to reach the speaker. On the other hand, *right now* does not refer to the time at which the speaker records the message. Instead, it refers to the time—merely fictive when the message is recorded—at which some unknown person is imagined as placing a call and hearing the message. The situation described by the sentence represents a blend that combines elements of the situations at the time of recording and at the time of the call, as well as the standard phone-call scenario. This blend represents the imagined situation of the speaker and caller communicating directly at a time that corresponds to both the time of recording and the time of the call. Of course, this blend is contradictory because these two times actually are distinct. That is the nature of blends, however: Literally they often are inconsistent; their coherence derives from correspondences to other mental spaces (*cf.* figure 2.3). Hence, the time constructed in the blend is simultaneously identified with the other two times. From the time of recording, the expression inherits the characterization of the specified location as being *here*. From the time of the call, the expression inherits the characterization of the situation as one in which the speaker is not at that location.

Although sentence (16) is very simple and readily understood, the mental construction supporting it is quite elaborate. This conceptual substrate hardly can be excluded from the scope of linguistic semantics because it determines the expression's form and is responsible for the coherent meaning that emerges. The example differs only in degree from canonical uses. An expression is always understood relative to a real or imagined context, one aspect of which is a conception of the very interaction in which it is embedded. The interaction often is conceptualized in terms of mental constructions with fictive components.

Among the conventional units of a language are cognitive models of the various speech acts that are standard in the culture—such as stating, ordering, promising, requesting, advising, and so forth. These models are abstracted scenarios representing conventionalized patterns of speaker-hearer interaction. In schematized form, they make reference to the interlocutors, the utterance, the social context, the result of performing the act, the conditions required for it to be successful, and so on. These idealized scenarios have different linguistic uses. They can function as the meaning of speech-act verbs (e.g., *say*, *order*, *promise*). These verbs can be used either descriptively or performatively. In performatives, the speaker, hearer, and utterance evoked by the speech-act model as generalized (hence fictive) entities are **strongly identified** with the actual speaker, hearer, and utterance of the current speech event (Langacker 2004c). Hence, the speech act itself is put onstage as the profiled occurrence, as shown in figure 2.7(b). The actual speech event then constitutes an **enactment** of the conventional scenario.

In other linguistic uses, these interactive scenarios remain covert, although they do have formal consequences. The scenarios of stating, asking, and ordering represent the prototypical import of declarative, interrogative, and imperative clauses. Importantly, these speech acts are not part of the meaning of these clause types per se. As we observe in (17), they all have uses in which they do not represent the speech act in question. Uttering the initial clause in sentence (17)(c), for instance, does not constitute an act of ordering.

(17) (a) *It's not the case that **pigs are more intelligent than cats**.*   [declarative clause]

    (b) *They don't know **who falsified the documents**.*   [interrogative clause]

    (c) ***Show him that letter** and I'll kill you.*   [imperative clause]

When such utterances **are** used to perform these speech acts, as in (18), the expression results from embedding the clause in the appropriate scenario—which, however, remains implicit. The resulting configurations, sketched in figure 2.9, are highly entrenched linguistic units representing the typical uses of these types of clauses. The expression's meaning then comprises both the overtly manifested clause and the covert scenario that incorporates it.

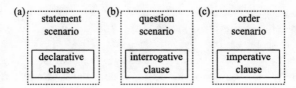

Figure 2.9 Speech Act Scenarios

(18) (a) *Pigs are more intelligent than cats.*

(b) *Who falsified the documents?*

(c) *Show him that letter!*

The units in figure 2.9 are embedded in still more elaborate scenarios representing conventional interactive patterns. Three such patterns are exemplified in (19). As shown in figure 2.10, each invokes a complex interactive frame in which one scenario is embedded in another. Thus, sentence (19)(a) is indeed a question, but it also is a request, as indexed by *please*. Similarly, sentence (19)(b) is basically a statement, but it is put forth to elicit confirmation, so at a higher level of conceptual organization it amounts to a kind of question (as well as an offer to help if needed). The statements in (19)(c) instantiate an established ironic formula. The first sentence appears to be a genuine statement. The following sentence, however, is so blatantly false that, given their juxtaposition as co-equal expressions, the first is inferred to be false as well.

(19) (a) *Can you pass me the wine list, please?*

(b) *You can't get that open?*

(c) *Bush is wise, informed, and intellectually honest. And I'm the president of Iraq.*

Although these phenomena usually are considered pragmatic rather than semantic, cognitive grammar regards the distinction as a matter of degree rather than absolute. A pattern is semantic (as well as pragmatic) to the extent that it is psychologically entrenched and conventionally established. As standard patterns used in speaking and understanding, reflected in the form of expressions and required for

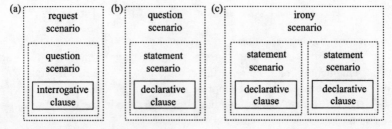

Figure 2.10 Embedding of Speech Act Scenarios

their semantic coherence, it seems to me that such phenomena can be excluded from what we call the "language" or "linguistic system" only arbitrarily.

Be that as it may, the examples in (19) also can be described in terms of fictivity. With respect to sentence (19)(a), for instance, we can say that the speaker's apparent enactment of the question scenario proves to be only apparent when it is construed in relation to the pattern overall. The act of questioning is subordinated to the act of requesting, so sentence (19)(a) is taken as expressing a desire for the wine list, not a genuine desire for information. (This construal continues with the answer: *Yes* or *Of course* indicates not the ability to pass the wine list but that the request is being granted.) More obviously, with the first sentence in (19)(c) the speaker merely pretends to make a valid statement. This fiction continues with the second sentence—where, however, the conflict with acknowledged reality is so obvious that the true intent is revealed.

Language use is replete with subtle interactive fictions, so frequently and easily used that we are hardly aware of them. The pattern in figure 2.10(c) is a special case of the fictive enactment of speech-act scenarios for ironic purposes. Examples like those in (20) are so prevalent that in some circumstances they almost amount to the default means of expression. If I do something ill-advised, I am more likely to utter sentence (20)(a) than to explicitly describe the move as stupid. In the context, a pretend assertion of its brilliance is not mistaken for an actual assertion; instead, it makes its stupidity stand out in sharp relief. Similarly, when time obviously is short we can heighten the sense of urgency by fictively asserting its absence. In sentence (20)(b), we invoke a situation in which the hearer's current pace would be appropriate, thereby providing a reference point for assessing how far the actual situation deviates from it. This mental construction provides the basis for inferring the extent to which the current pace is deemed inappropriate. The false profession of shock in sentence (20)(c) is comparable. It invokes a less imperfect world in which shock, rather than jaded acceptance, would be the actual reaction to the lying. This fiction, as well as the obviousness of its fictiveness, highlights the extent to which the actual world departs from our ideals.

(20) (a) *That was a brilliant move.*

(b) *Don't rush—we have all the time in the world.*

(c) *I'm shocked—absolutely shocked—that he would lie to us.*

As a final example, we might consider some alternate ways of giving an order:

(21) (a) *Shred those documents!*

(b) *You shred those documents!*

(c) *I (hereby) order you to shred those documents.*

(d) *I'm (hereby) ordering you to shred those documents.*

(e) *I regret that I must (hereby) order you to shred those documents.*

The first three patterns are ways of giving an order directly. They all constitute enactments of the order scenario, the idealized cultural model supporting the prototypical meanings of the verb *order* and imperative clauses. In true enactments

of the scenario, the actual speaker, addressee, and speech event are strongly identified with the fictive ones the scenario incorporates. The patterns differ with regard
to how much of this interaction is put onstage and explicitly coded, as opposed to
being left implicit as part of the supporting conceptual substrate. The difference between sentences (21)(a) and (21)(b) is that the former construes the addressee primarily as an interlocutor (typically not expressed), whereas the latter construes the
addressee primarily as an agent (expressed as clausal subject). This conception of
the addressee as an "other" that needs to be explicitly mentioned generally translates
into greater imperative force. The performative in sentence (21)(c) goes one step
further by putting the entire interaction onstage as the profiled clausal process. By
being fully explicit about the nature of the interaction, it lends itself to description as
being "formal," "official," or "contractual." Explicit mention of the speech act
makes possible the use of *hereby*—a legalistic term that specifies that the act in
question is carried out by the utterance itself.

True performatives, such as sentence (21)(c), occur in the simple present tense.
What, then, do we make of the progressive in sentence (21)(d)? The possibility of using *hereby* indicates that the sentence itself constitutes the giving of an order. I suggest, however, that the imperative force is softened somewhat by being cast in the
form of a description. The construction represents a kind of blend, in which the
speaker engages in the fiction of merely describing an act of ordering rather than performing it; hence the progressive—just as in (22), the true description of an ongoing
event. Blended with the fiction of merely describing the act, however, is the reality of
it actually being used to convey the order—hence the possibility of *hereby*.

(22) *She is ordering him to shred the documents.*

The fiction of mere description is more evident in sentence (21)(e), in which the
clause with *order* contains a modal and functions as a complement to the verb *regret*.
Nevertheless, this grammatical subordination does not prevent the speaker, the addressee, and their interaction from being identified with those invoked as part of the
speech-act scenario coded by *order*. Their identification is responsible for interpretation of the expression as an actual enactment of the order scenario, despite its grammatical form.

The account I offer in terms of fictive scenarios does not necessarily conflict
with other approaches that are based on notions such as politeness, face, relevance,
or implicature. I do not deny, for example, that expressions such as sentence (19)(a)
represent a politeness strategy: The force of making a direct request is softened by
posing it in the form of a question. Likewise, the force of giving an order is softened
by disguising it as a mere description. The implicit social reasoning behind such
strategies is part of the overall characterization of the patterns. The notion of fictive
scenarios does provide a link, however, to a wide range of other phenomena, only a
few of which I have examined here. They span traditional dichotomies such as lexicon and grammar, semantics and pragmatics, structure and use, and individual expressions and connected discourse. This suggests the wisdom of a unified approach
to these varied domains, as contemplated in cognitive grammar and cognitive linguistics generally.

What about pedagogical implications? Given my lack of experience in language teaching, I hesitate to make any specific suggestions. If the descriptive notions I propose seem appropriate and revelatory, they are pedagogically relevant at least in the sense of offering a new and radically different perspective on the nature of linguistic structure, linguistic meaning, and the conceptualizations they embody and reflect. They would seem most relevant for advanced instruction, as a way of elucidating the conceptual basis for standard modes of expression that initially may be opaque because they rest on implicit mental constructions. I wonder, however, whether explicit instruction actually is needed. The conceptual factors involved—such as blending, scanning, fictivity, and imagined scenarios—are basic, prevalent, and presumably universal. Mere exposure to the patterns may be enough for learners to grasp what is going on and learn to use them, with no need for analysis or reflective awareness of their basis. Hence, the role of the analyses I propose may be limited to guiding the instructor in making sure that students have sufficient exposure to representative examples. On the other hand, I can imagine that explicit awareness of these conceptual phenomena might lead to more thorough learning and greater ability to exploit them productively. Such awareness also would be educationally valuable in its own right, as insight into the nature of language and cognition. I leave these matters to the experts, however.

REFERENCES

Achard, Michel, and Susanne Niemeier, eds. 2004. *Cognitive linguistics, second language acquisition, and foreign language teaching*. Berlin: de Gruyter.

Austin, J. L. 1962. *How to do things with words*. Cambridge, Mass.: Harvard University Press.

Barcelona, Antonio. 2004. Metonymy in discourse-pragmatic inferencing. In *Linguagem, cultura e cognição: Estudos de linguística cognitiva*, vol. 2, ed. Augusto Soares da Silva, Amadeu Torres, and Miguel Gonçalves. Coimbra, Portugal: Almedina, 159–74.

Barsalou, Lawrence W. 1999. Perceptual symbol systems. *Behavioral and Brain Sciences* 22:577–660.

Croft, William. 2001. *Radical construction grammar: Syntactic theory in typological perspective*. Oxford: Oxford University Press.

Fauconnier, Gilles. 1985. *Mental spaces: Aspects of meaning construction in natural language*. Cambridge, Mass.: MIT Press.

———. 1997. *Mappings in thought and language*. Cambridge: Cambridge University Press.

Fauconnier, Gilles, and Eve Sweetser, eds. 1996. *Spaces, worlds, and grammar*. Chicago: University of Chicago Press.

Fauconnier, Gilles, and Mark Turner. 1998. Conceptual integration networks. *Cognitive Science* 22:133–87.

———. 2002. *The way we think: Conceptual blending and the mind's hidden complexities*. New York: Basic Books.

Fillmore, Charles J., Paul Kay, and Mary Catherine O'Connor. 1988. Regularity and idiomaticity in grammatical constructions: The case of *let alone*. *Language* 64:501–38.

Goldberg, Adele E. 1995. *Constructions: A construction grammar approach to argument structure*. Chicago: University of Chicago Press.

Goldsmith, John, and Erich Woisetschlaeger. 1982. The logic of the English progressive. *Linguistic Inquiry* 13:79–89.

Johnson, Mark. 1987. *The body in the mind: The bodily basis of meaning, imagination, and reason*. Chicago: University of Chicago Press.

Johnson-Laird, Philip N. 1983. *Mental models*. Cambridge, Mass.: Harvard University Press.

Kövecses, Zoltán, and Günter Radden. 1998. Metonymy: Developing a cognitive linguistic view. *Cognitive Linguistics* 9:33–77.

Lakoff, George. 1987. *Women, fire, and dangerous things: What categories reveal about the mind*. Chicago: University of Chicago Press.

————. 1990. The invariance hypothesis: Is abstract reason based on image-schemas? *Cognitive Linguistics* 1:39–74.

Lakoff, George, and Mark Johnson. 1980. *Metaphors we live by*. Chicago: University of Chicago Press.

————. 1999. *Philosophy in the flesh: The embodied mind and its challenge to western thought*. New York: Basic Books.

Lakoff, George, and Rafael E. Núñez. 2000. *Where mathematics comes from: How the embodied mind brings mathematics into being*. New York: Basic Books.

Langacker, Ronald W. 1984. Active zones. *Proceedings of the Annual Meeting of the Berkeley Linguistics Society* 10:172–88.

————. 1986. Abstract motion. *Proceedings of the Annual Meeting of the Berkeley Linguistics Society* 12:455–71.

————. 1987. *Foundations of cognitive grammar*, vol. 1, *Theoretical prerequisites*. Stanford, Calif.: Stanford University Press.

————. 1990. *Concept, image, and symbol: The cognitive basis of grammar*. Berlin: de Gruyter.

————. 1991. *Foundations of cognitive grammar*, vol. 2, *Descriptive application*. Stanford, Calif.: Stanford University Press.

————. 1997. Generics and habituals. In *On conditionals again,* ed. Angeliki Athanasiadou and René Dirven. Amsterdam/Philadelphia: John Benjamins, 191–222.

————. 1999a. *Grammar and conceptualization*. Berlin: de Gruyter.

————. 1999b. Virtual reality. *Studies in the Linguistic Sciences* 29, no. 2:77–103.

————. 1999c. Losing control: Grammaticization, subjectification, and transparency. In *Historical semantics and cognition,* ed. Andreas Blank and Peter Koch. Berlin: de Gruyter, 147–75.

————. 2001a. Dynamicity in grammar. *Axiomathes* 12:7–33.

————. 2001b. The English present tense. *English Language and Linguistics* 5:251–71.

————. 2003. Dynamicity, fictivity, and scanning: The imaginative basis of logic and linguistic meaning. *Korean Linguistics* 18:1–64.

————. 2004a. Metonymy in grammar. *Journal of Foreign Languages* 6:2–24.

————. 2004b. Possession, location, and existence. In *Linguagem, cultura e cogniçáo: Estudios de linguística cognitiva,* vol. 1, ed. Augusto Soares da Silva, Amadeu Torres, and Miguel Gonçalves. Coimbra, Portugal: Almedina, 85–120.

————. 2004c. Aspects of the grammar of finite clauses. In *Language, culture and mind,* ed. Michel Achard and Suzanne Kemmer. Stanford, Calif.: CSLI Publications, 535–77.

————. 2005. Construction grammars: Cognitive, radical, and less so. In *Cognitive linguistics: Internal dynamics and interdisciplinary interaction,* ed. Francisco J. Ruiz de Mendoza Ibáñez and M. Sandra Peña Cervel. Berlin: de Gruyter, 101–59

Matlock, Teenie. 2001. *How real is fictive motion?* Ph.D. diss., University of California, Santa Cruz.

Matlock, Teenie, Michael Ramscar, and Lera Boroditsky. 2004. The experiential basis of motion language. In *Linguagem, cultura e cogniçáo: Estudios de linguística cognitiva,* vol. 2, ed. Augusto Soares da Silva, Amadeu Torres, and Miguel Gonçalves. Coimbra, Portugal: Almedina, 43–57.

Matlock, Teenie, and Daniel C. Richardson. 2004. Do eye movements go with fictive motion? *Proceedings of the Annual Conference of the Cognitive Science Society* 26:909–14.

Matsumoto, Yo. 1996. Subjective-change expressions in Japanese and their cognitive and linguistic bases. In *Spaces, worlds, and grammar,* ed. Gilles Fauconnier and Eve Sweetser. Chicago: University of Chicago Press, 124–56.

————. 1997. Linguistic evidence for subjective (fictive) motion. In *The locus of meaning: Papers in honor of Yoshihiko Ikegami,* ed. Kei Yamanaka and Toshio Ohori. Tokyo: Kuroshio, 209–20.

Panther, Klaus-Uwe, and Günter Radden, eds. 2004. *Metonymy in language and thought*. Amsterdam/Philadelphia: John Benjamins.

Pütz, Martin, Susanne Niemeier, and René Dirven, eds. 2001a. *Applied cognitive linguistics I: Theory and language acquisition*. Berlin: de Gruyter.

————, eds. 2001b. *Applied cognitive linguistics II: Language pedagogy.* Berlin: de Gruyter.

Reddy, Michael J. 1979. The conduit metaphor—A case of frame conflict in our language about language. In *Metaphor and thought,* ed. Andrew Ortony. Cambridge: Cambridge University Press, 284–324.

Searle, John R. 1969. *Speech acts: An essay in the philosophy of language.* Cambridge: Cambridge University Press.

Sweetser, Eve. 1996. Mental spaces and the grammar of conditional constructions. In *Spaces, worlds, and grammar,* ed. Gilles Fauconnier and Eve Sweetser. Chicago: University of Chicago Press, 318–33.

————. 1997. Role and individual interpretations of change predicates. In *Language and conceptualization,* ed. Jan Nuyts and Eric Pederson. Cambridge: Cambridge University Press, 116–36.

Talmy, Leonard. 1988. The relation of grammar to cognition. In *Topics in cognitive linguistics,* ed. Brygida Rudzka-Ostyn. Amsterdam/Philadelphia: John Benjamins, 165–205.

————. 1996. Fictive motion in language and "ception." In *Language and space,* ed. Paul Bloom, Mary A. Peterson, Lynn Nadel, and Merrill F. Garrett. Cambridge, Mass., and London: MIT Press, 211–76.

Traugott, Elizabeth Closs. 1989. On the rise of epistemic meanings in English: An example of subjectification in semantic change. *Language* 65:31–55.

Turner, Mark. 1987. *Death is the mother of beauty: Mind, metaphor, criticism.* Chicago: University of Chicago Press.

3

The Impact of Grammatical Temporal Categories on Ultimate Attainment in L2 Learning

CHRISTIANE VON STUTTERHEIM AND MARY CARROLL
University of Heidelberg

FOREIGN LANGUAGE TEACHERS are familiar with the following experience of reading a paper written by a very advanced non-native speaker: Although it is impossible to point to a single lexical or grammatical error, information flow in the paper somehow does not meet expectations. In most of these cases, even describing what is unusual about the text is difficult—other than noting that native speakers do not write or speak like this. Is there something systematic in these manifestations of subtle inconsistencies that we might trace to the structure of the language itself? When speakers of different languages face a communicative task that requires production of a coherent text—as in the case of a narrative, a description, or a set of directives—are they guided in language-specific terms in the selection, organization, and expression of relevant information? If so, at what level in the process of language production do these inconsistencies occur—at the stage of conceptual planning, at the level at which concrete lexical or grammatical devices are selected, or at both? In Levelt's terms (1989, 1999), can we expect language specificity to play a role already within the *conceptualizer* or within the *formulator* only? Furthermore, can answers to these questions help us in understanding the specific problems that very advanced learners encounter in construing coherent texts?

Questions of this sort were the incentive behind a long-term research project at the University of Heidelberg, carried out in cooperation with several research groups at other European universities.[1] This project focuses on cross-linguistic differences in text production in standard as well as very advanced learner languages. Studies carried out within this frame have combined linguistic methods, including qualitative and interpretative corpus analysis, with psycholinguistic experiments that encompass chronometrical methods and eye-tracking studies. To date, these methods have not been systematically applied in second language acquisition research. The languages studied in this context have included Semitic (Modern Standard Arabic), Germanic (English, German, Dutch, Norwegian), and Romance languages (French, Italian, Spanish), as well as several learner languages both within and across these language groups (see Carroll and Lambert 2003; Carroll, von Stutterheim, and Nüse

2004). The gist of the findings is that information organization in language production follows distinct patterns that correlate with typological differences. More specifically, principles of information organization are perspective driven and are linked to patterns of grammaticization in the respective language.

In the context of these studies, we assume that to convey meaning through language, speakers have not only acquired a set of lexicogrammatical elements, they also have discovered the principles whereby representations of states of affairs typically are paired with certain lexicogrammatical structures that languages provide. The principles in question allow speakers to organize and shape the flow of information in context with respect to a given communicative goal. Language users learn to establish a conceptual framework that guides the kinds of decisions required in anchoring what is to be expressed in the domain of discourse. In particular, this framework means setting up the required viewpoints from which the material at issue will be presented for expression—for example, specification of a spatiotemporal frame, segmentation, topic focus assignment, or selection of a linearization principle. In this sense, the information at issue is transformed into units that can be expressed in a given context.

Against this background, the question of whether very advanced learners are able to discover these principles of construing what one might call "reportable content" in a foreign language—and, if so, how—is challenging. Do they identify the implications of specific grammatical means in the L2 for information organization—just as they do in L1 acquisition and use—or do they continue to rely on the principles of their respective L1?

In this essay we address these questions by looking at one specific domain—the conceptual domain of event construal—as the empirical basis for comparison and within that domain the grammatical feature of verbal aspect. We first present evidence for the interrelation between grammaticized means and specific principles of information organization by analyzing the language production of speakers from languages that differ in the way in which aspectual distinctions are coded. In the second part of this essay we investigate learner languages with respect to learning problems related to construction of meaning and selection of temporal perspective.

Background: Contrastive Text Analysis

The starting point of our research was an observation Carroll (1993) and Klein and von Stutterheim (1989) made in analyzing English and German texts of different genres: (re)narrations, descriptions, and directives. The analyses revealed significant differences in the way speakers of the two languages construed a coherent stretch of discourse. These differences relate to the domains selected for establishing coherence at the microstructural as well as the macrostructural level and can be linked to grammaticized means in the two languages.

Consider, for example, film retellings. The main tasks for the narrator lie in segmenting and selecting information stored in memory, anchoring information referentially, and connecting the events depicted in temporal terms. Each event will have to be represented by a dynamic predicate and its arguments. Starting with event structure, the situation referred to may be viewed, for example, as composed of three phases: an onset phase, an intermediate phase or nucleus, and an endphase or point of closure. In addition to event structure (which may or may not take the form described), there is the concept of a timeline that is structured as an abstract sequence of intervals. In linking these elements, speakers not only have to decide on a specific anchoring point, which will allow them to link the "substance" to the timeline at the level of the single event; they also must decide how events linked in this way should be related to each other. All of these components form part of the "referential frame" that is structured with respect to a set perspective. This fixed perspective ensures that the type of information that is mapped into the different units making up a proposition can be linked in a coherent form. In other words, perspective-taking allows coherent integration and interrelation of principles that guide selection of units at the microstructural level and principles of information flow at the macrostructural level.

Given different options for construing the flow of information, the question is whether speakers of different languages prefer one set of options over another. We do not detail here the analyses of the film renarrations (for details, see Carroll and von Stutterheim 2003; von Stutterheim and Lambert 2005; and chapter 4 in this volume);[2] instead we provide a summary of the findings to serve as background for the studies we do present here. For English and German speakers, the analyses show significant cross-linguistic differences in film re-narrations with regard to the events selected for mention and, within identical events, with regard to different aspects of the situation (see von Stutterheim and Nüse 2003). The basis for these differences resides in the perspective taken: German speakers present events holistically—that is, events are represented as bounded, with an endpoint or a resultant state—whereas English speakers select a temporal perspective that incorporates ongoing events. In contrast to the German texts, in English many events are presented as unbounded, as evidenced in patterns of information selection. With respect to patterns of coherence, German speakers tend to segment complex dynamic situations into a set of events that are presented as occurring in sequence on the basis of the temporal relation y after x, which is established by explicitly linking the current time span or "topic time" to the preceding time of situation (for details see Klein 1994). Thus, the reference point provided by the preceding time of situation involves a bounded event.

In other words, this linking strategy requires a holistic view of events and entails expression of points of completion or the results of an event. A bounded event creates a "post time"—and with it the conditions for opening up a new interval on the timeline (temporal shift). Temporal shift therefore entails a sequence in strict terms (situation x is completed before y begins) and is coded by expressions such as *dann* (then), which relate to the post time of a preceding event (anaphoric relation). This perspective follows the event line from within—as a participant, as it were. In film retellings in English, on the other hand, speakers typically represent the narrative sequence by linking the current time span—the topic time—to the time of utterance, not to the preceding time of situation. The relevant relation is a relation of inclusion because the time of situation includes the topic time and overlaps with the time of utterance, given by a deictically anchored "now." A deictic point of view (external viewpoint) allows speakers to anchor events that are ongoing; in this temporal frame there is no need for one event to be represented as completed or bounded before another one is introduced. The actual sequence often is implicit, and speakers also exploit other means—such as causal relations (x leads to y)—to show how events proceed (for details, see Carroll and von Stutterheim 2003; von Stutterheim, Carroll, and Klein 2003; von Stutterheim and Lambert 2005; and chapter 4 in this volume). Table 3.1 gives the number of bounded events as an indicator of the differences found in film re-narrations.

Why, however, should speakers of different languages rely on different principles of perspective-taking in solving the same communicative task? Although the differences between the two groups of subjects are related to the variable "native language," language as an abstract system may not be the only factor responsible for the differences at issue. After all, nothing in English *grammar* prohibits mentioning endpoints, nor is German lacking in means for referring to the notion of ongoingness (e.g., lexicalized means such as *dabei sein etwas zu tun*, "there-at be something to do," are available). Aside from the influence of grammaticized means, there may be a variety of possible nonlinguistic causes for the differences, ranging from individual stylistic differences or different learning traditions in constructing a text to deeply rooted cultural differences of various kinds.

To address the question of cultural differences, the study includes a group of speakers with a clearly different cultural tradition—namely, speakers of Arabic. Modern Standard Arabic (MSA) shares the critical grammatical feature of verbal aspect with English; in that regard, both languages contrast with German. If the construal of events in Arabic followed patterns other than those observed for English speakers, the result would support an explanation that relates contrasts to cultural tradition. If events were represented in similar terms in Arabic and English, however, the result would underscore structural linguistic factors. Given the results for the three languages, we can conclude that differences in construing event-time relations in narrative contexts are rooted in structural differences between the languages, with temporal morphology as the "trigger."

As it turns out, this posited co-relation was supported by another study that included speakers of Norwegian—a language that is similar to German with respect to verbal morphology. The results for Norwegian re-narrations were very similar to those for German speakers with respect to information selection, perspective-taking, and temporal linkage—underlining the hypothesis that grammaticized conceptual categories play a predominant role in how conceptual material is organized for verbalization. That factor previously had been attested cross-linguistically for spatial descriptions (Carroll 1997; Carroll et al. 2000). We further tested this hypothesis,

Table 3.1
Bounded versus Unbounded Events

	No. of propositions	Bounded (%)
L1 English	2,206	27.4
L1 German	2,189	51.4

Note: Numbers do not include utterances with inchoative aspect (e.g., *he starts*), modals (e.g., *he wants*), and states.

which runs counter to the widespread universalist position in cognitive linguistics and psycholinguistic research in language production, with a series of more controlled studies in which speakers of different languages were asked to verbalize a series of decontextualized individual events, presented as film clips.

Verbalization of Individual Events in L1

Reflecting the results of the text production studies, the languages we selected for further investigation had to exhibit structural contrasts that are relevant for the domain of event construal. Tense-aspect-systems seem to be crucial in this respect. Table 3.2 summarizes the temporal morphological means of the languages we studied for the present tense.

The Endpoint Study

The design of the empirical study was as follows. Subjects (twenty speakers per language) saw a series of individual situations (eighty items). These situations were presented in film clips that mainly depicted the initial or intermediate phases (or both) of a dynamic situation; the stage at which a possible endpoint was reached was not shown. Speakers were asked to tell what was happening and to verbalize the event as soon as they recognized what was going on. Their responses were audiotaped and transcribed.

The present tense is the preferred tense and is used across all languages studied. The following examples illustrate the individual situations described in the data.

	English	German
– endpoint	*a car is driving along a country road*	*ein Auto fährt auf einer Landstraße*
– effected object	*a man is painting*	*jemand malt*
+ endpoint	*a car is driving along a country road toward a house*	*ein Auto fährt auf einer Landstraße zu einem Haus*
+ effected object	*a man is painting a picture*	*ein Mann malt irgendwas*

Table 3.3 lists the frequency with which endpoints are mentioned across the four languages. Of the eighty situations shown, eighteen could be conceptualized as bounded; they form the basis of the analysis.

▓ Table 3.2
Language Overview

Morphological Tense and Aspect Features (x)		**Modern Standard Arabic (MSA)**	English	Norwegian	German
Tense		[periphrastic]	x	x	x
Aspect	Imperfective	x	x	[serial verbs]	[lexical]
	Perfective	x	—	—	—

Table 3.3
Percentage of Cases in which Endpoints Are Mentioned (averaged over 20 subjects per group, 18 items)

L1 German	L1 Norwegian	L1 English	L1 Arabic (MSA)
76.4	69.8	25.2	23.8

Note: Both types of event closures are plotted together: literal endpoints in terms of goal information in a motion event, and results of actions that imply a change in state (either for the subject or the object) and thereby closure of the causative action.

Our focus on dynamic scenes that mainly depict initial and intermediate phases of an event was intentional in that it allowed us to investigate two issues. First, speakers of languages in which phasal decomposition is grammaticized, such as Arabic and English, in theory could refer to any one phase; the question was whether they actually would do so. Second, for German speakers the absence of scenes that depicted an endpoint pushed the preferences observed in the re-narrations to the limits; in their case, the question was whether the focus on endpoints would lead them to scan the visual input for likely (or even less likely) endpoints in dynamic scenes in which no endpoint is actually shown.

We can interpret the results as a confirmation of the initial hypothesis. In the languages in which phasal decomposition is grammaticized—in this case, Arabic and English—speakers related to the phases of the events that were depicted in the scene. As we have noted, the majority of the scenes we selected depict either the beginning or an intermediate phase of an event, and verbalizations related to these phases were less likely to include an endpoint. In both languages, speakers used the aspectually marked form—that is, the progressive (English) and imperfective (MSA). By contrast, the nonaspect languages, Norwegian and German, cluster together, in that speakers construe events under a holistic perspective. Endpoints are expressed, even if they have to be inferred or invented.

Speech Onset Times: Time Course of Production

Because analyses of linguistic *products* do not allow for conclusions with respect to language-related differences in *processing*, other methods are required to gain insights into the planning phase—that is, the conceptualization phase in speech production. To measure speech onset times, we adopted a psycholinguistic tool that allows for tracking of differences that reflect the cognitive load involved in a verbal task.

Our hypothesis is as follows. Speech production data show that what constitutes *a reportable event* differs in accordance with the linguistic system. If language-specific principles are already at work at the level of conceptualization, one could expect a time effect, depending on the different requirements for information selection. For German and Norwegian speakers, having to include an endpoint to form a reportable event would mean that they could either start speaking before they have all relevant information about the final phase of the event depicted or they could wait until the endpoint of an action or an activity could be identified and then start with speech production. For the English and Arabic speakers, the temporal properties of the scenes presented would have different implications for the planning process because they encode the initial or intermediate phase, as depicted in the film clip. This pattern can be attributed to the fact that any phase of an event is a reportable unit in languages in which phasal decomposition is grammaticized. In other words, speakers of English or Arabic do not need to construe a final phase or endpoint to have a reportable unit. Therefore, if language-specific constraints already drive processes at the level of conceptual planning, we can expect a delay in speech onset times for German and Norwegian speakers, relative to Arabic and English speakers, in cases in which the endpoint of an action is not immediately evident in the visual input. We analyzed the same data that formed the basis for the endpoint study we describe above for speech onset times with German and English speakers. Our results indicate speech onset times of 4.6 seconds for L1 German and 3.5 seconds for L1 English.

An item-based analysis of the types of events represented in relation to the pattern of speech onset times (SOT) revealed that German speakers waited for an endpoint in situations in which the endpoint cannot be easily inferred or cannot be inferred at all. We observed significant cross-linguistic differences in relation to these items (*cf.* comparison to learner languages below).

The results confirm the findings in the analyses of the verbal productions: To conceptualize what can function as a reportable event, German speakers show a clear preference for a holistic perspective, which implies having to wait before speaking until the scene as a whole has unfolded. By contrast, because any phase of a motion event constitutes a reportable unit (taking the scenes presented) for speakers of English, these speakers can relate to the initial or intermediate phase of a situation, such as *a boat is sinking* or *a boy is running,* without having to wait for a possible outcome.

Eye Tracker Study

In the search for a window into planning processes in the phase of preverbal conceptualization—that is, in organizing information for expression—these results prompted another psycholinguistic experiment, using the method of eye tracking with the same stimuli. Although the study is still in progress, the results show significant processing differences for speakers of languages that code aspect grammatically relative to speakers of languages with lexical means.

The hypothesis underlying the eye tracking study is as follows. In dynamic scenes that show goal-oriented motion events—a person or thing on its way from one place to another—German speakers can be expected to scan the scene for the endpoints of such events. Furthermore, they may search the scene for possible candidates when an endpoint is not immediately evident. Because speakers of English typically code the initial or intermediate phase of the respective event, they can be expected not to fixate regions at which possible endpoints could be identified to the same extent as German speakers do. Again, we selected eighteen scenes from a set of eighty items as test items. These eighteen scenes depicted goal-oriented motion events in which the goal was not reached but could be inferred or construed. An example is a car driving down a country lane that goes past a farmhouse; the farmhouse is in the background of the scene depicted, so speakers can wait while they consider the farmhouse as a possible endpoint.

To determine whether subjects look at endpoints before they start speaking and, thus, before they finish planning the first part of the utterance or whether they attend to endpoints only while they already are articulating the first part of the clause and then possibly producing the corresponding locative prepositional phrase, we distinguish between fixations *before* and fixations *after* speech onset (SO). Subjects started speaking before the film clips ended, so fixations after speech onset were always possible. Table 3.4 gives the results for the two language groups.[3]

With regard to fixation before SO, we found that German speakers focus on the endpoint of an action before they start to speak, whereas English speakers start to speak before they look at this particular region. This finding indicates that in conceptualizing content to form a verbal representation of the scene depicted, German speakers attend to other—in this case, more—components of the visual input relative to English speakers.

Why is there such a pronounced difference between fixations before and after SO for the English group? English speakers apparently start to speak before they focus on the endpoint. This finding can be linked to the fact that events that are treated as ongoing have been decomposed into phases (inchoative, intermediate, and terminative phase). Thus, any phase of an event, as depicted in the stimuli at issue here, is a reportable unit in itself. Significantly, these speakers can conjoin one phase with another so that the encoding of the final phase with an additional verbalization of an endpoint can occur thereafter: *A car is going along the road . . . to the station* clearly is possible in English.[4] As with SO, the underlying phasal structure can explain why English speakers—in contrast to speakers of German—do not have to scan the scene for an endpoint to arrive at a conceptual unit that corresponds to a reportable event. The eye tracking results show, however, that in the course of the scanning process these speakers visually control for possible endpoints. Speakers can add the terminative phase and easily integrate it into the sentence that is already underway: *a car is going down a lane . . . to a farmhouse*. Although the findings are tentative, the results point to a language-specific effect at the level of conceptualization.

Information Organization in Advanced Learner Languages

These findings open new aspects and foreground longstanding questions for L2 acquisition research. Can we find support for our claim that linguistic knowledge not only covers lexicon, syntax, morphology, and phonology but also encompasses a

Table 3.4
Number of Fixations of Endpoints before and after Speech Onset (SO)

	L1 German	L1 English
Fixations before SO	6.9	2.9
Fixations after SO	9.5	8.5

specific set of principles of information organization? Are these principles particularly difficult to detect and acquire, resulting in problems that are related not so much to form as to factors governing their use? Might some problems of ultimate attainment—such as the subtle inconsistencies mentioned in the introduction to this essay—find an explanation in this context? To address these questions, we extended the foregoing empirical studies to very advanced learners. We used the same type of stimuli and elicitation method to carry out production experiments with learners of German and English, with the other language as the respective L1. The results for film re-narrations are reported in detail elsewhere (see Carroll and von Stutterheim 2003; von Stutterheim and Lambert 2005; and chapter 4 in this volume). In the following analyses, we again focus on patterns of event construal with respect to the category of boundedness.

Verbalization of Individual Events

In the first study, twenty advanced English learners of German and twenty advanced German learners of English were shown the eighty short scenes on a monitor and asked to tell "what is happening."[5] As in the L1 study, the analyses of endpoints were based on eighteen relevant items where an endpoint could be mentioned. Table 3.5 lists the percentage of endpoints mentioned for twenty speakers for these items; L1 results are repeated for comparison.

Broadly speaking, both learner groups are moving toward the target language norm. As the results indicate, however, this trend holds to a lesser degree for English learners of German than for their German counterparts. In other words, for the domain of events, learners of English seem to acquire the underlying linguistic knowledge associated with a form such as the progressive more easily, compared to the holistic perspective required of learners of German. Further data analysis, however, reveals a noteworthy additional difference. Data analysis of the German learners of English shows that references to an endpoint are omitted in scenes where the endpoint can be inferred—that is, where it is implicitly given. By contrast, where endpoints cannot be inferred, German learners of English tend to mention them. This finding brings us back to the principal difference between English and German: Speakers of German will wait to uncover the endpoint in cases where it is not evident, thereby allowing conceptualization of the situation in holistic terms; speakers of English do so to a significantly lesser degree because any phase is reportable.

To specify the differences even more closely, we carried out a more fine-grained analysis. In light of the preceding results, we divided the items into two groups: those in which the endpoint of the events depicted was inferable—in the sense of being highly predictable—and those where this was not the case. Two examples illustrate the distinction:

(a) Inferable endpoint: a boy jumping off a cupboard **onto the floor**.
(b) Endpoint not easily inferred: a car driving along a country road that goes past **a house**.

Table 3.6 provides an overview of the results for scenes of category (a).

Table 3.5
Endpoints Mentioned (average values, in percent, for 20 speakers per group), L1 and L2

L1 English	L1German–L2English	L1 German	L1English–L2German
25.2	36.7	76.4	31.6

Table 3.6
Endpoints Inferable: Percentage of Cases in which Endpoints Are Mentioned (averaged over 20 subjects per group), L1 and L2

L1 German	L1English–L2German	L1 English	L1German–L2English
50.0	29.4	25.0	13.0

L1 German users show a clear tendency to mention endpoints in these cases, but German learners of English omit their mention almost completely. In keeping with the general pattern for English learners of German, the frequency with which the endpoint is mentioned does not differ markedly from that for English L1 speakers.

Comparison with items of the category (b), where endpoints are not easily inferred, revealed a clear cross-linguistic difference. German learners of English clearly relate to an endpoint in cases of this kind, as shown in table 3.7, whereas English learners of German do not mention endpoints in this case and thus do not proceed on the basis of target language principles of information organization.

Distribution of the endpoints specified shows that L1 principles remain dominant for advanced L2 learners when they are conceptualizing what is considered to be a reportable event. German learners of English omit reference to an endpoint in situations in which it can be easily inferred, and reference to this type of situation accounts for most of the cases in which endpoints were not mentioned; they do refer to endpoints, however, where these endpoints are not implied by the predicate used. The English learners of German have not uncovered the holistic pattern of construal in German by which events are viewed as bounded. For both learner groups, the L2 productions are in accordance with principles of event construal in their respective L1.

Speech Onset Times: Time Course of L2 Production
Findings with respect to SOT in the learner data also support the general tendency observed in the production data. Measuring SOT with the same stimuli selected for the L1 speakers, we again note a significant difference between the two learner groups. As table 3.8 shows, German speakers move toward the target language, whereas English speakers show the same patterns in both the L1 and the L2. These

Table 3.7
Endpoints *Not* Readily Inferable: Percentage of Cases in which Endpoints Are Mentioned (averaged over 20 subjects per group)

L1 English	L1German–L2English	L1 German	L1English–L2German
25.0	70.6	68.0	20.0

▨ Table 3.8
Speech Onset Times (seconds)

L1 German	L1German–L2English	L1 English	L1English–L2 German
4.3	3.0	3.6	3.8

findings support the general tendency observed to date, in that German speakers move toward the target language to a greater extent.

The results of this analysis of preferences in event construal in learner languages support the conclusion that even very advanced learners retain the principles of event construal of their L1 in certain functional contexts. The data show that speakers draw on preferences for construing meaning for speaking developed in the course of L1 acquisition to solve verbal tasks in the L2. Language-specific preferences in information organization can be traced to meanings that are grammaticized in the respective languages. A close interrelation between patterns of grammaticization and principles of information organization at the text level also has been attested in a cross-linguistic study with respect to other syntactic domains (role of syntactic subject) and other communicative tasks (spatial descriptions). Here too, grammatical features such as the syntactic subject, word order (verb-second constraint in main clauses in German, for example), and the morphosyntactic structure of spatial expressions could be shown to lead to language-specific patterns in information organization (see Carroll et al. 2000; see also chapter 4, this volume).

One particularly interesting result in the data lies in the differences between German and English L2 speakers in the domain selected for analysis. The data suggest that English learners of German are further away from the target language pattern, compared to German learners of English. In other words, even assuming that the formal features have been acquired, moving to the English pattern of use still seems easier than the other way around. This finding may be attributable to the fact that English has a salient grammatical form that encodes the specific perspective of ongoingness—the progressive. By acquiring this form, the learner of English is led to find the function served by this form. For the learner of German, by contrast, there is no device for the expression of "holisticness." In analyzing the input, learners have to identify this concept and its function on the basis of inference processes that will span different informational components in a sentence, such as complements or adjuncts. The differences in acquisition of target language principles may lie in the complexity of that process.

Conclusion

Analysis of how the languages we investigated cluster with respect to the features we investigated provides clear evidence for the assumption that grammaticized meanings play a crucial role in determining how speakers proceed in solving the manifold tasks in language production. Speakers of Arabic and English share the same grammaticized feature (progressive aspect, imperfectivity), which is crucial in event construal, and they follow similar principles in the tasks we studied in construing content for speaking. Speakers of English, MSA, German, and Norwegian organize information under different perspectives and these perspectives also correlate with grammaticized features of the languages in question. The differences we observed are significant for the language pairs English–German and MSA–German. Contrasts are manifested both in selection of aspects of a situation for explicit representation (components of factual knowledge left for inferencing, components left unspecified) and the way information selected for mention is structured. Our observations confirm the hypothesis that given different grammatical systems, speakers develop specific overarching principles in the construction of referential frames and hence the types of event-time relations they incorporate. These underlying principles allow for integration of structural requirements across different conceptual domains and ensure a high degree of coherence across the means selected.

One could argue that in the course of acquiring one's first language, acquisition of grammatical structures and lexical forms results in principles that determine how information organization proceeds in context. After a long process of elaboration of the basic system, lasting until the age of fourteen or fifteen, native speakers finally achieve full competence in organizing information not only at the sentence level but also with respect to macrostructural organization (Halm 2007). We can assume that this development results in a specific level of linguistic knowledge that consists of general principles or strategies that determine what counts as a reportable informational unit in a given context. Reliance on these principles of information organization provides speakers with a set of criteria that enables them to carry out the complex set of tasks in text production in a coherent fashion. We can regard these results as a specification of what Slobin (1991, 1996) has called "thinking for speaking."

Returning to the main question we outline at the beginning of this essay— namely, the nature of the final steps in acquisition—the data provide evidence that in adult L2 acquisition these principles are no longer "automatically" constructed on the basis of the relevant formal categories. Instead, L2 speakers, even at a very advanced stage, also draw on L1 principles in construing reportable content. Indeed, identification and activation in the production process of target language principles seem to be extremely difficult and pose a persistent problem in the L2 even at advanced stages. Reasons for that difficulty may lie in the fact that these principles are essential in the interpretation and conceptualization of reality. They are extremely powerful in that they are abstract enough to enable the speaker to treat all kinds of situations within a consistent conceptual framework. Inasmuch as the evidence required to construct this conceptual network comes from many domains, it presents a degree of complexity that L2 learners will find difficult to process. Taking all these aspects into account, we conclude that the central factor impeding the acquisitional process at advanced stages ultimately is grammatical in nature, in that learners have to uncover the role accorded to grammaticized meanings and what their presence, or absence, entails in information organization.

NOTES

We would like to thank the Deutsche Forschungsgemeinschaft for financing the project described in this chapter.

1. In addition to the authors, the Heidelberg group includes Barbara Schmiedtova, Abbassia Bouhaous, and Natasha Sahonenko; cross-linguistic research has been carried out in cooperation with Monique Lambert (University of Paris VIII), Marianna Starren (Katholieke Universiteit Nijmegen), and Bergljot Behrens (University of Oslo). The eye tracking study was carried out by a former project member, Ralf Nüse.

2. The film is a silent animation (11 minutes long) with the title *Quest* that tells the story of a clay figure who has to face several obstacles in five different worlds.

3. Eye tracking studies with Arabic speakers and advanced L2 learners currently are being carried out; results are not yet available.

4. This is not the case in Dutch, where the progressive can be described as on its way to grammaticalization. In Dutch the progressive is incompatible with endpoints *de trein is **naar de station** an het rijen*. Eye tracking results for Dutch underline this difference in that Dutch speakers do not look at endpoints after speech onset.

5. Determination of whether learners can be classified as advanced is based on formal proficiency and lexical repertoire for the German learners of English; the latter measure was assessed in relation to the lexical means used by native speakers of English (thirty-five speakers in all) in the same task. English learners of German are classified on the basis of formal accuracy in their L2 productions with respect to nominal and verbal morphology.

REFERENCES

Carroll, Mary. 1993. Deictic and intrinsic orientation in spatial descriptions: A comparison between English and German. In *Cognition and culture: A cross-cultural approach to cognitive psychology,* ed. Jeanette Altarriba. Amsterdam: North-Holland, 23–44.

————. 1997. Conceptualization of spatial relations. In *Language and conceptualization,* ed. Jan Nuyts and Eric Pederson. Cambridge: Cambridge University Press, 137–61.

Carroll, Mary, Christiane von Stutterheim, and Ralf Nüse. 2004. The language and thought debate: A psycholinguistic approach. In *Approaches to language production,* ed. Christopher Habel and Thomas Pechmann. Berlin: de Gruyter, 183–218.

Carroll, Mary, and Monique Lambert. 2003. Information structure in narratives and the role of grammaticised knowledge: A study of adult French and German learners of English. In *Information structure and the dynamics of language acquisition,* ed. Christine Dimroth and Marianne Starren. Amsterdam/Philadelphia: John Benjamins, 267–87.

Carroll, Mary, and Christiane von Stutterheim. 2003. Typology and information organisation: Perspective taking and language-specific effects in the construction of events. In *Typology and second language acquisition,* ed. Anna G. Ramat. Berlin: de Gruyter, 365–402.

Carroll, Mary, Jorge Murcia-Serra, Marzena Watorek, and Alessandra Bendiscioli. 2000. The relevance of information organization to second language acquisition studies: The descriptive discourse of advanced adult learners of German." *Studies in Second Language Acquisition* 22:441–66 (special issue, ed. Clive Perdue).

Halm, Ute. 2007. Zum Ausdruck temporaler Kategorien im Diskurs: Die Entwicklung narrativer Kompetenz in Filmnacherzählungen von Kindern zwischen 7 und 14 Jahren. Ph.D. diss., University of Heidelberg.

Klein, Wolfgang. 1994. *Time in language.* London: Routledge.

Klein, Wolfgang, and Christiane von Stutterheim. 1989. Referential movement in descriptive and narrative discourse. In *Language processing in social context,* ed. Rainer Dietrich and Carl Friedrich Graumann. Amsterdam/Philadelphia: John Benjamins, 39–76.

Levelt, Willem J. M. 1989. *Speaking: From intention to articulation.* Cambridge, Mass.: MIT Press.

————. 1999. Producing spoken language: A blueprint of the speaker. In *The neurocognition of language,* ed. Colin M. Brown and Peter Hagoort. Oxford: Oxford University Press, 83–122.

Slobin, Dan I. 1991. Learning to think for speaking: Native language, cognition and rhetorical style. *Pragmatics* 1:7–26.

———. 1996. From "thought and language" to "thinking for speaking." In *Rethinking linguistic relativity,* ed. John J. Gumperz and Stephen C. Levinson. Cambridge: Cambridge University Press, 70–96.

Stutterheim, Christiane von, and Monique Lambert. 2005. Crosslinguistic analysis of temporal perspectives in text production. In *The structure of learner varieties,* ed. Henriette Hendriks. Berlin: de Gruyter, 203–30.

Stutterheim, Christiane von, and Ralf Nüse. 2003. Processes of conceptualization in language production: Language-specific perspectives and event construal. *Linguistics* 41:851–81 (special issue: Perspectives in Language Production).

Stutterheim, Christiane von, Mary Carroll, and Wolfgang Klein. 2003. Two ways of construing complex temporal structures. In *Deictic conceptualization of space, time and person,* ed. Friedrich Lenz. Berlin: de Gruyter, 97–133.

4

Reorganizing Principles of Information Structure in Advanced L2s:
French and German Learners of English

MARY CARROLL AND MONIQUE LAMBERT
University of Heidelberg and University of Paris VIII

THE STUDY ON WHICH WE REPORT in this essay is part of a series of empirical investigations that focus on the nature of linguistic knowledge underlying text structure (von Stutterheim 1997; von Stutterheim and Klein 1989). By comparing French, English, German, and associated L2s cross-linguistically, it looks at the extent to which language-specific preferences in information structure are driven by grammaticized means. More specifically, it investigates the extent to which very advanced L2 learners apply the principles of information structure of their target language, as contrasted with their native language (L1), in producing stretches of connected discourse such as telling a story, giving route directions, or describing the layout of their home. We highlight three areas of study in both native and learner language use: the role of grammaticized means for expressing time-event relations, information selection, and management of entities in reference introduction and management. The extent to which differences exist should provide us with important information about the nature of text and information structuring; it also should illuminate the particular challenges very advanced L2 learners face in restructuring a complex linguistic system.

Text structure has been studied under expansive headings such as *macrostructural planning* or *mental models* (Garrod and Sanford 1988; Kintsch and van Dijk 1978; Ochs et al. 1992). This analysis also takes a global perspective in that it focuses on factors that determine information selection and information structure across related domains in narrative tasks. The underlying principles have a multidimensional complexity because information organization spans the conceptual domains of time, space, entities, and events. In a narrative task, information structure reflects the means speakers use to order events in sequence, as expressed by time-event relations. The larger question we pursued is this: How do adult L2 learners derive the appropriate structures from the input, and how do they learn to put this knowledge into practice?

Approaching information structure broadly and drawing on Levelt's (1996, 1999) model of text production, we characterize the decisions speakers are required to make in producing a text such as a film retelling in terms of breaking down the information flow given by an extended series of dynamic situations and organizing relevant information into units that are suited for linguistic expression. To link events in sequence, speakers must choose a temporal frame of reference—a core aspect of performing a narrative task. Specifically, events can be regarded as ongoing (*they are walking*), reaching a point of completion (*they walk to the bus stop*), or overlapping. As speakers retell the content of a film, they have to decide how events with different temporal structures can be related to form a sequence. In doing so, speakers set up a frame of reference that draws on concepts such as that of a timeline, with structuring principles that define how events can be treated in relational terms (see Klein 1994; von Stutterheim, Carroll, and Klein 2003). With regard to the domain of entities, the participants in the events, speakers must assign them informational status, in that entities can be mapped as subject of a main versus a subordinate clause. Finally, in reference maintenance the options range from reference to the entity by means of a full noun phrase or a pronoun all the way to zero anaphora.

Analyses of the contrasts in the selection, ordering, coding, and linking of information across different domains of reference show that information structure is language-dependent; that is, it correlates with the specific system of grammaticized means in the language. Concepts that are mapped into grammatical form in one language are coded lexically in another. This finding has consequences for both information selection (considering what to say) and information structure (see Carroll and Lambert 2003; Carroll, von Stutterheim, and Nüse 2004; von Stutterheim, Nüse, and Murcia-Serra 2002). For example, children acquiring English as a first language need to learn to mark whether an event is ongoing or not. This feature is acquired at an early age; two-thirds of all present tense forms at age three take progressive aspect (retelling based on a picture storybook). Berman and Slobin (1994) take this finding as suggesting that for young children, progressive aspect is treated as the basic way of describing events, which are construed as applying at the time of speaking. In German, by contrast, the first explicit morphological marker children acquire relates to the perfect tense (*gelaufen, gegangen*). Accordingly, the perfect also is the form used most frequently in the film retellings of six- to ten-year-old children, compared to the simple past (Praeteritum) (Halm 2007).

The fact that grammaticized concepts play a determining role in the organization of information for expression in a given language (Slobin 1991, 1996; Talmy 1988) can be expected to pose considerable challenges for adult learners in the acquisitional process in that they may fail to recognize the role that grammaticized means of the target language play in shaping information structure. The following questions further specify the nature of those challenges: At what level in language production do L2 learners' decisions regarding information structure compare with those of native speakers? Do they differ at the conceptual level, in selecting and organizing information (conceptualizer), or do they deviate at the level where the selection of linguistic forms is carried out (formulator)? Answers to these questions should shed light on the nature of the linguistic knowledge that may hinder or foster attainment of near-native levels of proficiency in the target language.

We can assume that the adult learners participating in the study know how to construct complex texts such as narratives. In a lengthy process in their L1, which continues well into puberty (age fifteen or sixteen), they have acquired a network of form-function relations and abstracted the relevant principles that guide information structure in their L1 (see Halm 2007; Hickmann 2005). Structuring principles of the respective source languages therefore could play a central role in the hypotheses L2 learners generate when they analyze the language they are learning (see Perdue 1993), particularly as they progress beyond the earliest stages of L2 development that Klein and Perdue (1997) have termed the Basic Variety. We describe the continuing development of the learner language in terms of processes of reorganization, during which speakers may implement knowledge associated with their L1 as part of the developing L2.

To investigate these issues one must be able to compare the information structure speakers choose in the same communicative task across the source and target languages and then analyze learners' productions for emerging differences. Specifically, with regard to the role of grammaticized meanings in determining information structure (for example, the role of a form such as –ing, which is marked morphologically on the verb in English to express an ongoing event), languages with a similar set of grammaticized means should show similar patterns in information selection and information structure for the same kind of task. The posited relation between grammaticized means and information structure enables formulation of testable hypotheses once languages have been analyzed for relevant structural similarities and contrasts.

The study we report here took such an approach. All speakers in the study were asked to carry out a film-retelling task, in which temporal information and the way it is structured play a key role. The target language (English) and source languages (French and German) vary in the means provided to code time-event relations. Beyond the present tense shared by the three languages, English offers means to code the concept of ongoingness morphologically on the verb; this coding is not possible in either French or German, in which these means are lexicalized rather than grammaticized. The three languages also differ with respect to structural features of the syntactic subject: English and French share a fixed position for the syntactic subject (subject-verb-object [SVO]), whereas in German word order in main clauses is determined by the "V2" constraint: Finite verb forms take up second position in main clauses and can be preceded by one constituent only.

Participants were asked to retell an eleven-minute silent film, *Quest*, that features a single protagonist, a clay figure, on a quest for water. In that search, which takes the figure from one hostile world to another (five in all), the figure is successively confronted with inanimate elements such as rocks, sand, wind, and papers. Each speaker first saw the film as a whole and then episode by episode, and both native speakers and learners were asked to tell "what happened." Although the elicitation question was formulated in the past tense, almost all speakers retold the story in the present tense. The analysis we present here is based on the first three episodes, which take place in a desert world, a paper world, and a stone world, respectively.

The database consists of twenty speakers for all three native groups (L1 German, L1 English, and L1 French), and the L2 pairings L1French–L2English and L1German–L2English. All informants, L1 and L2, were university students or individuals who have graduated from university. L2 learners had studied English at school for a period of eight to ten years; the majority majored in English at college and also spent at least one year in the target language environment. Advanced learner status was ascertained on the basis of command of formal features and lexical repertoire; the latter measure was assessed in relation to the lexical means used by native speakers of English (a total of thirty-five speakers) in the same task.

Frames of Reference for Time-Event Relations: The Role of Grammaticized Means

As we have noted, different languages provide different linguistic means for expressing time-event relations. To frame our subsequent discussion of the challenges L2 learners face, we first investigate how native speakers of English, German, and French realize these relations in native-language retellings. In so doing, we build on a set of studies that compared film retellings in different languages, some of which code the aspectual distinction for ongoingness morphologically on the verb (English, Modern Standard Arabic) whereas others (such as Dutch, French, and German) code it by lexical means. Particularly relevant for German and French learner languages of English is the fact that English speakers often view dynamic situations in the narrative sequence as ongoing, in contrast to speakers of French or German.

Time-Event Relations in Film Retellings by L1 English Speakers

For the English retellings we focus on the role grammaticized aspect, as given in the form *be* + *-ing*, plays in the construction of an underlying temporal frame of reference. For the narrative sequence, the majority of English speakers (75 percent) follow a deictic frame of reference in telling what happened first and what happened next in the film, such that the point of reference is external and the events are organized for expression on the basis of "what you can see." As we have noted, almost all speakers in the study used the present tense, even though the question was posed in the past tense.

More specifically, relations between the events that are bundled deictically follow two patterns: *now you see. . .* or *then you see. . . .* ; these points of reference occur in succession in the narrative. In the first option, which can be phrased as "it is now the case that x is happening," the time span that the speaker views as "now" can cover a set of events that are hooked up to this point of reference. With the reference point "now you see," the concept of ongoingness, as expressed by *be* + *-ing*, plays a central role. The following excerpt from one of the retellings illustrates this mode of organization: a time span is given by (01).[1]

Example 1   Deictic organizing principle: it is **now** the case; **now** you see

01   he's looking around   (it is now the case)

02   and there is nothing but sand dunes everywhere
03   and he hears the sound of thunder
04   and he gets excited
05   a rain storm is going to start

If we consider the temporal relations holding between the utterances, the time span given by utterance (01) includes that of (03) and (04). These relations can be paraphrased as follows: What is happening now? He's looking around (01); while doing so, he hears the sound of thunder (03), and while doing so (04) he gets excited (for details, see Carroll and von Stutterheim 2003; von Stutterheim, Carroll, and Klein 2003; von Stutterheim and Lambert 2005). To indicate how events progress, English uses the contrast between the simple form (*hears*) and the progressive form (*-ing*): Events coded in the simple form can be interpreted in more holistic terms because they are not explicitly marked as ongoing. Thus, although events (03) (*hears x*) and (04) (*gets excited*) can be regarded as happening while the protagonist is looking around, his hearing the thunder and getting excited take place in succession. This interpretation is supported by the simple tense form, as well as inherent verb meaning; the contrast with the *-ing* form holds even though the simple tense form is "neutral" in morphological terms.

This short example provides a first indication of what acquisition of this frame of reference entails for learners. Not only must they learn to use the *-ing* form and hook ongoing events up as a succession of "nows" that move the storyline. As illustrated, events often are bundled in a complex way, and learners must uncover how the simple and progressive forms are integrated into the narrative sequence to move the storyline forward.

The learner's problem of analysis is further confounded by the fact that there are two options: Although the point of reference is linked to an external anchor in both cases, in the second option the temporal frame includes a more explicit form of sequentiality, and the dynamic situations perceived by the speaker are segmented and ordered in the retelling as "**then** you see."

Example 2   Deictic organizing principle: **then** you see
01   and **you see** a form in the sand
02   and there's a bottle lying near to the form
03   **and then you see** an eye
04   an eye opens
05   **and then** a figure stands up
06   and **you realize**
07   it's some sort of animal or person
08   he reaches out (. . .) for a bottle
09   that's lying near to him
10   and lifts up the bottle

11   and tries to get something out of it (. . .)
12   **and then you hear** the sound of water dripping / one drop
13   and the figure tries to find the drop
14   **and then** as the figure starts to dig
15   the sand starts to flow downwards

This system of temporal ordering is based on relations defined across the left boundary. For example, in *you see a form in the sand, and then you see an eye*, precedence of the event *you see a form* can be defined with respect to when this event started (its left boundary); that is, one may still see the form while taking a closer look at the eye. Thus, the preceding event (*you can see a form*) need not have reached a point of completion to mark the relation coded by *then* (*and then you see an eye*). Table 4.1 illustrates the role of the temporal form *then* in the film retellings in English and shows the extent to which the preceding event has reached a point of completion or not.

As the numbers show, the feature of completion—that is, boundedness defined with respect to a right boundary of the preceding event—is not relevant for the use of *then* in English. Instead, this form encodes precedence of the prior event without necessarily entailing that it has come to an end before the next one starts. In this sense, *then* does not relate back to a specific feature of the preceding event—its right boundary; instead, sequentiality is defined over the left boundary. A core feature of this system is the external reference point (*then you see*) given by the narrator because this point of reference can be reinstated where necessary throughout the narrative, as illustrated in example 2. In other words, frames of reference in English are not organized on the basis of a temporal shift with respect to events that reach a stage of completion with a right boundary. Although the retellings do incorporate events of this kind, such events are not a core feature of the temporal frame. We assume that the absence of this feature as a core element is driven by the *–ing* form: For the narrative sequence, the absence of temporal shift as a core organizing principle allows systematic integration of events that are conceptualized as ongoing.

As we show below (see table 4.2), events in retellings in German are more likely to have reached a stage of completion (bounded); a similar case applies in French (*et puis, donc*). Accordingly, French and German learners of English have to recognize that boundedness does not play the same role in the temporal frame in narratives in English that it plays in their native languages. A further aspect learners must recognize is how events marked as ongoing are integrated into the narrative frames, in contrast with the temporal ordering of events as they are organized in French or German.

▒ Table 4.1
Use of *then* in Film Retellings in L1 English (%)

Preceding event completed	53.7
Preceding event not completed	46.3

▓ Table 4.2
Bounded versus Unbounded Events (%)

	L1 English	L1 French	L1 German	L1German– L2English	L1French– L2English
Bounded	27.4	48.6	51.4	34.4	43.2
Unbounded	44.7	29.2	20.2	33.9	30.1

Note: Percentages do not include utterances with inchoative aspect *he starts*, modal *he wants,* and states.

Time-Event Relations in Film Retellings by L1 German Speakers

Speakers of German segment complex dynamic situations, such as those presented in the film, into individual events that have reached some point of completion. This process leads to a "post time"—and with it a new interval on the timeline. Temporal features of this kind locate a subsequent event. In German narratives, events are temporally linked as shifts on a timeline that relate to the right boundary of the preceding event:

Example 3   L1 German

01   wacht **dann** so langsam auf
     *and wakes **then** slowly up*
02   und schaut sich um
     and looks around
03   und sieht **dann** die Flasche vor sich liegen
     *and sees **then** the bottle lying in front of him*
04   nimmt die Flasche
     takes the bottle
05   und guckt
     and looks
06   ob da Wasser drin ist
     if there is water in it
07   **dann** steht er so langsam auf
     ***then** he gets slowly up*
08   und kniet so
     and kneels down
09   und guckt sich um
     and looks around
10   und **dann** donnert es plötzlich
     *and **then** there is suddenly thunder*

The excerpt in example 3 illustrates the contexts in which *dann* (then) occurs: in the preverbal slot (*Vorfeld*), as in (07), or directly following the finite verb

(*Mittelfeld*), as in (01) and (03). This contrast is not optional because *dann* in the Vorfeld codes a temporal shift, whereas *dann* in the Mittelfeld suspends a temporal shift defined over the right boundary of the preceding event and codes a causal relation between the events at issue (see Roßdeutscher and von Stutterheim 2006). With *dann* in the Vorfeld, the time span given for the event in (05) is coded as terminated before that of (07) starts, whereas this is not the case for (03) and (04).

Thus, we can say that a formal contrast exists in German between "occurrence in the Vorfeld" versus "occurrence in the Mittelfeld." The function of *dann* in the Vorfeld is clearly marked, and the right boundary of the preceding event serves as a reference point in creating a new interval on the timeline. This pattern signals a temporal sequence that is based on the principle "x completed before y started": *dann* in the Vorfeld follows an anaphoric sequencing perspective.

In other words, German learners of English are familiar with a system in which the same "form" *dann* occurs in two functions with respect to the temporal frame: In one case it is anaphoric (Vorfeld); in the other (when it is used in the Mittelfeld), causal relations between the relevant events are prominent.

Time-Event Relations in L1 French Film Retellings

In French, the overall temporal frame also is based on anaphoric sequencing. Speakers differ, however, with regard to the extent to which they link events predominantly by temporal or by causal relations (*donc*, so).

Example 4   French

01   et il aperçoit un endroit humide
      and he perceives a humid spot

02   **donc** il s'en approche
      so he approaches it

03   il commence à tâter
      he starts to tap

04   il sent que c'est humide
      he feels that it is humid

05   et **donc** il lève ses mains vers le ciel
      and so he lifts his hands towards the sky

French speakers frequently mention the protagonist's intentions, goals, and states relevant to his actions. In contrast to German speakers, French speakers mostly leave temporal relations implicit and express causal links by different means, such as connectors, subordinate clauses, and relative clauses that specify circumstances underlying actions.

Therefore, French learners of English have to successfully analyze the fundamentally different role of temporal shift in frames of reference in English, compared to their linguistic knowledge of such systems of reference in the L1. Analysis of the use of the -*ing* form is a core issue for frames of reference set up by advanced learners, given the role of ongoingness in the English narratives and the absence of grammatical means in French or German to code this aspectual distinction. The question is: Have the learners uncovered the specific functions of the role of *–ing* in the temporal frames of reference developed in English for a retelling task?

We begin by comparing the number of occurrences of the progressive in the first three episodes. In the English L1 narratives, 21 percent of the total number of propositions (with differences ranging from 32 percent to 14 percent) is coded with the progressive form. For the L2s, numbers are higher in the German learners' group (26 percent) and identical with L1 English narratives in the French group (21 percent).

Time-Event Relations in Film Retellings in Learner Languages: L1German–L2English and L1French–L2German

The following examples illustrate the frame established to express time-event relations in the narratives of L2 learners. As in English, French, and German, the content of the film is retold in the present tense. On the whole, focus is placed on temporal shift in the frame of reference used by learners:

Example 5   L1German–L2English
07   and **then** he hears water drop
08   and tries to localize
09   where it comes from
10   and **then** he starts digging in the sand
11   and as he digs in the sand
12   **suddenly** the sand starts moving underneath him
13   and forms a hole
14   and **then** he falls into that hole

Example 6   L1French–L2English
01   and **then suddenly** you can hear water dripping
02   and he thinks
03   that there is water underneath
04   and he starts digging for water madly
05   and **then (at) once** there's a hole in the sand
06   and the hole gets bigger and bigger
07   the sand slides down
08   he gets caught in it

Table 4.2 summarizes the extent to which the narrative sequence includes events that are viewed as reaching a stage of completion and thus are bounded in some form. The percentages show an evolution toward target language usage for the L1German–L2English narratives, whereas French learners of English remain closer to the source language options.

Management of Events and Their Interrelation

L1German–L2English   Although German learners of English tend to rely on sequential ordering and mark temporal relations with the adverbial shifter *then*, they have discovered that *then* in utterance initial position codes precedence but does not entail that the preceding event has reached a point of completion—in contrast to the use of *dann* in this position in their L1. Because the frame they use is closer to "then you see," however, the narratives show that they have not learned how ongoing events, marked by the *–ing* form, are integrated into the narrative sequence and overgeneralize their role by introducing them without the necessary point of reference.

Example 7   L1German–L2English

01   at first he is little bit amazed

02   but after a few seconds he gets up

03   and is looking around

The ongoing event *is looking around* does not have an appropriate anchor, given the fact that the two previous events form a sequence. In the L1 English texts there are the following options: The narrator as the deictic reference point is reactivated—*after a few seconds he gets up, and you see him looking around, and then he starts walking across the desert*—or the point of reference can be given by a state ("it is now the case"; see example 9, line 89, below) to which the ongoing event can be hooked up.

L1French–L2English   French learners construct a frame of reference on the basis of temporal shift, which is defined anaphorically. Moreover, French learners of English express not only temporal but also causal relations, as in their L1. Thus, the influence of the predominant options of their L1 is readily apparent. Analyses of learners' narratives reveal that they have uncovered certain features of their target language. The learners are sensitive to the concept of ongoingness. Examination of the role of the progressive in its context of occurrence, however, shows learners using these forms for restricted functions: to provide information on the setting (by locating the protagonist or other entities such as a bottle), to introduce referents, or to exclude events from the storyline (in main clauses, subordinated temporal clauses, or relative clauses). In this learner language, events are not organized deictically so that selected activities, coded by means of the progressive, open up a temporal span as a point of reference for a set of events. Such activities sometimes are selected for expression and coded as ongoing, but they are mapped into a subordinate clause and thus are excluded from the storyline.

For French learners of English, as for their German counterparts, ongoing events are not integrated as required. In the following excerpt, for example, the transition in (82) to an ongoing event is not appropriate given the fact that the preceding events form a sequence (80, 81), and there is no point of reference to which it can be linked.

Example 8   L1French–L2English
77   and as he is walking
78   there are rocks emerging from the floor around him
79   and as he keeps on walking
80   one of these big piles of rock rises up under his feet
81   so he ends up at the summit of the rocks
82   and he is just trying to look around
83   to see what's happening

In a similar context in L1 English, integration of the ongoing situation is carried out by using a state as a reference point.

Example 9   L1 English
85   all the time these rocks are pushing up from under the ground
86   and he hears the water again
87   but suddenly he's pushed up into the air by one of these towers
88   that comes up out of the ground
89   and he's up on top of this tower (state: it is now the case)
90   and he's looking around for the water

Integration also can proceed by reactivating the external deictic anchor (*and you see him up there looking around for the water*), as noted above.

These short examples indicate the nature of the task advanced learners confront in analyzing the system of temporal reference in the target language. They show how both groups of learners use the progressive but have not uncovered the principles whereby events coded as ongoing can form an integral part of the reference frame.

Information Selection in Native and L2 English, French, and German

Given the different underlying principles in the temporal frames of reference, we carried out analyses on the extent to which the requirements for the temporal frame affect information selection in general for the task. Because the temporal frames are similar in French and German, with similar preferences in event construal (events that reach a stage of completion), an interesting question is whether both languages also compare with regard to information selection as a whole.

Answering that question requires us to consider a further set of grammaticized features that are relevant at this level: the syntactic subject and word order constraints. English and French are similar with respect to the grammatical status of the syntactic subject: Both languages have fixed word order with respect to the position of the syntactic subject (SVO). They differ, however, in another core feature—the absence of grammaticized aspect in French (for the present tense) and its associated temporal frames. Here French and German form a cluster.

In German, however, word order in main clauses is subject to the verb second constraint for the finite element of the verb (V2 constraint). This constraint creates a preverbal slot that can be filled in ways that differ from French and English because the position of the syntactic subject is not fixed. This constellation opens the possibility of investigating how these clusters of grammatical features influence information selection. Specifically, if the temporal frame is the sole determining feature, one should find similar results for French and German with regard to the types of entities and associated events that speakers select for mention (relevant feature completion or some telic component). As we note at the beginning of this essay, these questions form one of the core tasks in the analyses: the extent to which information structure in any of the referential domains (time, space, entities, events, possible worlds) provides evidence of structural interdependency.

Two types of entities can be distinguished in the film: the protagonist and inanimate entities that the protagonist encounters in his quest for water (the forces of wind, sand, water, rocks, and machines). The analysis focused on dynamic situations in which the entities occur as agents and experiencers and thus are potential candidates for inclusion in the narrative sequence (wind blows paper into the protagonist's face; water is dripping down; a rock is headed toward the protagonist). Inanimate entities are relevant for this comparison because they often are involved in events that are not bounded and thus do not deliver on the conditions required for a temporal shift (water drips down/is dripping down, the wind blows/is blowing).

Taking the average value for twenty speakers in each native speaker group, the results show that the frequency of reference to inanimate forces in a dynamic role is similar in English and French (as well as in Italian and Spanish): 34.5 percent in L1 English and 37.1 percent in L1 French. L1 German, by contrast, shows a significantly lower frequency: 24.5 percent (as does Dutch—like German a V2 language—at 23.6 percent) with a value of $p = 0.006$ (see Carroll and Lambert 2003). In contrast to L1 French, L1 speakers of German (and Dutch) tend to focus attention in their narratives on the protagonist, often omitting reference to prominent inanimate forces. For example, comparing values for German and English for a scene in which the protagonist is exposed to an inanimate force—a huge rock dropping from the sky—90 percent of L1 English speakers referred to this incident, but only 45 percent of L1 German speakers chose to do so. Furthermore, mention of inanimate forces versus the protagonist generally is low in L1German–L2English learner narratives (26.7 percent), corresponding to the pattern of selection in the L1. In L1French–L2English the figure is 34.1 percent, which is similar to both the L1 and the target language.

To summarize, the two languages in which the syntactic subject has a fixed position (French and English) show similar preferences in information selection. Agents of different kinds qualify for mention in the SVO languages, whereas in German there is a tendency to focus attention on one candidate—the protagonist. In other words, because the languages differ at this level, preferences in information selection in French and English cannot be attributed to the nature of the temporal frame. Instead, this preference correlates with a feature these languages have in common: a syntactic subject in fixed position (SVO). If the temporal frame and narrative sequence were a driving factor, French and German would have shown similar preferences because they have similar temporal frames. As Carroll and Lambert (2003) show, differences in informational status become evident at a later stage in the planning process in French, compared to German, in that inanimate entities are selected for mention but are later evaluated for their eligibility as subjects of a subordinate rather than a main clause. For French, this is the level at which the temporal frame comes into play: Inanimate entities are downgraded within the narrative sequence and are more likely to be mentioned as subjects of a subordinate clause. In German, by contrast, they are downgraded at the level of information selection. Neither of these cases applies in English, where any agent and the associated event can bring the story forward (because completion is not a core requirement); thus, inanimate entities can be both selected for mention and mappable as subject of a main clause in the narrative sequence.

Values for inanimate entities as the subject of a main clause are 26.0 percent for L1 English, 10.4 percent for L1 French, and 14.7 percent for L1 German. For German learners of English the value is 24.3 percent, and for French learners of English it is 13.2 percent—a figure that compares with the L1 (for details, see Carroll and Lambert 2003). Although the value for main clauses is close to that of the target language, German learners of English still tend to downgrade the status of these entities, inasmuch as they often occur as the subject of a subordinate clause (L1 English 2.5 percent; L1German–L2English 29.0 percent).

Overall results so far show that German learners of English are slowly fitting the pieces together, in that temporal shift is not contingent on events that have reached a stage of completion and agents within the narrative sequence sometimes are mapped as the subject of a main clause. Thus, in contrast with the L1, mapping patterns at this level are not preferentially confined to a specific candidate. Information selection continues to follow L1 patterns, however (for similar conclusions, see Slobin 1991, 1996).

Management of Entities in Reference Introduction and Maintenance

As a final topic in this intricate network of linguistic features available for information structuring, we turn to the management of reference—particularly reference introduction and maintenance. In keeping with the foregoing results, the way inanimate entities are introduced to the domain of reference correlates with their eligibility for mention as the subject of a main or subordinate clause. In English they are introduced mainly by means of presentationals—that is, existentials that predicate their existence, as in *there are huge sheets of paper flying around*, or perception verbs, such as *you can see sheets of paper flying around*. In French and German they are more likely to appear as an argument in a clause in which the protagonist is the agent or experiencer: *he falls into a new world with huge sheets of paper*. In the latter case, entities are less salient compared to the prominence they are accorded by presentationals. The preferences observed in both learner languages in reference introduction remain closer to the options of their source languages (Carroll and Lambert 2003).

With regard to reference maintenance, the most important indicator is how reference to the protagonist is maintained—for example, through use of a full noun phrase, a pronoun, or zero anaphora. Because English and French share similar features at the level of word order (SVO) but differ with regard to grammaticized aspect—where German is similar to French—we can investigate whether and how these clusters of grammatical features pair with patterns of reference maintenance.

Reference Maintenance in L1 English, L1 French, L1 German, and the L2s

French and English follow a similar pattern in that subject maintenance across adjacent utterances does not license zero anaphora (*cf.* lines 19, 20, and 21; 23 and 24; and 28 and 29 of example 10).

Example 10   L1 English

10   **and you see**
11   he is eh like a clay man
12   he's made out of brown clay
13   and he's just got eyes
14   and that's all really
15   **you can see** like big hands
16   like a sort of plasticene man
17   or something
18   and he wakes up
19   and he reaches out
20   and he can feel a bottle
21   and he picks it up
22   but there's nothing in there
23   and he stands up
24   and he can hear thunder
25   and then he hears raindrops
26   just falling
27   plop / plop
28   and he sort of looks around
29   and he sees
30   they're falling on the sand

Similar patterns of maintenance in L1 French are shown in example 4. By comparison, use of zero anaphora is restricted in English and French to contexts in which events are very closely related. They may relate to the intentions of the protagonist on his quest for water, as in (34) and (35), or causal relations, as in example 11.

Example 11   L1 English

31   and he can still hear the sound of eh water
32   falling

33   and dripping onto the ground

34   so he gets up

35   and Ø goes towards the sound

Zero anaphora also occurs when one action clearly leads to the next (example 12).

Example 12   L1 English

09   and then he tries to climb down

10   and <u>he</u> falls

11   and Ø <u>hits his head</u>

The pattern in German differs in that zero anaphora is clearly licensed with maintenance of the protagonist over adjacent utterances (provided that certain structural features of the utterance also are kept constant). This pattern was illustrated in example 2. Table 4.3 relates to all cases with reference maintenance to the protagonist in a main clause (see line 11 in example 12, for example). In L1 German, more than half of all sentences (54.2 percent) in which the protagonist is the subject of a main clause show zero marking in reference maintenance; the remaining cases are clauses with pronouns. In comparison to German, zero anaphora is markedly lower in L1 English: Only 16.4 percent of the sentences with reference maintenance to the protagonist show zero anaphora because L1 speakers of English mainly use pronouns in this context (see occurrence of pronouns in reference maintenance in example 10). The percentages give the average value for twelve speakers.

Reference Maintenance in L1German–L2English

Because reference maintenance is similar in L1 English, L1 French, and L1French–L2English, we focus here on L1German–L2English. Zero anaphora occurs in 30.7 percent of the clauses showing reference maintenance in the learner retellings. Although the percentages are lower than in L1 German (54.2 percent), there is evidence of the influence of the L1 in that reference maintenance occurs across a series of events in which the protagonist is maintained as subject, if there are no interruptions by comments or other side structures.

▓ Table 4.3
Use of Zero Anaphora in Main Clauses Showing Reference Maintenance (protagonist) (%)

L1 English	16.4
L1 German	54.2

Note: Mean values for twelve speakers (sand and paper scene).

Example 13   L1German–L2English

100   and suddenly he is between two machines

101   one is always putting steel plates on the ground

102   the other one is fixing it to the ground

103   so he runs away very fast

104   Ø is scared

105   and Ø stumbles over something

106   it's a kind of screw

107   and Ø falls right onto a kind of a fence on the ground

108   where he can see the next level / the next world

We note an increase in the number of comments that may reflect an emerging shift in organization to a deictic perspective, leading to a lower number of events in which the protagonist holds the stage at a stretch. Despite these tendencies, none of the learners has recognized that zero anaphora is confined in tasks of this kind in English to a series of events that are very closely linked in semantic terms. Thus, with respect to the question of ultimate attainment, learners depart from the pattern found for native speakers in reference maintenance. In assigning informational status to entities that are eligible for mention as the subject of a main clause, German learners of English show clear evidence of the influence of their L1 in that informational status accorded to the protagonist in information selection and reference maintenance is closer to the L1 and thus not (yet) nativelike.

Although the criterion of nativelikeness may have its drawbacks in identifying L2 learning processes that do not lead to the same outcome as in monolingual first language acquisition, it is a testable benchmark for investigating ultimate attainment and learner potential in adult L2 acquisition, as long as relevant features can be well defined (see Birdsong 2004; Singleton and Ryan 2004).

Subject and Topic in German (V2) as Opposed to French and English (SVO)

The study results show how zero anaphora is less constrained in the V2 language (German) than in the SVO languages (French and English). In German, zero anaphora is licensed on the basis of maintenance of the same entity as subject (in this case, the protagonist) over adjacent utterances, provided that several structural constraints hold. In English and French, zero anaphora occurs only when a close semantic link is given for the information predicated in the adjacent utterances. That is, the V2 language assigns a status to the protagonist that is not found in the SVO languages, even in similar contexts (for French and German we have the same protagonist and similar events ordered on the basis of temporal shift).

In contrast to French and English, status assignment in German begins at the level of information selection: Agents that act on the protagonist (*a sheet of paper knocks him down*) are less likely to be selected for mention than in French and English, and those that are selected are passivized (*he is knocked down by a sheet of paper*). The passive form underlines the informational status accorded to the protagonist—a choice that is highly consistent in the German narrative task (see Murcia-Serra 2001). Can we assume that the V2 constraint requires speakers to rank candidates (e.g., agents of an action) with respect to eligibility for mention as the subject of a main clause in the narrative sequence? In other words, does the V2 constraint work as a filter and accord prominence to one type of agent, the protagonist, in the present task?

A comparison with French is relevant at this point: French also accords prominence to the protagonist for the narrative sequence because inanimate agents are not eligible for mention as the subject of a main clause; they typically occur as the subject of a subordinate clause. This cross-linguistic difference may be attributed to an additional factor: an interdependency between the constituents that typically may occur in the Vorfeld in German in a given task—for narratives these constituents are linguistic means that code temporal relations (such as *dann*); in German, entities that map into the syntactic subject may be ranked with respect to their ability to accommodate temporal relations such as shift. In the task investigated, one of these entities (protagonist) is accorded what may be called "topic" status on a global basis for the task as a whole because an intentional agent may be more likely to be involved in events that reach a goal or point of completion, thereby allowing temporal shift. In sum, the V2 filter acts from the outset in information selection in German. Topic assignment may proceed on the basis of interdependent factors that are structurally driven and are set on a global basis for the text as a whole.

With respect to the related question of patterns of reference maintenance, the first conclusion we can draw on the basis of the cross-linguistic comparison is that prominence—and with it a high degree of accessibility (entity maintained as subject of a main clause across adjacent utterances)—in itself does not provide conditions that allow widespread use of zero anaphora. If prominence and accessibility were the significant factors, we should find no difference between French and German. The informational status expressed by zero anaphora, as found in German, appears to be conferred by other factors, such as structural features created by the V2 constraint. Thus, differences in patterns of reference maintenance between the SVO languages and the V2 language point to the limits of notions such as "accessibility" in explaining the conditions observed in the use of zero anaphora and pronouns.

Subject and Topic in L1German–L2English

No structural feature in English accords a similar ranking in information structure to temporal shift and associated participants in related events. As the foregoing analyses show, however, German learners of English have maintained these grammatically driven foundations in their L2. For them, semantic constraints that determine zero anaphora are operable at the outset in language planning—that is, at a level of decision making in language production when they are considering "what to say." Here German learners of English proceed as in their L1. Thus, the conditions holding for English in licensing zero anaphora cannot be considered unless German learners of English begin to question these foundations and initiate the process of reorganization at this level. Because the learner has to confront a linguistic system in its own right, with a hierarchical organization in information structure and a complex set of interdependencies rather than a loose collection of coding options, this level of information organization may be the most difficult to reorganize.

Discussion and Conclusion

As this cross-linguistic study on narratives shows, differences in information selection cannot be explained by a single feature; they are determined by a coalition of grammaticized features—particularly temporal concepts, the role of the syntactic subject, and word order constraints. Structural features—which affect the domains of time, events, and entities—interact in different ways in information organization and information structure in the languages studied.

The choices learners make at various levels in information organization indicate the nature of their linguistic knowledge when they are asked to retell the content of a film and order events in sequence. Some of the principles of information organization that drive speakers' decisions in selecting, ordering, linking, and coding information can be linked to grammatical form. Adult native speakers have gradually learned how to accommodate the requirements of a communicative task (establish a sequence of events) with the specific grammatical structure of their language. In this process, they have derived guidelines that determine choices in information structure at all levels of text construction. Because information structure and the choices speakers make are multidimensional and thus highly complex, second language learners tend to maintain the basic selection patterns of their source language (temporal shift); their coding options in the L2 reflect an interconnected set of choices. Adult learners approach the task with knowledge of information organization and information structure acquired together with their L1s. Cross-linguistic comparison reveals the extent to which this knowledge is implemented in the L2. The structure of the L2 systems shows that this process is not a simple transfer; it reveals an interconnected set of choices with a deeply rooted logic. This process may prove to be the major hurdle with respect to ultimate attainment, especially when evidence of incompatibility with the target language is subtle in nature. To reach nativelike proficiency, L2 speakers must discover the functions of grammatical features and unravel the implications for information structure. The linguistic underpinnings of this type of knowledge have long been neglected in the field of linguistics—or simply not recognized for what they are. Rather than attributing them to factors such as "style" or cultural preferences, we can identify the nature of this knowledge, thereby rightfully making it an integral part of language instructional programs that could be made available to adult learners from the outset. ▪

NOTE

1. In this and subsequent examples, the numbers in parentheses refer to actual sample lines.

REFERENCES

Berman, Ruth, and Dan I. Slobin. 1994. *Relating events in narrative: A crosslinguistic developmental study.* Hillsdale, N.J.: Erlbaum.

Birdsong, David. 2004. Second language acquisition and ultimate attainment. In *The handbook of applied linguistics,* ed. Alan Davies and Catherine Elder. Oxford: Blackwell, 82–105.

Carroll, Mary, and Monique Lambert. 2003. Information structure in narratives and the role of grammaticised knowledge: A study of adult French and German learners of English. In *Information structure and the dynamics of language acquisition,* ed. Christine Dimroth and Marianne Starren. Amsterdam/Philadelphia: John Benjamins, 267–87.

Carroll, Mary, and Christiane von Stutterheim. 2003. Typology and information organisation: Perspective taking and language-specific effects in the construal of events. In *Typology and second language acquisition,* ed. Anna Giacalone Ramat. Berlin: de Gruyter, 365–402.

Carroll, Mary, Christiane von Stutterheim, and Ralf Nüse. 2004. The language and thought debate: A psycholinguistic approach. In *Approaches to language production,* ed. Christopher Habel and Thomas Pechmann. Berlin: de Gruyter, 183–218.

Garrod, Simon, and Anthony Sanford. 1988. Thematic subjecthood and cognitive constraints on discourse structure. *Journal of Pragmatics* 12:519–34.

Halm, Ute. 2007. Zum Ausdruck temporaler Kategorien im Diskurs: Die Entwicklung narrativer Kompetenz in Filmnacherzählungen von Kindern zwischen 7 und 14 Jahren. Ph.D. diss., University of Heidelberg.

Hickmann , Maya. 2005. Determinants in first and second language acquisition: Person, space, and time discourse across languages. In *The structure of learner varieties,* ed. Henriette Hendriks. Berlin: de Gruyter, 230–62.

Kintsch, Walter, and Teun A. van Dijk. 1978. Toward a model of text comprehension and production. *Psychological Review* 85:363–94.

Klein, Wolfgang. 1994. *Time in language.* London: Routledge.

Klein, Wolfgang, and Clive Perdue. 1997. The basic variety (or: couldn't natural languages be much simpler?). *Second Language Research* 13:301–47.

Levelt, Willem J. M. 1996. Perspective taking and ellipsis in spatial descriptions. In *Language and space,* ed. Paul Bloom, Mary A. Peterson, Lynn Nadel, and Merrill F. Garrett. Cambridge, Mass.: MIT Press, 77–107.

———. 1999. Producing spoken language: A blueprint of the speaker. In *The neurocognition of language,* ed. Colin M. Brown and Peter Hagoort. Oxford: Oxford University Press, 83–122.

Murcia-Serra, Jorge. 2001. *Grammatische relationen im Deutschen und Spanischen.* Frankfurt am Main, Germany: Lang.

Ochs, Elinor, Carolyn Taylor, Dina Rudolph, and Ruth Smith. 1992. Story-telling as a theory-building activity. *Discourse Processes* 15:37–72.

Perdue, Clive, ed. 1993. *Adult language acquisition: Cross-linguistic perspectives.* Cambridge: Cambridge University Press.

Roßdeutscher, Antje, and Christiane von Stutterheim. 2006. Semantische und pragmatische Prinzipien bei der Positionierung von *dann. Linguistische Berichte.*

Singleton, David, and Lisa Ryan. 2004. *Language acquisition: The age factor,* 2nd ed. Clevedon, England: Multilingual Matters.

Slobin, Dan I.1991. Learning to think for speaking: Native language, cognition and rhetorical style. *Pragmatics* 1:7–26.

———. 1996. From "thought and language" to "thinking for speaking." In *Rethinking linguistic relativity,* ed. John J. Gumperz and Stephen C. Levinson. Cambridge: Cambridge University Press, 70–96.

Stutterheim, Christiane. 1997. *Einige Prinzipien der Textproduktion: Empirische Untersuchungen zur Produktion mündlicher Texte.* Tübingen, Germany: Niemeyer.

Stutterheim, Christiane von, and Wolfgang Klein. 1989. Referential movement in descriptive and narrative discourse. In *Language processing in social context,* ed. Rainer Dietrich and Carl F. Graumann. Amsterdam: North-Holland, 39–76.

Stutterheim, Christiane von, and Monique Lambert. 2005. Crosslinguistic analysis of temporal perspectives in text production. In *The structure of learner varieties,* ed. Henriette Hendriks. Berlin: de Gruyter, 203–30.

Stutterheim, Christiane von, Mary Carroll, and Wolfgang Klein. 2003. Two ways of construing complex temporal structures. In *Deictic conceptualisation of space, time, and person,* ed. Friedrich Lenz. Berlin: de Gruyter, 97–133.

Stutterheim, Christiane von, Ralf Nüse, and Jorge Murcia-Serra. 2002. Cross-linguistic differences in the conceptualisation of events. In *Information structure in a cross-linguistic perspective,* ed. Hilde

Hasselgård, Stig Johansson, Cathrine Fabricius-Hansen, and Bergljot Behrens. Amsterdam: Rodopi, 179–98.

Talmy, Leonard. 1988. The relation of grammar to cognition. In *Topics in cognitive linguistics,* ed. Brygida Rudzka-Ostyn. Amsterdam/Philadelphia: John Benjamins, 165–205.

5

Language-Based Processing in Advanced L2 Production and Translation:
An Exploratory Study

BERGLJOT BEHRENS
Department of Linguistics and Nordic Studies, University of Oslo

IN THIS CHAPTER I EXPLORE the possibility that particular features of language use in advanced L2 production and translation into L1 may reside in the same or similar underlying constraints. The reasoning behind the study is that both types of text production—L2 speech production and translation into L1—exhibit features that do not quite meet target language conventions. By target language I mean for L2 users their L2 and for translators normally their L1. The features in which I am interested, which typically are not errors at the sentence level, nonetheless make a text somewhat odd or "marked" for an observant native reader or listener.[1]

Recent contrastive research into narrative text production of native speakers and advanced L2 speakers indicates that some of these marked features in L2 production can be explained by assuming that grammaticized typological features of language are so deeply rooted in the mind of speakers that they affect the way they conceptualize their knowledge or observations in preparing to talk about them. This suggests that conceptualization for speaking is language specific, not language independent. In this chapter I report on the findings of research with such an orientation and explore the possibility that certain features of translation into L1 and advanced L2 production reveal the same underlying language-specific constraints on conceptualization.

The Conceptualizer and the Deverbal Message
Online L2 production and translation into L1 consist of verbalizing messages or thoughts, conceived as selected from knowledge in long-term memory or on the basis of interpretation of another text. Research has suggested that the message to be verbalized is language-independent. For example, Levelt's (1989) influential model of speaking postulates a cognitive module, the conceptualizer, in which the message is conceived in terms of its nonverbal substance. The output of this module is the deverbal message, which is fed into the linguistic formulator—the module from which lexical items are accessed and mapped onto syntax, morphology, and phonology (graphology).

Similarly, Seleskovitch and Lederer's (1984) interpretive approach to successful translation also models the cognitive operation of translation as a process of deverbalization and reverbalization. The translator transforms the linguistic input signals into chunks of pure, language-independent meaning. These deverbalized chunks or units subsequently are combined with immediate and more global contexts prior to the output phase. In other words, the input signals are linguistically decoded and their interpretation is "reconceived," as it were, before it is reformulated in the target language. Such reconceptualization must take place in the conceptualizer and thus bears close resemblance to the "thinking for speaking" (Slobin 1996) that is postulated for monolingual language production.

One question that has been raised with respect to Levelt's model is just how language independent the conceptualizer is. Although this question is not easy to answer—not least because processes of conceptualization are difficult to pin down and describe—careful crosslinguistic research with this focus has been performed by Christiane von Stutterheim and her research group (referred to here as the von Stutterheim project). That research indicates that information organization at the conceptual level follows language-specific constraints (Carroll and von Stutterheim 1993; von Stutterheim, Nüse, and Murcia-Serra 2002; von Stutterheim and Nüse 2003).

The goal of the von Stutterheim project is to identify language-specific features of the "deverbal message." To this end, the researchers have devised test methods that are based on the hypothesis that typological differences between languages put constraints on how native speakers organize the information they are in the process of verbalizing (Slobin 1991). Using identical tests for native speakers and very advanced L2 speakers, the researchers have found that the two groups of speakers organize information differently. Even very advanced L2 speakers who can be expected to know all the "rules" of the target language tend to miss out on dynamic information organizing principles that are dictated by typological features of the target language. One possible explanation for why this happens is that information organization, which takes place in the conceptualizer, is itself language-specific.

Information Organization, L2 Production, and Translation

I focus in this chapter on advanced L2 speakers, who can be expected to know all the "rules" of the L2 but do not always make use of them (Carroll and von Stutterheim 1993; von Stutterheim, Nüse, and Murcia-Serra 2002). There are grounds, then, for comparing features of L2 production with production of L1 in a bilingual setting— that is, a setting in which speakers use their L1 while having the L2 active in memory. Translation into the L1 would appear to be such a setting. Indeed, inasmuch as translated text differs in certain ways from text that was originally produced in that same language, an interesting inquiry would be to see whether translation into the L1 demonstrates any similarity with advanced L2 production and, if so, whether the shared features are related to similar processes of "source language" (i.e., L1) influence on L2 use.

Von Stutterheim and her research group have made careful comparisons among discourse organizational principles revealed in data elicited from subjects engaged in retelling an eleven-minute silent film, *Quest*. Analysis reveals differences across several languages with respect to various dimensions of the planning process. Speakers of English and German, for example, segment the situations presented in the film differently. Whereas German speakers select a relatively broad level of granularity in their retellings, English speakers systematically opt for a finer level of granularity throughout the texts, and the events they select often are phasally decomposed. Speakers of English and German also select different components of the external situation for verbal representation. English speakers frequently do not talk about the endpoint or result reached in a given situation, whereas inclusion of such endpoints is the general pattern in the German as well as the Norwegian retellings— indicating that German and Norwegian native speakers tend toward more holistic event organization. The differences are in line with typological differences between these languages: English is an aspect language, and German and Norwegian are not. Despite their high level of German, EnglishL1–Advanced GermanL2 speakers exhibit patterns of information organization that follow their L1 rather than the target language. According to the von Stutterheim studies, restructuring the knowledge component that relates to principles of information organization seems to be extremely difficult (Carroll and von Stutterheim 2003; see also chapters 3 and 4 in this volume).

Results from advanced L2 speakers are interesting as well from the point of view of translation norms. Although professional translation is performed by native speakers of the target language, readers of translations often note subtle oddities in these texts, which mark them off as different. Could these marked phenomena be the result of language-specific perspectivization on the thoughts formulated? To explore that possibility I present data on different phenomena in translation as well as in advanced L2 production. The data come from comparable corpora of texts of two origins: texts originally produced natively in the language and translations into that same language. The basis for comparison of a particular category of use is monolingually produced texts by native speakers. In general, deviation from the norm may entail either overuse or underuse of that category in the translation data. Of course, the occurrence of marked features in translation may or may not show affinities with the same (or even different) marked features of advanced L2 use. In that sense, my study represents exploratory work in progress; no firm conclusions can be drawn at this point. If such affinities could be established, however, they would open an intriguing window into the human language capacity, particularly if they should turn out to be traceable to the same underlying constraints.

Marked Features in Translation into L1 and L2 Production

I present data from translation and L2 production and discuss their potential underlying sources in view of the foregoing questions about language-specific information selection and perspectivation in the conceptualizer. I check data from findings in the von Stutterheim project against translations, and I consider translation data as potentially similar to L2 production. The translation data are extracted primarily from comparable corpora of authorized translations.

Marked Phenomena in Translation into L1

Published translations that, presumably, have undergone careful editing nevertheless often reveal oddities of various kinds. When these oddities reflect the influence of the structure of their L2 source text, including its language use, they generally have been put into two categories: oddities that reflect a lack of source text understanding on the part of the translator and textual features that lead to problems in finding L1 target language formulations. Both types of oddity may result in expressions that are influenced by source language wording and appear clumsy in the L1. One can also detect, however, marked features that do not seem to reside in a lack of source or target language competence. To account for these occurrences, researchers typically adduce situational/psychological circumstances in the translation process. Among these circumstances are the following possibilities:

- The source text is present and source language wording is unintentionally active in short-term memory.
- The translator does not have time for in-depth interpretation of the text and does not follow careful steps in translation from source to target text.
- The translator has no communicative intention—that is, the text being reproduced is not truly internalized as a thought (Ydstie 1998).

With regard to the last possibility, communicative intentions are considered crucial inasmuch as they generate utterances that come with a guarantee of textual relevance that is based on the desire to communicate certain thoughts, intentions, or beliefs. Indeed, the foregoing situational circumstances are an obstacle to good translation practices because of their ability to undermine the creation of genuine communicative intentions.

Studies conducted by von Stutterheim and her collaborators on conceptualization in language production raise the question of whether certain marked tendencies in professional translation indicate truly internalized thoughts—the deverbalized thought in Levelt's sense—or whether they are generated on the basis of source text conventions. In that case, they could result in violations of certain typologically based, crosslinguistically different conventions, or what I have here called features of markedness. Such marked phenomena may manifest themselves in overuse of L1 conventions, with certain grammaticized meanings in L1 taking precedence over other, less-conventionalized alternatives. I discuss below examples pointing in that direction.

Marked Phenomena in L2 and Translation into L1

We can reasonably expect differences in marked language use in translation into L1 and advanced L2 production. Thus, certain odd uses in L2 would not appear in translations precisely because translation typically occurs into one's L1, and the norms for its use are well established in adults, including translators. For example, Norwegian distinguishes between prepositions denoting *to a place* and *at a place*, as in (1) and (2), respectively:

(1) Han klatret **opp** på taket   (*He climbed up on the roof*)

(2) Han satt **oppe** på taket   (*He sat up on the roof*)

A nonissue in translation into L1 Norwegian, this distinction is a frequent source for inappropriate language use in L2 Norwegian.

On the other hand, instances of the same marked use of language exist both in translation into L1 and in L2 production. Examples can be found through careful analysis of at least two sources, marked uses identified through close reading of a translation, and marked uses drawn from frequency counts between texts produced monolingually and translations. The latter are of interest for this study, particularly if they also coincide with documented instances of marked L2 use, as differentiated from errorful L2 use. This interest derives from the fact that ultimately both occurrences (in advanced L2 use and in translation into the L1) might derive from the same underlying constraints.

Two primary reasons have been adduced for why marked phenomena might occur in translation: unstable norms in the target language that allow for some variation in use and overuse of either a source or target language norm. To the extent that both of these phenomena also can be observed in very advanced L2 use, a careful analysis of the operative constraints should prove insightful.

Unstable Norms in the Target Language   Norwegian distinguishes between predicative noun phrases with and without a quantifier (countable nouns), as exemplified in (3) and (4):

(3) Han er lege   (*He is doctor*) (*He is a doctor by profession*)

(4) Han er en lege   (*He is a doctor*) (*He is one of a group of people who are doctors*)

The quantified/nonquantified distinction also is possible with other verbs, as in (5) and (6), in which the nonquantified object may be read as incorporated into the verb—that is, it forms a compound with the verb, as suggested by the translation into English:

(5) Han bygger hus   (*He builds house*) (*He is house-building, builds houses as a profession*)

(6) Han bygger et hus   (*He builds a house*) (*He is building a particular house*)

We find marked uses in this area of Norwegian grammar in L2 and in translation into Norwegian L1. For example, the Norwegian text in (7)b is a translation from English; (8) is an attested example from Norwegian L2:

(7) a. Tunisia was **a one-party state** under the Neo-Destour party

    b. Tunisia var **ettpartistat** under Neo-Destour-partiet

    Tunisia was one-party-state under the Neo-Destour party

(8) Han er venn av meg (*He is friend of me*)

The Norwegian translation in (7)b would be considered somewhat unnatural by many Norwegian speakers, who would prefer that the predicative noun were preceded by the indefinite article. The L2 Norwegian is similarly unnatural to many Norwegians, although neither (7)b nor (8) represents a definite error.

Marked use of a phenomenon in L2 might be explained by referring to its nonoccurrence in L1—a factor that presumably contributes to its difficulty, as attested by (8). However, its marked occurrence in translation into L1 from a language that does not make the distinction, as in (7), suggests that we should seek an explanation instead in the L1 target language. Thus, Ydstie (1998) suggests that the norms for this structure are "on the move," so to speak, based on the fact that there are native speaker vacillations and native speaker divergences with respect to the acceptability of such examples. As an aside, such vacillations also would make the L2 learners' task more difficult.

Another explanation is in terms of simultaneous activation of two languages that influences the speaker/translator's general language intuition. Thus, an English/Finnish study looking for Anglicisms in a translation into Finnish (Mankkinen 1999) pointed to marked uses of two Finnish verbs denoting two different senses of the English "take" but was unable to find an explanation for the markedness in transfer from the English source. Mauranen (2004) suggests that this outcome was not a case of the English source text directly influencing the Finnish target text but a matter of the language system underlying the source text indirectly influencing the target system and the target text. This line of thinking appears to accord with the view in Carroll and von Stutterheim (2003) regarding online L2 production: In the translation case, the underlying L2 system influences L1 production; in L2 production, the reverse is true.

The differences among conceptualization, lexical access, and syntactic formulation, however—as fleshed out in Levelt's model—would require us to explain the marked uses as residing in different modules of the mind: The unstable rule for using the indefinite article in Norwegian incorporation constructions (as in [5] and [3] above) properly would reside in the target language formulator, and the problem would be the same for L1 and L2 users of Norwegian. The lexical access problem could be explained only with an organization of the lexicons in the two languages that we do not yet fully understand. In Levelt's model, the lexicon interacts with the formulator but not with the conceptualizer, and lexical access problems therefore would not be related to language-specific conceptualization in L1 translation or in online L2 production.

Overuse and the Target Language Perspective   Two types of overuse have been distinguished in translation studies. The first arises when a particular form/structure is more common in the source language than in the target language. One might call such cases true *interference* phenomena, or a "shining through" of the source language. The other type of overuse occurs when a language phenomenon is more common in the target language than in the source. Such overuse entails (*over*)*normalization* of the target norms (Teich 2003). The same categories of markedness are known in L2 acquisition. My particular interest lies with the latter category.

Translation data demonstrate that the consequential connective *dermed* in Norwegian (German cognate *damit*) is overused in Norwegian translations relative to originally produced Norwegian texts (Behrens 2004). Some examples demonstrate that a consequential structure is chosen where the source has a temporal structure—that is, target language construal differs from that of the source, as in (9):

(9) a. Andrew led her into the picturesque thatched bungalow they had moved into the day before and which was to be theirs for ten days more. "I don't want to share you with the ants and land crabs, and if that makes me a prude, okay." **He slipped off his swim trunks as he spoke.** (Arthur Hailey, *Strong Medicine*)

The Norwegian translation of the bolded sentence is in the form of a consequential structure:

(9) b. Dermed rev han badebuksen av
With that/Therewith tore he the swim trunks off
Damit riss er sich die Badehose herunter.

The anaphor appears right after a direct quote, indicating that the protagonist's action takes place as a consequence of what he says. The consequential relation also is overtly expressed in the German translation.

In view of language-specific differences in the underlying perspectives taken on event construal, as discussed in the von Stutterheim project, there is a possibility that Norwegian—like German but unlike English not an aspect language—construes narrative structures according to consequential frames more often than English and that a temporal frame in English is more common. The translator in (9) has followed native speaker conventions in changing the structure. To a native ear the Norwegian translation is not marked. Clearly, further research is necessary to uncover potential differences between English and Norwegian conventions in narrative. Furthermore, only by comparing frequencies of reliable language data in larger corpora can we uncover a possible overuse of such patterns in translation.

Parallel Corpora and Marked Features

Development of parallel corpora has facilitated comparison of translations with originally produced text in the same language.[2] This method allows detection of marked phenomena in translations that are not easily found in individual text excerpts (see also Baker 1993; Eskola 2004). The Oslo Multilingual Corpus (OMC), developed at the University of Oslo, includes four source languages and parallel translations into three languages, based on an original corpus of English and Norwegian texts (the English Norwegian Parallel Corpus [ENPC]; S. Johansson, www.hf.uio.no/iba/prosjekt/intro.html) that was subsequently expanded to include German and French texts (see www.hf.uio.no/forskningsprosjekter/sprik/english/index.html). A corpus related to the crosslinguistic von Stutterheim project also exists in Oslo. We have collected Norwegian L1 retellings of the silent film *Quest*, thereby making L1 Norwegian available for comparison with the other L1 data in the von Stutterheim project. Although collection of Norwegian L2 data awaits funding, the L1 and L2 data in German already can be compared with the English-German translations in the OMC at this stage, and the von Stutterheim findings may be correlated with findings in the translation data. Such work on overuse of a form/structure in translation ultimately may lead to an explanation in terms of language-specific conceptualization.

The star lines in figure 5.1 illustrate the possible paired comparisons of texts within the OMC corpus.

In the following section I present some marked phenomena in translation into L1 that the OMC corpus has revealed, with a view to similar marked phenomena in advanced L2. Again, phenomena that appear in both translations and advanced L2 are of particular interest in the search for an explanation for their occurrence.

Although some of the marked elements in translation are not related to source language influence—in the sense that the norms of the source language shine through in translation—others clearly are. Traits that do reflect deviation from norms would not be immediately recognizable by the reader of the individual translated text but become visible through frequency counts in larger corpora. One such trait is the use of consequential connectives.

Consequential Connectives in Translation and L2
A study of L2 Norwegian demonstrates that appropriate use of connectives of various kinds is difficult to acquire (Selj 1999): Learners of Norwegian not only struggle with placement of connectives, they also tend to make little use of them. This is true although subjects in the study had spent from five to twenty-four years in Norway, after arriving in Norway as adults who had been educated in their native country.

Consequential connectives seem to be used with varying frequency across English, Norwegian, and German. Translators tend to follow source language norms (L2) more than the norms of their native tongue targets—that is, interference or "shining through" is more common than normalization. Thus, we find an overall reduction in frequency in Norwegian translation from English but an overuse in Norwegian translation from German of two typical connectives that denote consequentiality. A closer study of anaphoric adverbial connecting devices (Behrens

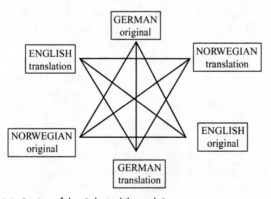

Figure 5.1 Crosslinguistic Design of the Oslo Multilingual Corpus

2004) demonstrates an overuse of the connective *"dermed"* in Norwegian, in translation from both German and English. Because such connectives generally are more frequent in German than in Norwegian and the translations from German therefore point to interference, translations from English would demonstrate a case of (over)normalization, given that consequential relations often are derived only implicitly in English. More important for this discussion, in Norwegian the consequential relation is deemed felicitous, whereas a temporal relation is used in the English source, as (9) demonstrates. A possible relation between (over)normalization and grammaticized information structural patterns in L1 seems worthy of further study.

Pro-Adverbial *"dann"* in German Source and German Translation: Correlation between Translations and L2

Another interesting case is the use of the temporal shift operator *dann* in German texts (Roßdeutscher and von Stutterheim 2006). In texts originally produced by German native speakers, *dann* in narratives is used in initial position to indicate a temporal shift— that is, the event preceding *dann* has reached a stage of completion. L2 speakers of German with L1 English use *dann* in the left periphery in their narrative retellings, as in L1 German; in 45.8 percent of the cases in which *dann* occurs, however, the preceding event has not reached completion (see chapter 4 in this volume). These findings suggest that English advanced L2 speakers of German do not recognize the operative native German information structural principle in their L2 production.

Translation data between English and German reveal significant overuse of initial *dann* in the German target texts. Thus, the English–German–English subcorpus of comparable texts within the Oslo corpus, which presently comprises thirty English–German and eighteen German–English texts of the same length, demonstrates a much higher frequency of initial *dann* in translation than in originally produced texts (302 occurrences in German translations, 109 in German source texts). Balancing the frequency yields an average of 201 occurrences of initial *dann* in twenty texts of German translations, compared with 121 in German source texts—that is, 160 percent of the source frequency.

These frequency counts are even more surprising because the German translations were produced by native German translators: They clearly indicate that the translators have not adhered to information structural conventions that otherwise hold for German. Simultaneous activation of the two languages involved in the translation may block native speaker intuition, resulting in translations with an element of "difference" that is reminiscent of advanced L2 German. Although frequency itself is a strong indicator, further analysis of the actual examples is necessary to ascertain whether these subtle markedness phenomena and the L2 phenomena reside in the same crosslinguistic differences. The L2 phenomenon derives from a mismatch in temporal structuring. If the translations demonstrate the same type of mismatch, there is reason to point not only to instability in the system itself but to a lack of awareness on the part of the translator of the deeper discourse structural principles of the target language, even though it is the translator's L1.

Complicating Factor: "dann" Used as a Temporal
Anaphor Denoting Simultaneity

If one were to take the description of narrative *dann* as a temporal shift operator at face value, occurrences of "misuse" in German translations should be extractable by way of Norwegian. In Norwegian, temporal shift is marked by the temporal adverbial *så*, which corresponds to German *dann* from the standpoint of discourse pragmatics, whereas simultaneity is expressed by the temporal adverbial *da*. Thus, the two Norwegian connectives distinguish between two interpretations of English temporal *then*, of which only one corresponds to German *dann*. A search of the corpus for occurrences of initial *then* in English texts with *da* in Norwegian translations and *dann* in the German translations should yield examples of interest for our queries. Instead, several occurrences did not mark a temporal shift in narrative but used *dann* to relate events as taking place at a time or times defined by some event(uality) in the preceding utterance, as in (10).

(10) a. From time to time we had a weekend off. Usually once a fortnight, or once in three weeks, depending on the work. **Then** we'd leave for Vienna in an ambulance on the Friday, come back on Sunday night, by train, third class, by which time one wouldn't have a bloody groschen left. (André Brink, *The Wall of the Plague*)

(10) b. Von Zeit zu Zeit hatten wir ein Wochenende frei. Normalerweise einmal in zwei, drei Wochen, das kam auf die Arbeit an. **Dann** fuhren wir am Freitag mit einem Krankenwagen nach Wien und kamen Sonntagabend per Bahn dritter Klasse zurück; und bis dahin hatte man keinen lumpigen Groschen mehr.

This normal use of *dann* probably should be taken into consideration in the discussion of English advanced L2 speakers of German, inasmuch as a more comprehensive understanding of the connective beyond the temporal shift interpretation may affect the use and misuse of this connective in L2.

In (11) *dann* has been used to translate not only Norwegian *så*—which indicates temporal succession in the penultimate sentence—but also Norwegian *da* in the last sentence, where the time of the running away coincides with the bad days' coming, as related in the penultimate sentence. The coming of the bad days is not understood as temporally bounded, and *da* does not mark a temporal shift. The German rendering invites a temporal succession reading, which is not the reading of the Norwegian source, whereas the English translation with *that's when* is in line with the source meaning. The German translation could count as an example of overuse—that is, not a case of shining through but a winning out by the German pattern for narrative temporal succession over other means.

(11) a. Det er jo ikke lenger så vanlig å love hverandre evig troskap. Man holder sammen i de gode dagene. Men **så** kommer de onde dagene. **Da** er det mange som bare stikker av. (Jostein Gaarder, *Maya*)

b. Es ist ja nicht mehr so üblich, einander ewige Treue zu geloben. In guten Zeiten hält man zusammen. Aber **dann** kommen die schwierigen Zeiten. Und **dann** laufen viele einfach davon.

c. It's rare to promise eternal fidelity these days. People stay together while the going's good. But **then**, there are the bad times as well. **That's when** a lot of people just cut and run.

Unambiguous Cases of Shining Through in Translation

The V2 feature of German and Norwegian, in contrast with English, has been shown to affect left periphery phenomena in L2. The strong position of the subject in English makes English more of an object-framed language, in that event descriptions focus on the objects involved in the event, whereas German—a V2 language that pushes the subject to the right of the finite verb when another feature appears first—is more focused on the spatiotemporal localization of the event (Carroll 1997). Norwegian is a V2 language, like German, and one therefore may expect spatiotemporal localization to be a stronger topical feature in Norwegian than in English.

Table 5.1 demonstrates the differences in frequency of initial prepositional phrases in original Norwegian and original English texts.

Table 5.1
Initial Prepositional Clauses Anchoring Events in Context

Initial Position	Norwegian Original	Norwegian Translation	Initial Position	English Original	English Translation
PÅ (on/at)	223	165	ON	97	144
I (in)	975	616	AT	80	157
VED (by)	114	57	IN	499	951
OVER (over)	20	9	OVER	6	13
UNDER (under)	38	30	UNDER	11	19
FØR (before)	22	19	BEFORE	21	22
ETTER (after)	134	78	AFTER	50	106
UTPÅ (toward)	4	1	TOWARD	3	0
MED (with)	64	59	WITH	47	61
AV (of/by)	58	39	OF	24	36
TIL (to)	129	94	TO	53	50
			BY	54	35
SUM	**1,781**	**1,167**		**945**	**1,694**
	decreasing			increasing	

Note: Frequency counts on the basis of thirty texts of equal length translated into/from English/Norwegian (ENPC subcorpus of the OMC).

Initial prepositional phrases are far more common in Norwegian (1,781 occurrences of prepositions used for temporal and spatial adverbials) than in English (945 occurrences of English counterparts). The relative frequency of initially placed prepositional phrases and their translations suggests that translations deviate from originally produced text in the same language. The shining through in translation, established on the basis of these frequency counts, indicates that even professional translators do not appropriately recognize information structural conventions of the target language. Because the German subcorpus is not a balanced corpus, comparison with German data awaits further expansion. Nevertheless, interpretation of the data even now suggests that the complexity of the translation task and the simultaneous presence of two languages in active memory block recognition of information structural principles in the target language, even if the target is the translator's L1.

The phenomenon encountered here—a case of transfer—does not mean that the problem is not one of conceptualization. Topic/focus assignment, thematic assignment, and referential framing in terms of spatiotemporal anchoring are all steps in the thinking-for-speaking process. These aspects of language planning are perspective driven and have to be solved in the conceptualizer. The fact that L2 conventions are transferred to the translations suggests that these organizing principles are textually very complex and very difficult to disentangle. Furthermore, because they are not disallowed in the target language, although their occurrence would be marked, they carry over into the target text, thereby contributing to the "oddness" of the translation. Because they are driven by information organizational principles in the conceptualizer, one would expect the same tendencies to appear in very advanced L2. This possibility merits further study.

Concluding Remarks

Some of the examples I present have demonstrated information structural organization according to source text norms; others tended in the direction of target-based solutions that may be overused; still others do not fall in either category, possibly because the norm itself is unstable. Similar structuring across the languages as well as lexical cognates may confuse translators to the extent that source language conventions in the L2 win out over target language conventions in the L1, however much the translator works to deverbalize the message. If the hypothesis that deverbalized messages are linguistic in nature is correct, as the work by von Stutterheim and her group claims, translators seem to have great difficulties retaining certain elements of the target language system that are partly blocked by the underlying source text system. On the other hand, examples discussed in this chapter also demonstrate that information structural principles underlying L1 may be so strong that they take precedence in translation into L1, indicating that such principles are deeply rooted in the conceptualizer. That conclusion would support the view that Levelt's hypothesis with respect to the language independence of the conceptualizer is incorrect. Further studies into phenomena that are affected by underlying language-specific grammaticized meanings in the conceptualizer may provide a window to a better understanding of textual markedness in translation into L1 and in L2 performance.   ▩

NOTES

1. In this chapter I use the term "marked" in the nontechnical sense, to indicate a construction that would strike a native user as somewhat unusual or even odd.
2. Norwegian L1 data have been collected under the Språk i Konstrast (SPRIK [Languages in Contrast]) project in Oslo; parallel L2 data remain to be collected, as do written L2 data, particularly from Norwegian L2 speakers of English and German.

REFERENCES

Baker, Mona. 1993. Corpus linguistics and translation studies: Implications and applications. In *Text and technology: In honour of John Sinclair,* ed. Mona Baker, Gill Francis, and Elena Tognini-Bonelli. Amsterdam/Philadephia: John Benjamins, 233–50.

Behrens, Bergljot. 2004. Cohesive ties in translation: A corpus-based study of the Norwegian connective "dermed." *Languages in Contrast* 5:3–33.

Carroll, Mary. 1997. Conceptualization of spatial relations. In *Language and conceptualization,* ed. Jan Nuyts and Eric Pederson. Cambridge: Cambridge University Press, 137–61.

Carroll, Mary, and Christiane von Stutterheim. 1993. The representation of spatial configurations in English and German and the grammatical structure of locative and anaphoric expressions. *Linguistics* 31:1011–41.

———. 2003. Typology and information organisation: Perspective taking and language-specific effects in the construal of events. In *Typology and second language acquisition,* ed. Anna G. Ramat. Berlin: de Gruyter, 365–402.

Eskola, Sari. 2004. Untypical frequencies in translated language. In *Translation universals: Do they exist?* ed. Anna Mauranen and Pekka Kujamäki. Amsterdam/Philadelphia: John Benjamins, 83–99.

Levelt, Willem J. M. 1989. *Speaking: From intention to articulation.* Cambridge, Mass.: MIT Press.

Mankkinen, Marika. 1999. Manifestations of translatedness: A case study of Anglicisms in the novel *Trainspotting.* Unpublished master's thesis, Savonlinnan School of Translation Studies, University of Joensuu, Finland.

Mauranen, Anna. 2004. Corpora, universals and interference. In *Translation universals: Do they exist?* ed. Anna Mauranen and Pekka Kujamäki. Amsterdam/Philadelphia: John Benjamins, 65–82.

Roßdeutscher, Antje, and Christiane von Stutterheim. 2006. Semantische und pragmatische Prinzipien bei der Positionierung von *dann. Linguistische Berichte.*

Seleskovitch, Danica, and Marianne Lederer. 1984. *Interpréter pour Traduire.* Paris: Didier.

Selj, Elisabeth. 1999. Uttrykk for logiske relasjoner i norsk som andrespråk. *NOA* no. 22. Oslo, Norway: University of Oslo.

Slobin, Dan I. 1991. Learning to think for speaking: Native language, cognition and rhetorical style. *Pragmatics* 1:7–26.

———. 1996. From "thought and language" to "thinking for speaking." In *Rethinking linguistic relativity,* ed. John J. Gumperz and Stephen C. Levinson. Cambridge: Cambridge University Press, 70–96.

Stutterheim, Christiane von, and Ralf Nüse. 2003. Processes of conceptualization in language production: Language-specific perspectivization and event construal. *Linguistics* 41:851–81.

Stutterheim, Christiane von, Ralf Nüse, and Jorge Murcia-Serra. 2002. Cross-linguistic differences in the conceptualization of events. In *Information structure in a cross-linguistic perspective,* ed. Hilde Hasselgård, Stig Johansson, Cathrine Fabricius-Hansen, and Bergljot Behrens. Amsterdam: Rodopi, 179–98.

Teich, Elke. 2003. *Cross-linguistic variation in system and text: A methodology for the investigation of translations and comparable texts.* Berlin: de Gruyter.

Ydstie, Jo Terje. 1998. Oversatt norsk—unaturlig norsk? *Working Papers in Applied Linguistics* 4, no. 98: 170–87. Oslo, Norway: University of Oslo.

6

Learning and Teaching Grammar through Patterns of Conceptualization:
The Case of (Advanced) Korean

SUSAN STRAUSS
Pennsylvania State University and Center for Advanced Language Proficiency Education and Research (CALPER)

IN THIS CHAPTER I PROVIDE a brief overview of conceptual grammar to propose it as an alternative analytic and pedagogical approach to the study of grammar that derives from a combination of three theoretical-methodological paradigms: cognitive linguistics, discourse analysis, and corpus linguistics. Fundamental to the approach is the twofold view that linguistic structure is motivated by, dependent on, and reflective of underlying conceptual structures and conceptual categories that emerge in discourse and interaction—in other words, that grammar, as a patterned system of symbolic structures, is largely fluid, dynamic, and strongly influenced by the discursive construction of context—and that cognitively based pedagogical treatments of grammar can draw the attention of foreign and second language learners (and teachers) toward a novel way to understand certain linguistic rules. Although I demonstrate the approach by using examples from Korean, with a focus on the advanced learner, its applicability to virtually any foreign or second language learning context should be clear.[1]

Conceptual grammar is similar in part to what Tomasello (1998, xiii) refers to as cognitive-functional linguistics. Scholars within that paradigm (predominantly cognitive linguists and functionalists) essentially have the following in common: They examine all aspects of natural language use, privilege naturally occurring discourse as a primary object of study, and relate all components of linguistic structure (e.g., phonology, morphology, semantics, syntax) to cognition, imagination, symbolization, and metaphor (e.g., Chafe 1994, 1998; Croft 1998; Goldberg 1995, 1998; Langacker 1987, 1998, 2001; Talmy 1975, 1985, 2000; and Taylor 1993, among others).

Within cognitive linguistics, form, meaning, and use all converge in systematic ways, providing insights into the human mind through linguistic expression and close analysis of that expression. In contrast to traditional approaches to grammar, in cognitive linguistics meaning is "not objectively given, but reflects our apprehension of situations" (Langacker 2001, 8). Furthermore, meaning is not limited to a single lexical item, a particular morpheme, or strings of lexical items and morphemes:

Every linguistic structure carries meaning as a symbolic unit or "conceptual tool" (Langacker 2001, 7), through which users of language conceptualize, perceive, and make sense of their own experiences and their surrounding environments; meaning is located and identified through linguistic patterns and then schematized (meta-linguistically, graphically, or both) to reflect a generalizable, unified representation of the conceptual structure.

Such generalizable, unified representations of conceptual structure are discovered through in-depth, micro-level analysis of corpora of naturally occurring discourse. Unlike in some frameworks in cognitive linguistics, use of contextually bound discourse is crucial. For the Korean constructions I present here to exemplify such an approach, the corpora consist of a variety of discourse samples—including spoken, written, and hybrid modes (e.g., computer-mediated discourse); scripted and spontaneous speech; everyday conversation (both face-to-face and telephone); narratives; monologues; and public discourse (e.g., television and radio broadcasts, religious sermons).

In addition, each of the constructions I present in this chapter consists of one pair of potentially competing linguistic structures that are pervasive markers of stance and speaker/writer attitude in addition to being subtly similar in terms of meaning, function, and basic syntactic properties.[2] Such frequency of use, coupled with a surface-level semantic and pragmatic similarity between target forms, makes the receptive task of accurately discerning the difference between the two challenging at best, especially at advanced levels of language study. Learners at the advanced level have enough linguistic (i.e., syntax, semantics, morphology, and pragmatics) and cultural knowledge to recognize the degree to which the target forms might overlap in structure, meaning, and function, yet they probably would be unable to pinpoint precisely how the forms differ and why. Even more challenging is the productive task of intentionally selecting one form over the other to express a particular communicative intent.

Grammatical exercises and explanations developed with this approach are constructed from an abundance of situated, context-bound language excerpted from the corpus, combined with elements of cognitive linguistics. The exercises are designed to systematically guide learners, both inductively and deductively, to focus on crucial, micro-level textual components and their patterns—ultimately leading learners to deduce the underlying conceptual meaning for each form. This text-based approach to language and conceptualization provides a means for advanced learners to disambiguate such seemingly competing grammatical constructions through in-depth investigation of conceptual structure and, more important, to make meaning-driven choices in their own language production (see also Byrnes and Sprang 2004). Thus, a primary goal of the approach is to discover conceptual meanings that underlie linguistic structures to disambiguate one form clearly from its seemingly similar counterpart and to discern systematic distinctions that may be covert, intricate, and not easily deduced.

To illustrate the notion of seemingly competing linguistic structures with subtly similar meanings and functions in English, note the following three example pairs juxtaposing modals (i.e., "will") versus phrasal modals (i.e., "be going to"), demonstratives "this" versus "that" versus "it," and the "be" passive versus the "get" passive. Each pair was culled from corpora of naturally occurring English discourse that parallel our corpora of Korean data.

(1) modals and phrasal modals—e.g., "will" vs. "be going to" (The Weather Channel, 8 July 2004)

You're **gonna** have that high humidity, you're **going to** have those temperatures close to or at ninety degrees.

. . . maybe just a touch cooler, though, in some places. That**'ll** feel a little bit better.

(2) demonstrative pronouns "this" vs. "that" vs. "it" (Icy Hot Sleeve television commercial—Shaquille O'Neal)

You've never seen anything like **this** before. (does a layup)

Not **that. This.** (pointing to his elbow w/an Icy Hot Sleeve)

(3) "be" passives vs. "get" passives (Screen message when checking e-mail through Pennsylvania State University's Webmail)

You will **be redirected** to your inbox in 5 seconds. If you do not **get redirected**, click here.

With respect to the foregoing sentence pairs, the ways in which one member of the pair systematically differs from the other, and why, probably are not immediately evident, even to native speakers of English or highly proficient advanced learners. One way to disambiguate these meanings would be through a conceptual grammar approach.

A skeletal outline of the methodology is as follows:

1. Identify the target construction(s) for study.
2. Locate, tag, and tabulate their distributions within the corpora.
3. Conduct a brief macro-level study of frequencies and distributions across corpus types.
4. Analyze macro-level patterns of the target form(s) (e.g., through questions such as the following: In what specific discourse genre does the form appear? Who is the speaker/writer? Who is the addressee/reader? What epistemic/affective stances emerge in the discourse through these patterns?).
5. Using the macro-level findings, begin the micro-level analysis.

This final analytic step is the most challenging and time consuming because the ultimate goal of the analysis is to discern a generalizable, unified representation of the target construction(s). The microanalysis for each form or set of forms varies and often requires a recursive series of formulating and reformulating hypotheses, with a view to accounting for the greatest number of instances of the target constructions, ultimately to attain generalizability. Questions that may arise within this phase include the following: Are there syntactic constraints influencing the form(s)? What are the discursive patterns surrounding the target form(s)? What are the secondary patterns that emerge with respect to co-occurring or surrounding linguistic markers (e.g., verb classes and other characteristics of verbal semantics, temporal adverbials, intensifiers, concessive or contrastive markers, modals)? Such secondary patterns of co-occurring structures are particularly helpful in discerning the unified representation of the target forms.

Instructional materials developed through this approach initially are intended to raise students' (and language teachers') awareness of discursive patterns—particularly those that are not transparent or easily deduced. These materials can be designed to lead users sequentially through a small-scale analysis of the target forms, much like the inductive analytic processes originally employed by the linguist, though simplified and purposefully ordered to build incrementally on the various stages of analysis. The goal is to engage learners through scaffolded instruction, provided as a combination of inductively and deductively designed exercises; to guide learners' discovery of the generalizations underlying the grammatical patterns; and to help them recognize the intricate relationships among meaning, communicative intent, speaker stance, and the linguistic representation of cognition. Ideally, language learners who work with the materials ultimately will internalize the target patterns and use them creatively, productively, and naturally on their own.

Although this approach is applicable to any language at any level of instruction, the types of grammatical issues presented for English in examples (1)–(3) and those I present for Korean in the section that follows are geared to the needs of advanced language learners. That is, the types of grammatical constructs and the contextually based communicative goals of the discourse under consideration here presuppose a sophisticated level of familiarity with the target language and culture, as well as with its various discourse genres (Swaffar 2004). Not only do advanced learners possess a robust vocabulary and repertoire of connectives, discourse markers, adverbials, intensifiers, and other nominal and verbal descriptors in the target language, they also are familiar with more fine-grained, language-specific phenomena. Among these phenomena are subtleties in aspectual meaning; gradient degrees of referential force; and linguistic representations of agency, power, and control. The approach appeals to combinations of such features of language use, drawing on the relevant linguistic patterns that surround the target forms. Using authentic discourse in the manner proposed here makes such distinctions more salient and raises students' awareness of the complex ways in which language encodes meanings well beyond the type of "literal" meaning that appears in dictionary entries and glossaries.

Furthermore, the findings from studies such as these can fill the gap in reference materials for advanced level foreign/second language study—especially true for less commonly taught languages such as Korean, which suffer from a serious limitation of discourse/context-based pedagogical materials. The reference materials that do exist tend to be descriptive in nature: Although they are insightful and thorough (Lee 1993; Martin 1992; Sohn 1994, 1999), illustrative examples often are both invented and limited to isolated sentences. As such, they disregard the crucial relationship that exists between discourse, interaction, cognition, and grammar.

Two Completives in Korean: V-a/e pelita versus V-ko malta

Two auxiliary constructions exist in Korean that serve as markers of completive aspect: V-a/e pelita versus V-ko malta. I use "completive aspect" here in the sense of

Bybee, Perkins, and Pagliuca (1994, 54), who define the completive as expressing the notion of doing "something thoroughly and to completion." They subsequently extend the definition by stating "the object of the action is totally affected, consumed or destroyed by the action" (57). Completive aspect in English can be expressed through particles such as *up, out,* and *away,* as in the following verb pairs: "eat" versus "eat up" (completive), "fly" versus "fly away" (completive), "dry" versus "dry up" (completive) or "dry out" (completive), and so forth. The concept of completion also is expressed crosslinguistically through adverbials generally meaning "all," "completely," "finally," and "totally," in addition to markers of middle voice such as Spanish *se,* French *se,* and German *sich* (Kemmer 1993). Conceptually, in natural discourse, completion or perceived completion is a typical means for expressing emphasis or affective stances of surprise, regret, disappointment, counterexpectation, excitement, and the like (Strauss 2003). A study that centers on completive aspect as a marker of stance and speaker/writer attitude in the target language has the potential of revealing subtle, yet powerful, perspectives on the complex interrelationships among grammar, meaning, conceptualization, and speaker/writer intent. Korean has two auxiliaries that mark affective stance, which renders the issue more significant.

Explanations of the two constructions as they appear in existing reference grammars of Korean can be encapsulated as follows: Sohn (1994, 1999) indicates that both are markers of "terminative aspect." V-*a/e pelita* expresses the meaning of "finish up," "end up with," or "do completely." Martin (1992) treats V-*a/e pelita* as an exhaustive marker—expressing the idea of "do something completely," "finish up," "get through," and so forth—and V-*ko malta* as a terminative marker, expressing the idea of "ends up (by) doing" or "finally does something." Lee (1993) indicates that the meaning of V-*a/e pelita* is closely related to the meaning of *pelita* as a main verb, "to ruin or spoil." For Lee, V-*a/e pelita* expresses an abstract and extended meaning of "spoiling the speaker's expectation," which simultaneously carries the evaluative expressions "to my regret" or "to my relief"; he does not address the V-*ko malta* auxiliary construction.

Examples (4) and (5)—which are extracted from Lee (1993) and Sohn (1994), respectively—illustrate the meanings of each auxiliary. Coincidentally, both examples are structured around the main verb *ttenata* (to leave).

(4) [Adapted from Lee (1993)]

*ku yelcha-ka tten-**A-PELI**-ess-ta* [MAIN VERB: *ttenata* "leave" + *a-pelita*]

"The train left (to my regret)" / "The train left (to my relief)"

("The train ended up leaving" / "The train finally left")

(5) [Adapted from Sohn (1994)] [MAIN VERB: *ttenata* "leave" + -*ko malta*]

*Minca-nun ttena-**KO MAL**-ass-ta*

"Minca ended up leaving"

("Minca left to my regret / to my relief; Minca finally left")

What is noteworthy and potentially problematic here is that it is possible (and natural) to gloss the meanings of each Korean sentence with any one of the English meanings provided above for V-*a/e pelita* and V-*ko malta*. In other words, if one were to rely solely on existing literature, it would not at all be transparent to the learner of Korean how the two forms differ from each other and why.

Before I analyze the auxiliary constructions, I first consider the meanings of each of the two auxiliaries as lexical verbs. *Pelita* as a lexical verb means "to throw away, to ruin, to spoil," as in *Minaka piey cecunconkilul peliessta* (Mina **threw away** the paper that got wet from the rain), or *nanun nemwu maywun umsikul manhi mekese, wuicangul peliessta* (I ate too much spicy food and **ruined** my stomach). *Malta* as a lexical verb means "to stop doing something, to give up doing something," as in *kunun ku chaykul ilkta malassta* (He **stopped** reading the book [i.e., didn't finish]), or *nanun ku chaykul ilkulyeta malassta* (I planned to read the book, [but I] **gave up** [i.e., didn't finish]). These examples uncover an interesting semantic parallel as well as a semantic contrast between the two lexical verbs. With regard to the parallel, both verbs are telic—that is, both encode the endpoint of a particular action. However, p*elita* encodes an act of throwing something away or ruining something, which inherently signals total completion of that act, whereas *malta* signals the act of not doing something through completion—in fact, of stopping prior to completion of an ongoing action. Such semantic distinctions surrounding these verbs as lexical verbs become quite relevant to the aspectual distinctions that each expresses as an auxiliary.

Early steps in this approach involve location and tabulation of the target forms across the various discourse genres and modalities. The results from one such study on the current auxiliary verbs are abridged in table 6.1.

It is noteworthy that V-*a/e pelita* is the more frequent of the two and that V-*ko malta* rarely occurs in oral discourse. I consider one possible reason for this finding later in this chapter. With regard to the relative frequency of these auxiliaries vis-à-vis other auxiliaries, in a subcorpus of oral, written, and hybrid discourse data, Strauss,

▦ Table 6.1
Data Descriptions and Frequency and Distribution of Target Auxiliary Forms

Dataset	No. of words	V-*a/e pelita*	V-*ko malta*
I. Written			
A. Translated literary works	32,600	87	10
B. Korean short stories	5,700	8	6
C. Internet	12,400	24	26
II. Oral			
A. Television programs (7 hours)	70,000	45	1
B. Conversation (18 hours)	153,000	109	0
C. Sermons (2.5 hours)	21,250	10	1
Total: I and II	294,950	283	44

Source: Adapted from Strauss, Lee, and Ahn (2006)

Lee, and Ahn (2006) found that V-*a/e pelita* and V-*ko malta* each represents the third most frequently appearing auxiliary. For infinitive-derived constructions, V-*a/e pelita* (completive) followed the second-ranked V-*a/e pota* (to try; attemptive); the most frequent auxiliary deriving from a main verb infinitive was V-*a/e cwuta* (to do something for someone; benefactive). For gerund-derived auxiliaries, V-*ko malta* (completive) followed the second-ranked V-*ko siphta* (want, wish; desiderative); the most frequent gerund-derived auxiliary was V-*ko issta* (be + V-ing), the aspectual marker whose meaning and function broadly resemble the progressive.

V-*a/e pelita*

Examples (6) through (11) illustrate typical occurrences of V-*a/e pelita*; examples (12) and (13) illustrate typical occurrences of V-*ko malta*. The data excerpts have been ordered incrementally to reveal essential characteristics pertaining to the underlying conceptual structures of the target forms. In (6) through (10), one must pay particular attention to the main verbs with which the V-*a/e pelita* construction occurs. In (6) and (7) the main verbs are *icta* (forget) and *epsecita* (disappear). Both are telic in that they inherently encode the endpoint of the action:

(6) Face-to-face conversation—Main verb: *ICTA* "forget" [TELIC]

((topic of conversation: "school bullying" (*wangtta*) experiences in Korea))

kuliko cakinun ku kiekul meli sokeyse malkkumhi **icepelyesstalako** *sayngkak*

hako i nyenul cinaysseyo, cwung il, cwung i.

"And she thought she'd <u>completely</u> (lit. "clearly," "cleanly") **forgotten-PELITA** all the memories in her head, and spent two years (there), in the first and second grades."

(7) *Achim Matang* (TV program)—Main verb: *EPSECITA* "disappear" [TELIC]

((Samtek, Misen's aunt, is telling the story of how she came to lose her niece. The two remained separated for a number of years after the incident.))

Samtek: *sikol-ey iss-taka wuli-cip-ey han ithul iss-nuntey sicang-ul.*

pwa-ss-nuntey-yo <u>kumsay</u> *yay-ka* **epsecyi-e-peli-ess-e-yo.**

"(Misen) used to live in the countryside and visited and stayed at our house for a couple of days. When we looked around the market (for her), <u>suddenly</u> **she disappeared-PELITA.**"

In both (6) and (7), the V-*a/e pelita* construction underscores an inherent sense of totality expressed by each main verb—forgetting something completely and completely disappearing. Each of the foregoing sentences would be perfectly well formed without V-*a/e pelita;* for the most part, it is a grammatically optional construction. Utterances without V-*a/e pelita* tend to be framed as objective utterances, whereas those that include the construction contain some element of speaker emotivity or subjectivity. Here, both examples were extracted from extended narratives of past experience, and both depict emotionally charged situations.

Furthermore, both (6) and (7) contain emphatic stance-marking adverbials: *malkkumhi* (neatly) and *kumsay* (suddenly). This phenomenon illustrates the tendency that certain types of stance marking typically collocate with other stance-marking structures of the same type. In (6) the act of forgetting, or forgetting completely, is framed as a positive occurrence; the subject of the sentence had been a target of school bullying (*wangtta*) in the past. That she "neatly and completely forgot those memories" presumably would have afforded her some sense of relief. In (7) the act of disappearing, or completely disappearing, is framed as a strongly negative occurrence. The young girl, Misen, had disappeared one day at the market—suddenly and without warning.

In contrast with the telic events depicted in (6) and (7), the main verbs in (8) and (9) inherently encode motion, *kata* (go), and change of state, *maluta* (become dry), respectively. Both are inherently atelic; they do not, on their own, encode an endpoint reading with respect to the event.

(8) *nwunuy yewang* "The Snow Queen"—Main verb: *KATA* "go" [MOTION]

khai-nun cwuk-e-se meli **ka peli-ess-e**

"Kay is dead and he's **gone far-PELITA (gone far away)**."

(9) "LG Home Shopping" (television program)—Main verb: *MALUTA* "become dry" [CHANGE]

(item being advertised: food storage containers)

Program hostess: *cicebwunhan nayngcangkoan, yachaynun* **malla peliko** *swunapun engmangcinchang ttalkinun cismwuluki olsswuyessesscyo?*

"Inside the messy refrigerator, the vegetables **become dry-PELITA (dry out)** and storage is a total mess. Don't strawberries often go bad?"

In this second pair of examples, V-*a/e pelita* designates an endpoint that is not inherently encoded in the main verb, such that the motion verb "go" now encodes the sense of "go away" (completely) and "become dry" now points to the finality of the state change—that is, "dry out" (completely). By virtue of the V-*a/e pelita* construction, both examples also express a subjective reaction on the part of the speaker/writer/narrator.

The excerpt in (10), from Hans Christian Andersen's *ppalkan kwutwu* "The Red Shoes," contains the main verb *ccicta* (pull off)—an inherently telic verb. Unlike the telic verbs *icta* (forget) and *epsecita* (disappear) in (6) and (7), however, the verb *ccicta* (pull off) also encodes agency: The sentential subject has control over the action.

(10) *ppalkan kwutwu* ("The Red Shoes")—Main verb: *CCICTA* "pull off" [TELIC]

(Karen had put on the forbidden red shoes, and her feet began to dance uncontrollably; she was frightened and wanted to remove the shoes, and so she ripped off her socks, but the shoes remained on her feet.)

Kaleynun yangmalul ccicepeliesssupnita.
"Karen **tore off-PELITA** her socks."

As in (6) and (7), V-*a/e pelita* adds emphasis to an inherent endpoint; here, however, given the context and the fact that the verb *ccicta* (pull off) is agentive, it also strongly underscores the intentionality of Karen, the sentential subject: She had to get those socks off, tore them right off of her feet—deliberately, completely, and with all her might.

In the excerpt in (11), the main verb *taytap hata* (answer), which is atelic, is similar to *kata* (go) in (8) and *maluta* (become dry) in (9). *Taytap hata* (answer) also is inherently agentive, like *ccicta* in (10); the pragmatic implication emerging from the V-*a/e pelita* auxiliary does not underscore intentionality, however, but accidentality and a lack of control on the part of the narrator of the story (an airplane pilot).

(11) *elin wangca The Little Prince*—Main verb: *TAYTAP HATA* "answer"

   Elin wangcanun iltan cilmwunul hayssul ttaynun pokihanun ceki epsessta. Nanun polthuttaymwuney sinkyengi kontwuse issessumwulo toynun taylo amwulehkeyna **taytaphay pelyessta.**

   "The little prince never let go of a question once he had asked it. As for me, I was upset over that bolt. And **I answered-*PELITA*** with the first thing that came into my head."

In this example, the existence of the V-*a/e pelita* auxiliary emphasizes the endpoint of the action, but the words clearly were not what the narrator wanted to say; they just came out. He had been so distracted while attempting to repair his aircraft, his response was careless, and he regretted his behavior.

The foregoing excerpts provide sufficient evidence to posit an underlying conceptual representation for V-*a/e pelita:* The core meaning of this construction is **FINALITY with TOTALITY.** The core meaning of FINALITY also pragmatically implicates a secondary meaning of emphasis, accidentality, irreversibility, an event beyond the speaker's control, and deliberateness. That is, when an event is framed as complete and total or over and done with, there are two basic interpretations: The event either occurred accidentally and without the control of the speaker or sentential subject, or it occurred precisely because the speaker or sentential subject willed it to occur in that way, through deliberate actions and resolve. Finally, as exemplified in the foregoing excerpts, such pragmatic implications give rise to emotional/subjective overtones such as regret, relief, pride, surprise, disappointment, unexpectedness, strong resolve, and so forth. Figure 6.1 provides a schematic representation of the conceptual structure of V-*a/e pelita.*

V-*ko malta*

Like V-*a/e pelita,* V-*ko malta* is a grammatically optional form. When it appears, it also encodes FINALITY within event descriptions, and it, too, serves to underscore emphasis, accidentality, and deliberateness, as well as emotional overtones such as regret, relief, pride, or resolve. This auxiliary differs in conceptual meaning from V-*a/e pelita* in one crucial way, however. Examples (12) and (13), with V-*ko malta,*

UNDERLYING MEANING →	pragmatically implicates	→ pragmatically implicates
OF *V-A/E PELITA*	SECONDARY MEANINGS	EMOTIONAL/SUBJECTIVE OVERTONES
FINALITY W/ TOTALITY	EMPHASIS	relief, regret, pride
	accidentality	surprise, disappointment
	irreversibility	unexpectedness, strong resolve
	beyond control	
	deliberateness	

Figure 6.1 Schematic Representation of Conceptual Structure of V-*a/e pelita*

provide a telling contrast with the excerpts containing V-*a/e pelita*. In addition to the auxiliary verb, note also contrast markers such as -*nuntey* (but) and –*ciman* (however) and temporal adverbials such as *ku ttaymata* (each time) and *kyelkwuk* (finally).

(12) *kalmayki uy kkum Jonathan Livingston Seagull*—Main verb: *CHEPAKHITA* "crash down"

Yel penul sitohayse yel pen motwu sisok 112 khillomithelo nalass<u>ciman,</u> <u>ku ttaymata</u> penpenhi cwungsimul ilhko kistheli hantey engkhin chay patassokey **chepakhiko malasssupnita**.

"Ten times he tried, however, all ten times (lit. "<u>each time</u>"), as he passed through seventy miles per hour, he burst into a churning mass of feathers, out of control, **crashing down-***MALTA* into the water."

(13) Internet: diet and ramyen—Main verb: *MEKTA* "eat"

Taiethunun hanun tongan lamyenun toytolokimyen mekci malayaci ha<u>nuntey</u> mekko malassta. Sasil cengmal elmacenpwuthe lamyeni nemwunemwu mekko sipessta. chamassess<u>nuntey</u> <u>kyelkwuk</u> onul mekko malassta.

"While I am on a diet, I should try not to eat ramyen. <u>But</u> I **ate it—** *MALTA*. In fact, I have really, really been craving ramyen for a while. I've suppressed my cravings, <u>but</u> today, I <u>finally</u> **ate-***MALTA* ramyen."

Both (12) and (13) are narrative excerpts: (12) is from Richard Bach's (1970) allegorical novel *kalmaykiuy kkwum Jonathan Livingston Seagull*, and (13) is from an Internet posting about a young woman's attempt to diet. Both depict events with a focus on the endpoint or the outcome of that event, not unlike examples (6)–(11) for V-*a/e pelita*. The crucial distinction that emerges in (12) and (13), however—which does not appear in (6)–(11)—is that the speaker, writer, or narrator experiences a struggle (physical, psychological, or other) before the actual unfolding of that outcome. That is, the event is construed such that the outcome occurred in spite of an attempt to prevent it or in spite of the speaker's (or sentential subject's) strong desire to avoid it.

Both V-*a/e pelita* and V-*ko malta* express the concept of FINALITY. Whereas V-*a/e pelita* expresses FINALITY **with TOTALITY**, V-*ko malta* expresses

FINALITY with **RESISTANCE or STRUGGLE** to avoid an undesirable outcome. The conceptual representation of V-*ko malta* appears in figure 6.2.

V-*ko malta* signals a core meaning of FINALITY with RESISTANCE or STRUGGLE, and the secondary meanings implicated by V-*ko malta* and the subjective overtones are similar to those of V-*a/e pelita*, though they are significantly stronger. This intensified pragmatic strength carried by V-*ko malta* appears to account for its less frequent use overall, especially in oral discourse.

Practical Application/Materials Design

In this section I offer a proposal for the types of pedagogical materials and exercises that could be used to guide learners toward a grounded understanding of the two auxiliary constructions V-*a/e pelita* and V-*ko malta*. All such materials and exercises point out particular discursive patterns surrounding the forms and ultimately guide learners toward the formulation of their own "rules" with respect to the constructions. In materials for learning these constructions, explanations should progress from the simplest, most concrete images to progressively more complex and abstract images. Thus, these discourse-based exercises might begin with the V-*a/e pelita* auxiliary and include data excerpts that contain main verbs, which themselves inherently already encode an endpoint reading—verbs such as *icta* (forget), *ilhta* (lose), *kkunhta* (quit), and *cwukta* (die). Learners could be encouraged to try to locate the pattern underlying this class of verbs and verbalize the fact that they all somehow relate to an endpoint orientation. An excerpt or two also could be included containing an original version in which V-*a/e pelita* is juxtaposed with an altered version that includes only the bare main verb without the auxiliary, as in (14) and (14'). Example (14), from *Jonathan Livingston Seagull*, contains the verb *salacita* (disappear) with V-*a/e pelita*. Example (14') has been altered by removing the auxiliary.

(14) *conatahan lipingsuthenun nwunul kkampakiesssupnita.*

    Aphumto kyelsimto etilonka **salacie-peliesssupnita**.

    Jonathan Livingston Seagull blinked. His pain, his resolutions **vanished-PELITA.**

(14') . . . *Aphumto kyelsimto etilonka* **salaciesssupnita.**

    His pain, his resolutions **vanished.**

UNDERLYING MEANING →	pragmatically implicates	→ pragmatically implicates
OF *V-KO MALTA*	SECONDARY MEANINGS	EMOTIONAL/SUBJECTIVE OVERTONES
FINALITY WITH	EMPHASIS	relief, regret, pride
RESISTANCE OR	accidentality	surprise, disappointment
STRUGGLE	irreversibility	unexpectedness
	beyond control	very strong resolve
	deliberateness	

Figure 6.2 Schematic Representation of Conceptual Structure of V-*ko malta*

Students might be asked to read a larger passage of the data and then comment on which of the two excerpted lines sounds more subjective, which more objective, and why.

Other sentence pairs might be provided to illustrate how *V-a/e pelita* imposes an endpoint reading on events in which the main verbs do not themselves encode telicity—process verbs such as *mekta* (eat) or *ssuta* (use), motion verbs such as *kata* (go), and change-of-state verbs such as *pyenhata* (change) or *toyta* (become). Again, original passages could be chosen for co-occurrence of this verb type with V-*a/e pelita*. Learners could be asked first to locate the target construction and then to locate other co-occurring forms (particularly adverbials) within the passages that emphasize the finality or totality of the described event. The distinctions between the bare verbs—such as *mekta* (eat) and *meke-PELITA* (eat up) or *pyenhata* (change) and *pyenhay-PELITA* (change completely)—probably would become transparent to learners at this point.

The final sets of passages and exercises for V-*a/e pelita* could center on strongly intentional versus accidental readings, with examples similar to those in (10) and (11) but with extended passages of discourse. Again, co-occurring stance markers also might be noted.

The pragmatic content of the selected discourse excerpts proceeds first from an underscoring of inherent completion or totality in the main verb (*salacita* [disappear], *cwukta* [die], *icta* [forget], etc.), to the expression of totality in a process-type main verb where no endpoint reading exists (atelic) (e.g., *kata* versus *ka-pelita*, [go] versus [go away]; *mekta* versus *meke-pelita*, [eat] versus [eat up]), to an intentional reading of "to get something over and done with," and finally to an accidental reading of "the event happened in such a way that it was beyond my control, accidental, spontaneous, etc." At this point, students would be asked to synthesize the "rules" they progressively formulated by working through the exercises and to compare them with the schema of conceptual meaning in figure 6.1. The schema depicts a core conceptual structure of FINALITY with TOTALITY and visually links two sets of pragmatic extensions: the first illustrating concepts such as *beyond control, accidental,* and *spontaneous* that emerge from the core structure and the second illustrating the relationship between the core meaning and the expression of speaker/writer stance and affective overtones of *relief, surprise, pride, disappointment.* The schema also would be accompanied by a parallel set of explanations that explicitly make the link between core conceptual structure and pragmatic extensions.

Next, V-*ko malta* could be introduced with the same approach—using corpus-based excerpts and exercises with guiding questions for learners to gradually induce semantic/pragmatic "rules." These exercises would be followed by a schema of conceptual meaning similar to that presented for V-*a/e pelita* together with its accompanying set of explanations, where relevant pragmatic extensions are explicitly and systematically linked to the core conceptual structure. For example, in addition to more extended versions of sample passages such as those in (12) and (13), an excerpt similar to the one in (15), from Hans Christian Andersen's *ppalkan kwutwu* "The Red Shoes," could be used as a sample passage with guided exercises.

(15) From *ppalkan kwutwu* "The Red Shoes"

*Ku taum cwuileyn sengchansiki issesssupnita. Cipeyse naseki ceney khaleynun kemun kwutwulul naylyeta poko, tasi ppalkan kwutwuey nwunkilul cwuesseyo. Khaleynun ppalkan kwutwueyse nwunul tteyl swu ka epse hanchamul **mangselitaka kiei** <u>ppalkan kwutwulul</u> **sinko malasssupnita.**

"Next Sunday was communion, and Karen looked at the black shoes and she looked at the red ones—and then she looked at the red ones again and, **hesitating, finally put** <u>the red ones</u> **on-*MALTA*.**"

With respect to the examples illustrating V-*ko malta*, the crucial question to ask learners is the following: Did the speaker, writer, or sentential subject actually want the outcome of the event to happen in the way that it did? Learners could be asked to locate and comment on the linguistic cues that point to this interpretation. Then they could compare the two auxiliaries and verbalize on their own the similarities and differences, thereby formulating their own versions of the "rules" underlying these two constructions. They could then evaluate their own understandings vis-à-vis schematic representations of each, such as those in figures 6.1 and 6.2. Such similarities and differences would center on the essential conceptual differences as well as the pragmatic strength carried by each form.

Next, an example pair similar to that in (16) and (17) (though again with extended stretches of discourse, not simply one or two sentences for each) might be presented, so that students could analyze them and verbalize—now with more precision—how the two constructions differ and why. By this time, students should have gained a stronger awareness and appreciation of the importance of the more global context surrounding the discourse, including the linguistic expression of speaker stance:

(16) <u>Source: Internet</u>: Main verb: *WUSTA* "laugh" + **PELITA**

*honnay-l ttay-myen, ha-nun mal-mata ta ttala ha-nun thong-ey kkwucwung-ul ha-taka-to **wus-e peli-nta.***

"When my son is being scolded, he just does what I say. That's why **I laugh** while I reprimand him."

(17) <u>Source: Internet</u>: Main verb: *WUSTA* "laugh" + **MALTA**

*Cheli-nun tongsayng-uy thek-eps-nun kecismal-ey ei-ka eps-e **wus-ko mal-ass-ta.***

"Cheli **laughed** in blank dismay because of his brother's whopping lie."

Students by now should be able to notice stance-related differences between (16) and (17) and other such parallel excerpts, especially with regard to the event outcomes occurring in each and the intensity of feelings (by the speaker, writer, or sentential subject) associated with each.

For both completive constructions, learners are first guided through carefully designed discourse excerpts and exercises to inductively formulate their own "rules" with respect to the target forms by attending closely to the relationship between linguistic form and meaning making. These inductively driven exercises are then followed by visual schemas for each form. The schemata serve to simultaneously confirm or disconfirm learners' own set of "rules" formulated by the discourse data excerpts; guide learners into conceptualizing meaning in a novel way, beyond that of literal meaning and/or dictionary definitions; and visually link the concept of completion—that is, TOTALITY, with two possible structures in Korean: TOTALITY with FINALITY (V-*a/e pelita*) and TOTALITY with RESISTANCE or STRUGGLE (V-*ko malta*). In both cases, learners come to associate expressions of completion and totality with elements of accidentality, agency/control, and spontaneity, as well as with speaker/writer stance, affect, and subjective expression. Ultimately, in a later set of exercises students would be expected to choose correctly one form over the other, based on contextual cues, and to produce the constructions in their own written and oral discourse in contextually and pragmatically appropriate ways.

Conclusion

In this chapter I have provided a detailed account of two auxiliary constructions in Korean that superficially appear to express very similar aspectual meanings. My brief summary of how the two are treated and explained in existing reference materials emphasizes their functional similarities; explanations and sample sentences sometimes actually blur the two, potentially creating a false impression of interchangeability between one form and the other while failing to explain their semantic and discursive differences. The analysis I present here, by contrast, focuses on those subtle but important differences. This analysis originally emerged from my own experiences as an advanced learner of Korean and a desire to know how these forms differed and why (Strauss 2002). The analytical framework of cognitive grammar can uncover subtle but crucial linguistic patterns involving target constructions and other surrounding forms, elucidating with precision and systematicity the conceptual structures of each auxiliary. Although the work of empirical discovery through micro-level analysis may be both challenging and time consuming, the results could be invaluable in advanced language learning contexts. Finally, an approach such as this raises students' and teachers' awareness of linguistic form in general and especially the crucial relationships between grammar, cognition, imagery, and stance.

NOTES

Research for this project was partially funded by the Pennsylvania State University Center for Advanced Language Proficiency Education and Research (CALPER), through a grant from the U.S. Department of Education (CFDA 84.229A P229A020010), and by a faculty grant from the Liberal Arts Research and Graduate Studies Office (RGSO) at Pennsylvania State University.
    1. For a full discussion and illustration of the conceptual grammar approach for these auxiliary constructions, see Strauss, Lee, and Ahn (2006).

2. The two forms differ syntactically in that V-*a/e pelita* is formed with the infinitive verbal stem + auxiliary, whereas V-*ko malta* is formed with the gerundive verbal stem + auxiliary. Similar conceptual work on other competing forms in Korean completed to date under the CALPER project includes two honorific suffixes, –*yo* versus –*supnita*; two verbs of visual perception, both expressing the meaning of "to appear" or "come into view," *naota* versus *poita*; and three mirative sentence enders: –*kwun*, -*ney*, and –*tela*.

REFERENCES

Bach, Richard. 1970. *Jonathan Livingston Seagull: A story.* New York: Avon Books.

Bybee, Joan, Revere Perkins, and William Pagliuca. 1994. *The evolution of grammar: Tense, aspect, and modality in the languages of the world.* Chicago: University of Chicago Press.

Byrnes, Heidi, and Katherine A. Sprang. 2004. Fostering L2 literacy: A genre-based, cognitive approach. In *Advanced foreign language learning: A challenge to college programs,* ed. Heidi Byrnes and Hiram H. Maxim. Boston: Heinle-Thomson, 47–85.

Chafe, Wallace. 1994. *Discourse, consciousness, and time: The flow and displacement of conscious experience in speaking and writing.* Chicago: University of Chicago Press.

———. 1998. Language and the flow of thought. In *The new psychology of language: Cognitive and functional approaches to language structure,* ed. Michael Tomasello. Mahwah, N.J.: Erlbaum, 93–111.

Croft, William. 1998. The structure of events and the structure of language. In *The new psychology of language: Cognitive and functional approaches to language structure,* ed. Michael Tomasello. Mahwah, N.J.: Erlbaum, 67–92.

Goldberg, Adele. 1995. *Constructions: A construction grammar approach to argument structure.* Chicago: University of Chicago Press.

———. 1998. Patterns of experience in patterns of language. In *The new psychology of language: Cognitive and functional approaches to language structure,* ed. Michael Tomasello. Mahwah, N.J.: Erlbaum, 203–19.

Kemmer, Suzanne. 1993. *The middle voice.* Amsterdam/Philadelphia: John Benjamins.

Langacker, Ronald. 1987. *Foundations of cognitive grammar, volume I. Theoretical perspectives.* Stanford, Calif.: Stanford University Press.

———. 1998. Conceptualization, symbolization, and grammar. In *The new psychology of language: Cognitive and functional approaches to language structure,* ed. Michael Tomasello. Mahwah, N.J.: Erlbaum, 1–39.

———. 2001. Cognitive linguistics, language pedagogy, and the English present tense. In *Applied cognitive linguistics I: Language pedagogy,* ed. Martin Pütz, Susanne Niemeier, and René Dirven. Berlin: de Gruyter, 3–39.

Lee, Keedong. 1993. *A Korean grammar on semantic-pragmatic principles.* Seoul: Hankwuk Moon Hwa-sa.

Martin, Samuel. 1992. *A reference grammar of Korean: A complete guide to the grammar and history of the Korean language.* Rutland, Vt.: Charles E. Tuttle.

Sohn, Ho-min. 1994. *Korean.* London: Routledge.

———. 1999. *The Korean language.* Cambridge: Cambridge University Press.

Strauss, Susan. 2002. Distinctions in completives: The relevance of resistance in Korean V-*a/e pelita* and V-*ko malta* and Japanese V-*te shimau. Journal of Pragmatics* 34:143–66.

———. 2003. Completive aspect, emotion, and the dynamic eventive: The case of Korean V-*a/e pelita,* Japanese V-*te shimau,* and Spanish *se. Linguistics* 41:653–79.

Strauss, Susan, JiHye Lee, and Kyungja Ahn. 2006. Applying conceptual grammar to advanced level language teaching—The case of two completive constructions in Korean. *Modern Language Journal* 90:185–209.

Swaffar, Janet. 2004. A template for advanced learning tasks: Staging genre reading and cultural literacy through the précis. In *Advanced foreign language learning: A challenge to college programs,* ed. Heidi Byrnes and Hiram H. Maxim. Boston: Heinle-Thomson, 19–45.

Talmy, Leonard. 1975. Figure and ground in complex sentences. In *Proceedings of the first annual meeting of the Berkeley Linguistics Society*. Berkeley, Calif.: Berkeley Linguistics Society, 419–30.

———. 1985. Lexicalization patterns: Semantic structure in lexical forms. In *Language typology and syntactic description*, vol. 3: *Grammatical categories and the lexicon*, ed. Timothy Shopen. Cambridge: Cambridge University Press, 57–149.

———. 2000. *Toward a cognitive semantics*. Cambridge, Mass.: MIT Press.

Taylor, John R. 1993. Some pedagogical implications of cognitive linguistics. In *Conceptualizations and mental processing in language*, ed. Richard A. Geiger and Brygida Rudzka-Ostyn. Berlin: de Gruyter, 201–23.

Tomasello, Michael. 1998. *The new psychology of language: Cognitive and functional approaches to language structure*. Mahwah, N.J.: Erlbaum.

Descriptive and Instructional Considerations in Advanced Learning

7

Narrative Competence in a Second Language

ANETA PAVLENKO

Temple University and Center for Advanced Language Proficiency Education and Research (CALPER)

NARRATIVES ARE THE CENTRAL MEANS by which people make sense of their experiences. Their functions also include presentation of self, organization of autobiographical memory, socialization of children into cultural membership, and mediation of ways of thinking about problems and difficulties. These functions are crucial for adult second language (L2) learners who are looking for ways to become "meaningful" in the new environment because "the person can only be a meaningful entity, both to himself or herself and to others, by being 'read' in terms of the discourses available in that society" (Burr 1995, 142). A misunderstood narrative becomes an inappropriate presentation of self or of a sequence of events and may result in cross-cultural miscommunication.

Nevertheless, foreign language (FL) and L2 curricula and classroom practices continue to privilege acquisition of linguistic or, at best, pragmatic competence and rarely focus on teaching narration. Several factors explain this oversight, including the perennial lack of time and the mistaken belief that learners who can construct "correct" sentences should be able to string them together into narratives. Yet nothing could be further from the truth: Learners who are very skillful at the sentence level may still fail to construct language- and culture-appropriate narratives because narrative competence is not tantamount to linguistic competence and does not fully correlate with measures of syntactic complexity or vocabulary size (McCabe and Bliss 2003).

What is required to tell a story well? Even in one's native language narrative is not an easy task, and some of us are better storytellers than others. In a second language the task is even more challenging because of the ongoing search for the right word or the correct tense. Yet the American Council on the Teaching of Foreign Languages (ACTFL) Proficiency Guidelines, which emphasize narration and description as two critical features of advanced language proficiency, do not elaborate on what constitutes L2 narrative competence and offer only assessment guidance (Breiner-Sanders et al. 2000). The guidelines state that speakers at superior and advanced-high levels should be able to provide lengthy and coherent narrations; in all time frames; with ease, fluency, and accuracy; and without hesitation. They should exhibit good control of aspect; a variety of narrative strategies, such as paraphrasing, circumlocution, or illustration; and the ability to separate main ideas from supporting information through the use of syntactic and lexical devices and intonational features.

In this chapter I address two gaps in the field of applied linguistics: the gap in theorizing L2 narrative competence and the gap in teaching of L2 narrative skills in FL and L2 curricula. Because of space limitations, this discussion focuses mainly on oral narratives, leaving out the work on L2 reading and writing and on contrastive rhetoric. The discussion is based on a synthesis of three types of research: crosslinguistic studies of narrative construction, studies of narrative development in monolingual and bilingual children, and studies of second language acquisition (SLA) and bilingualism that involve elicited and spontaneous narratives. The need for triangulation of findings from distinct research paradigms stems from the fact that to date the construct of L2 narrative competence has not been elaborated in any of the paradigms, although each has something important to contribute to this enterprise.

Crosslinguistic studies offer important insights into similarities and differences in narrative styles among speech communities (Chafe 1980; Henkin 1998; Holmes 1998; Tannen 1980, 1982, 1993). Yet precisely because these studies focus on narrative construction in a single language by native speakers of that language, we do not learn from them which differences may cause problems for L2 learners.

Studies of narrative development of monolingual and bilingual children acknowledge cross-linguistic differences, advance a specific construct of narrative competence, and examine development of this competence in a variety of languages (Berman 1995; Berman and Slobin 1994; McCabe and Bliss 2003; Minami 2002; Pearson 2002). The focus of these studies, however, is on development of narrative competence in light of children's overall linguistic, cognitive, and literacy development. Not all of the narrative components examined in these studies are relevant for analysis of the stories told by adolescent and adult FL and L2 learners. Comparative studies of children's and adults' narratives show that narrative development in child L1 and adult L2 acquisition are qualitatively different processes because children are still in the process of acquiring the cognitive and linguistic skills necessary for competent storytelling, whereas adults already have the requisite skills (Berman 1999; Henkin 1998; Strömqvist and Day 1993). Consequently, in dealing with adult L2 learners we do not need to be concerned with all aspects of narrative competence outlined in the studies of narrative development; instead, we need to focus on aspects that are critical for competent storytelling in a second language. Yet studies of narrative development for the most part fail to inform us what these areas of difficulty might be.

On the other hand, studies of narratives in the fields of SLA and bilingualism (Bardovi-Harlig 2000; Berman 1999; Ordóñez 2004; Pavlenko 2002; Rifkin 2002; Rintell 1990; Verhoeven and Strömqvist 2001) focus on difficulties experienced by L2 learners in several aspects of the storytelling activity. These studies, however, fail to examine L2 narrative competence in a comprehensive manner, as studies of children's narrative development do, nor do they take into consideration cross-linguistic differences in narrative styles uncovered in cross-linguistic studies of narrative construction.

To date, the only attempt to describe components of L2 narrative competence comes from Berman (1999, 2001). Based on the studies of storytelling by L2 users of

Hebrew and English, Berman posited a four-tiered hierarchy of distance from native-like norms. At the first level in this model is core grammar and thus errors in word order, case marking, and grammatical inflections. The second level of difficulty lies in the domain of lexical selection—that is, the choice of specific and appropriate vocabulary. The third level involves rhetorical expressiveness: that is, competent expression of a variety of discourse functions. The fourth level involves register appropriateness—the ability to vary linguistic choices according to context, cultural norms, and genre conventions.

This hierarchy undoubtedly is useful for research purposes, but it is not specific enough to offer implications for FL and L2 curricula. In what follows I advance an alternative construct of L2 narrative competence that is applicable for classroom instruction. I begin with a definition of L2 narrative competence; then I outline three components of this competence that are particularly relevant for adolescent and adult FL and L2 learners and point to ways in which these components can be investigated and incorporated into FL and L2 curricula.

L2 Narrative Competence

The term *narrative*, as used here, refers to "all types of discourse in which event structured material is shared with readers or listeners, including fictional stories, personal narratives, accounts and recounts of events (real or imagined)" (Mistry 1993, 208). Narrative studies commonly differentiate between two broadly defined types of narratives: fictional and personal. *Fictional narratives* are stories about fictional events; in the study of L2 learning they can be elicited with verbal and nonverbal prompts, such as pictures or videos, that allow us to obtain comparable language samples from a variety of speakers. *Personal narratives* are stories that are based on speakers' personal knowledge and experience; researchers can examine both spontaneously told stories and those elicited with verbal prompts, such as interview questions or key words.

L2 narrative competence, in the view adopted here, refers to L2 users' ability to interpret, construct, and perform personal and fictional narratives similarly to a reference group of native speakers of the target language. The reference group involves speakers who are similar to the L2 users in age, gender, and socioeconomic and educational background because narrative styles have been shown to vary along these sociolinguistic parameters within speech communities (Henkin 1998; McCabe and Bliss 2003). Elsewhere I offer detailed recommendations on collection and analysis of L2 narratives (Pavlenko, in press). In what follows I focus exclusively on three interrelated components of the L2 narrative competence: (1) structure, (2) evaluation and elaboration, and (3) cohesion. In each section, I first discuss crosslinguistic differences in realizations of the component in question, then methods of analysis of this component, and finally, ways to incorporate this component in FL and L2 classroom activities.

Narrative Structure

Competence in terms of *narrative structure* involves the use of language-, culture-, and genre-appropriate narrative components.

Crosslinguistic Differences   Sir Frederic Bartlett, a celebrated British psychologist, was the first scholar to investigate and theorize crosslinguistic and crosscultural differences in narrative construction. In Bartlett's ([1932] 1995) classic study, Western subjects were read a Native American story, "The War of Ghosts," and then were asked to re-tell it. Because participants found the story structure and many accompanying details unfamiliar, they repeatedly transformed the tale in recall, both through omissions of details and through rationalizations, which made the story conform to a more famil-iar Western pattern. On the basis of these observations and experiments, Bartlett ([1932] 1995) developed his theory of schema that informs much of contemporary cognitive science, psychology, and narrative study.

Crosslinguistic studies show that narrative schemas or structures differ across languages and cultures in both fictional and personal stories. Western narratives—in particular those in the Anglo-American tradition—favor a *topic-centered* chronolog-ical structure that focuses on a single event. In contrast, Japanese narratives may combine two or three similar incidents into a single story (Minami 2002), and speak-ers of Spanish highly value performative *topic-associating* narratives that combine things that happened at different times and places and to different people (McCabe and Bliss 2003). Conventional Western narratives also require a resolution, whereas in Maori stories, for instance, the conflict is created but not necessarily resolved (Holmes 1998). Differences also have been observed within particular genres: Tradi-tional Western folktales, for example, posit a goal for the main character to achieve, whereas Japanese folktales do not require such a goal (Matsuyama 1983). Speech communities also may favor unique story genres: Contemporary Russian society, for instance, favors complaint stories or litanies that do not require problem-solving so-lutions (Ries 1997).

Speakers whose narrative styles diverge from the mainstream standard often are perceived as lacking narrative competence. Thus, Maori stories appear incomplete to the ears of white New Zealanders waiting for a resolution and a coda (Holmes 1998). Topic-associating narratives of Spanish speakers are perceived as incoherent leapfrogging by Anglo-American interlocutors who expect stories about a single event (McCabe and Bliss 2003; Riessman 1991). Americans who offer problem-solving solutions to Russian litanies find their contributions ignored by their Rus-sian interlocutors, who respond to complaint stories with similar complaints (Ries 1997).

Consequently, the first component of L2 narrative competence is knowledge of narrative structures that are conventional in the target language and the ability to ap-peal to these structures in a context-appropriate manner. Use of language- and cul-ture-appropriate structures contributes greatly to positive perception of story coher-ence by target language speakers. In turn, coherence, or the feeling that the text makes sense, often is regarded as a defining characteristic of a competent narrative.

Methods of Analysis   Five approaches commonly are used in analyzing narrative struc-ture: high point, story grammar, stanza analysis, narrative assessment profile, and form-function analysis. *High-point analysis* examines narrative functions of particu-lar utterances and episodes in terms of the structure outlined by Labov (1972) and

Labov and Waletzky (1967), based on a large sample of elicited personal narratives. This structure consists of an abstract (or narrative opening), an orientation (time, place, character identification), a complicating action (what happened and how), an evaluation, a resolution, and a coda (or narrative closing). This approach has been successfully applied to analysis of narratives told by L2 learners of English (Berman 1999; Ordóñez 2004; Rintell 1990), Hebrew (Berman 1999), Japanese (Maeno 1995), Spanish (Lafford 1998), and Swedish (Viberg 2001).

Story grammar analysis was developed by Mandler (1982) and Stein and Glenn (1979), based on Propp's (1968) analysis of Russian folktales. This approach investigates the degree to which the story is structured around the explicit goals of the protagonist and thus examines the following components: setting, initiating event, character's internal response and plan, character's attempts to solve the problem, and consequences. This approach has been successfully applied to analysis of L2 learners' narratives by Leppänen and Kalaja (2002).

Critics argue, however, that high-point and story grammar analyses may be biased toward Western narratives—more specifically, toward the European tradition (McCabe and Bliss 2003; Mistry 1993). This concern is addressed in the third approach, *stanza analysis*, which was advanced by Hymes (1981) and extended by Gee (1985). Stanza analysis breaks the narrative into lines and then groups the lines into hierarchical levels, such as verses (a simple sentence or clause), stanzas (a group of lines about a single topic), scenes, and acts—presenting the narrative as if it were a prose poem. This approach was used successfully by Maeno (1995) to examine narratives of American L2 learners of Japanese. Yet although stanza analysis is helpful in illuminating the structure of Japanese or Zuni narratives, it does not apply well to all cultures (McCabe and Bliss 2003).

The fourth approach, *narrative assessment profile*—advanced by McCabe and Bliss (2003) on the basis of many years of work with children from a variety of cultural and linguistic backgrounds—addresses cultural concerns through its multidimensionality. This approach, which was developed to evaluate discourse coherence, examines topic maintenance, event sequencing, informativeness, referencing, conjunctive cohesion, and fluency and has been successfully used by McCabe and Bliss in their analysis of bilingual children's narratives.

Finally, *form-function analysis* (Berman 1995; Berman and Slobin 1994) considers how linguistic forms are deployed to express narrative functions—that is, to encode temporal relations (temporality) or create textual cohesiveness (connectivity). This approach also has been successfully applied to L2 learners' narratives, particularly in analysis of deployment of tense and aspect (Bardovi-Harlig 2000).

Analyses of L2 learners' narratives conducted to date demonstrate that when the narrative structures of the L1 and L2 are similar, learners do exhibit appropriate narrative structure in target language stories (Berman 1999; Ordóñez 2004; Rintell 1990; Viberg 2001), and when the narrative structures of L1 and L2 are dissimilar, learners can acquire some new structures (Maeno 1995). The main weaknesses of the L2 learners' narratives identified in these analyses are lack of appropriate linguistic markers of particular narrative structures and functions and insufficient elaboration and evaluation (McCarthy 1991; Ordóñez 2004; Rintell 1990; Viberg 2001).

Incorporation in FL and L2 Classrooms   Among the most common exercises that allow students to practice narrative structure are sorting and sequencing activities, in which students are asked to put disconnected parts of a narrative (either pictorial or verbal) into a logical sequence (see, for example, Wajnryb 2003). Exercises such as "choose your own adventure" may be used to practice particular elements of narrative structure, such as complication, resolution, or a coda. Unfortunately, North American teachers often use these activities with an assumption that a conventional Labovian structure applies to all target languages. A variation on a sorting or sequencing activity would involve a larger array of pictures—so that Japanese and Spanish learners, for instance, also could create narratives that combine two or three similar events. Even more important for advanced narrative competence are consciousness-raising and noticing activities that have students analyze the structure of conventionalized narratives in the target language and notice linguistic markers of particular narrative components, including openings (e.g., "This reminds me of," "Did I tell you about the time when . . ."), complicating events (e.g., "Suddenly, out of the blue . . ."), and closings (e.g., "Makes you wonder") (McCarthy 1991).

Students also should be encouraged to experiment with unconventional and unfamiliar formats, such as topic-associating narratives in the Spanish class or litanies in the Russian class. This does not mean that they should be forced to produce narratives in these formats but that they should learn, at least, to recognize them as legitimate, follow them, and behave appropriately as interlocutors—for instance, providing adequate back-channeling or abstaining from offering problem-solving solutions to Russian litanies. McCarthy (1991, 140–42) offers several useful suggestions for teaching students how to be active listeners and how to participate in joint storytelling.

Evaluation and Elaboration

To capture listeners' attention and ensure their involvement, narratives have to be not only appropriately structured but also vivid and engaging. This function is accomplished through *elaboration*—that is, skillful uses of lexical choices, figurative language, reported speech, imagery, and descriptive details. *Evaluation* is an important function of elaboration and a prominent component of narrative structure in the Labovian model. The role of evaluation is to convey the narrator's attitude toward the events and to make the story worth listening to or reading. This narrative component differs from others in that it occurs throughout the story rather than at one point and is marked lexically, syntactically, and prosodically. Thus, at any point in the narrative, evaluation may appear directly as a lexical item (e.g., emotion words)—a separate clause or a set of clauses (e.g., causal explanations)—or indirectly as prosody, repetition, intensification, mitigation, metapragmatic descriptors, or figurative language.

Crosslinguistic Differences

Crosslinguistic studies demonstrate that narrative traditions vary in conventionalized uses of evaluation strategies. Classic studies by Tannen (1980, 1982, 1993) compared recalls of the same elicitation stimulus, the *Pear Film*, by Greek and American women. Tannen found that American women treated the recall as a memory task and attempted to report the events in the film in detail but without much added interpretation, except for comments on the film itself. On the other hand, Greek women did not say much about the qualities of the film but offered abundant evaluation and interpretation of the story line. Spanish speakers recalling the same film also tended to provide their own interpretations and inferences and appealed to a wide array of evaluative strategies (Blackwell 1998). Berman (1997) also showed that some narrative styles require more evaluation than others. In her study, stories elicited by the same stimulus from English- and Hebrew-speaking children contained a higher amount of evaluation than stories elicited from Turkish- and Japanese-speaking children, who avoided making explicit references to characters' psychological states.

Speech communities may differ not only in the conventionalized amount of evaluation and interpretation but also in preferred evaluation strategies. For instance, evaluation in Maori stories often is implicit, whereas in white New Zealanders' stories it often is made explicit (Holmes 1998). Personal stories by Palestinian Bedouin children and adults favor repetition and direct speech and make little use of other evaluation and involvement strategies (Henkin 1998).

These studies suggest that in the context of the same task, different narrative styles may require different amounts and strategies of evaluation and elaboration. L2 speakers who use an inappropriate amount of evaluation or inappropriate strategies may be misunderstood or even penalized, either for telling boring or incomplete stories or for telling overly dramatic stories and overinterpreting events. Consequently, the second component of L2 narrative competence involves familiarity with evaluation strategies that are common in a particular speech community and the ability to provide a language- and culture-appropriate—that is, conventional for a particular context—amount of evaluation.

Methods of Analysis

Elaboration and evaluation can be analyzed on four linguistic levels: prosodic, lexical, morphosyntactic, and discursive. On the prosodic level, evaluation can be signaled through three clusters of *prosodic cues*: frequency (pitch, tone, intonation), intensity (loudness, stress), and duration (rhythm, rate of articulation). The social meanings of these cues differ across languages and cultures (for a review, see Pavlenko 2005); thus, analysts must consider both L1 and L2 meanings in interpreting prosodic cues in L2 narratives.

On the lexical level, elaboration and evaluation are accomplished through lexical selection and lexical diversity. *Lexical diversity* typically is measured through a type-token ratio that compares the number of different words (types) with the number of total words (tokens) (for alternative measures, see Dewaele and Pavlenko 2003; Jarvis 2002). To analyze *lexical selection* in a particular domain, scholars identify all references to specific target denotata (e.g., deer, stag, antelope, elk), including circumlocutions (e.g., little animal), and analyze them in terms of context and register appropriateness.

The morphosyntactic level of narrative competence involves selection of appropriate *morphosyntactic options* for alternating between background information and foregrounded events (e.g., tense-aspect switches), for offering agent and patient perspectives (e.g., shifts in voice or valency), or for situating the narrative within appropriate temporal, spatial, and discursive frames (Berman 1999).

The discursive level involves the ability to choose appropriate *rhetorical options* to express various discursive functions and *strategic competence*—that is, the ability to select an appropriate register and use a variety of narrative strategies.

Studies of L2 learners' narratives conducted to date show that competent narratives are distinguished by appropriate lexical, discursive, and register choices and by skillful uses of paraphrasing and circumlocutions in cases of difficulties with lexical retrieval. Weaker narratives display insufficient elaboration and evaluation; an absence of figurative language, reported speech, epithets, and depersonalization; and overuse of compensatory strategies, such as repetition, pausing, lexical borrowing, code-switching, omission, and explicit attempts at word retrieval and requests for help (Berman 1999; Cenoz 2001; Lafford 1998; Ordóñez 2004; Pavlenko 2002; Pavlenko and Jarvis 2002; Rintell 1990; Viberg 2001). Lafford's (1998) cross-sectional study of American L2 learners of Spanish shows that the transition from intermediate to advanced level of proficiency involves an increase in the amount of narrative evaluation.

Incorporation in FL and L2 Classrooms
Several types of exercises promote the skills of evaluation and elaboration. In consciousness-raising and noticing activities, students may be asked to analyze the means of elaboration and evaluation in the stories they read or listen to (see, for example, Hatch 1992, 170–71). Then they can be given "bare bones" stories and asked to elaborate on these stories and make them more vivid and engaging. To make this exercise easier and more focused, students can be asked to do one thing at a time: creatively use a set of new lexical items, appeal to reported speech, incorporate specific types of figurative language, and so forth.

Students can then practice their newly acquired skills of elaboration in the context of personal storytelling, as illustrated in McMahill's (2001) study of a feminist English class in Japan. The researcher demonstrates that Japanese women in this class appeal to a wide array of elaboration strategies that increase the listener's emotional involvement: repetition; use of emphatic particles such as "very" and "just"; use of parallel structures; prosodic cues, particularly stress; and reported speech. McMahill then shows that the students' success in telling such emotional and dramatic stories stems from the fact that they have learned the strategies of emotional involvement in the context of telling narratives that are meaningful to them, the stories of their own lives, oppression, and resistance.

Narrative Cohesion
Constructing coherent narratives requires more than following a context-appropriate narrative structure and providing sufficient evaluation; coherence also relies on *cohesion*, or surface links between clauses and sentences. Two types of resources are used to create cohesion. *Lexical resources* include lexical ties (e.g., reiteration, collocation, synonymy) and deictic markers, which include personal deixis (e.g.,

pronouns), temporal deixis (e.g., temporal adverbs), spatial deixis (e.g., demonstratives, verbs of motion), social deixis (e.g., forms of address, kinship terms), and discursive deixis (e.g., context-dependent references, such as "next chapter"); *grammatical resources* include reference, ellipsis, substitution, conjunction, and tense and aspect (Halliday and Hasan 1976; Hatch 1992; McCabe and Bliss 2003; McCarthy 1991).

Crosslinguistic Differences

Crosslinguistic differences in means of cohesion are particularly apparent in three areas. The first area is *reference*—that is, identification of individuals, objects, features, locations, and events, most often expressed through personal, social, and discourse deictic markers such as pronouns or demonstratives. Differences in this area exist in the ways in which people and objects are divided into categories and in the ways in which these categories are invoked in narratives. For instance, Spanish-language narratives told by Puerto-Rican adults were found to contain a significantly greater percentage of reference cohesion than narratives produced by English-speaking adults (McCabe and Bliss 2003). The authors attribute this finding to Spanish speakers' preference for references to family members—a strategy that creates cohesion and grounds the narrator and the listener. In turn, Japanese storytellers tend to dispense with nominal references to entities they assume to be in the focus of the listeners' consciousness (Chafe 1980; Minami 2002).

The second important area is *temporality*—that is, tense and aspect deployment in the context of various narrative structures and functions. Tense and aspect systems vary significantly across languages and, as a result, are used differently in narrative construction. In Slavic languages, for instance, discussion of past events will encode whether the actions were accomplished or not (perfective/imperfective aspect), whereas in English the same events may be described in terms of "now-relevance" (present perfect) and "break with the present" (past simple) (Hatch 1992; McCarthy 1991).

Differences also exist in the area of *conjunctive cohesion*—that is, use of connectors (e.g., and, then, but, because) to mark a variety of semantic and pragmatic functions and relationships. Members of different speech communities may differ in patterns of connector use. For instance, Zambian L2 learners of English rarely use "and" and "but" in contexts where native speakers of English commonly do (McCarthy 1991).

Methods of Analysis

Studies of reference typically focus on *character introduction* and *reference continuation* and examine the lexical and morphosyntactic resources learners use to introduce characters, objects, or places (e.g., name, extensive description) and to maintain reference (e.g., personal pronouns that can be clearly interpreted) (McCabe and Bliss 2003; Nistov 2001; Ordóñez 2004; Strömqvist and Day 1993).

In studies of *temporality,* clauses are coded for anchoring tense, and patterns of tense maintenance and shift are considered in the light of narrative functions, such as foregrounding or backgrounding. Bardovi-Harlig (2000, 279–337) offers an excellent discussion of the distribution of tense and aspect across different narrative structures, types, and functions, as well as an overview of the studies of temporality in L2 narratives.

Studies of *conjunction* examine the uses of connectors that signal pragmatic functions and mark semantic relationships, such as coordination, subordination, causality, juxtaposition, or temporal sequence (Berman 1999; McCabe and Bliss 2003; Strömqvist and Day 1993; Viberg 2001).

Together, studies of narrative cohesion in L2 learners' narratives show that learners experience difficulties in acquiring language-specific patterns of reference continuation, temporality, and connectivity and that their choices are affected by universal and language-specific factors, such as L1 influence. In the beginning stages, L2 learners may favor one type of pronominal reference or connector over all others; even when they have acquired the other connectors, their patterns of use still may be different from those of native speakers of the language (Viberg 2001). Studies also have shown that when learners attempt to incorporate more advanced linguistic resources into their narratives, they may sacrifice narrative cohesion—in other words, with increases in linguistic competence, narrative cohesion may temporarily weaken before it becomes stronger (Strömqvist and Day 1993).

Incorporation in FL and L2 Classrooms
Classroom activities can offer learners multiple opportunities for practicing the use of cohesive devices in the context of narratives. In noticing and consciousness-raising activities, students may be asked to locate all connectors or particular deictic markers in the text and to identify their functions (see, for example, Hatch 1992, 213, 215–16, 227–28). Fill-in-the-blank activities may require students to fill in blanks in the narrative with particular types of cohesive devices, such as personal references, and explain their choices (see, for example, Hatch 1992, 212–13). To practice causality markers, students may be asked to argue a case or make a complaint (Wajnryb 2003).

Byrnes and Sprang (2004) offer interesting ideas in discussing teaching of narration in a college-level German classroom. The instruction offered students a variety of scaffolds to aid in retelling of authentic texts. For instance, to master the intricacies of temporal cohesion, students were offered visual aids that graphically represented temporal adverbs and adverbial phrases on a timeline. These aids allowed learners to move beyond minimal conjunction structures *und dann . . . und dann . . .* (and then . . . and then . . .) to use more complex linguistic means for signaling temporality and foregrounding some events while backgrounding others.

Rifkin's (2002) study of Russian narration by American learners suggests that use of cohesive devices benefits from classroom emphasis on narrative skills. Rifkin's analysis of narratives told by native speakers of Russian, American students in a traditional conversation class, and American students in a class designed to promote learning of narration established that learners from the experimental class produced more complex sentences than learners in the traditional class and approached native speakers of Russian in frequency and accuracy of relativization. The study made a convincing argument that conversation classes alone may not develop narration in a satisfactory manner and that more attention to development of narrative proficiency is needed to help students make the transition from intermediate to advanced level.

Conclusion

I have argued that FL and L2 curricula should incorporate activities that promote L2 narrative skills that are critical for assessment purposes and for interaction with target language speakers. I have outlined three components of L2 narrative competence—narrative structure, elaboration and evaluation, and cohesion—that often are not only language-specific but also culture-specific and thus particularly difficult to acquire. I also have provided recommendations on how these components can be analyzed and incorporated in the curricula. Further recommendations on narrative analysis appear in McCabe and Bliss (2003), and ideas for narrative activities in L2 classrooms appear in Wajnryb (2003).

REFERENCES

Bardovi-Harlig, Kathleen. 2000. *Tense and aspect in second language acquisition: Form, meaning, and use.* Malden, Mass.: Blackwell.

Bartlett, Frederic. [1932] 1995. *Remembering: A study in experimental and social psychology.* Cambridge: Cambridge University Press.

Berman, Ruth. 1995. Narrative competence and storytelling performance: How children tell stories in different contexts. *Journal of Narrative and Life History* 5, no. 4:285–313.

———. 1997. Narrative theory and narrative development: The Labovian impact. *Journal of Narrative and Life History* 7, no. 1–4:235–44.

———. 1999. Bilingual proficiency/proficient bilingualism: Insights from narrative texts. In *Bilingualism and migration,* ed. Guus Extra and Ludo Verhoeven. Berlin: de Gruyter, 187–208.

———. 2001. Narrative development in multilingual contexts: A cross-linguistic perspective. In *Narrative development in a multilingual context,* ed. Ludo Verhoeven and Sven Strömqvist. Amsterdam/Philadelphia: John Benjamins, 419–28.

Berman, Ruth, and Dan Slobin. 1994. *Relating events in narrative: A crosslinguistic developmental study.* Mahwah, N.J.: Erlbaum.

Blackwell, Sarah. 1998. A cross-gender and cross-cultural analysis of Spanish oral narratives: Revisiting "The Pear Stories." Paper presented at International Pragmatics Conference, Reims, France, July 20.

Breiner-Sanders, Karen, Pardee Lowe, John Miles, and Elvira Swender. 2000. ACTFL Proficiency Guidelines: Speaking Revised 1999. *Foreign Language Annals* 33:13–18.

Burr, Vivien. 1995. *An introduction to social constructionism.* London: Routledge.

Byrnes, Heidi, and Katherine A. Sprang. 2004. Fostering advanced L2 literacy: A genre-based, cognitive approach. In *Advanced foreign language learning: A challenge to college programs,* ed. Heidi Byrnes and Hiram Maxim. Boston: Heinle Thomson, 47–85.

Cenoz, Jasone. 2001. The effect of linguistic distance, L2 status and age on cross-linguistic influence in third language acquisition. In *Cross-linguistic influence in third language acquisition: Psycholinguistic perspectives,* ed. Jasone Cenoz, Britta Hufeisen, and Ulrike Jessner. Clevedon, England: Multilingual Matters, 8–20.

Chafe, Wallace, ed. 1980. *The pear stories: Cognitive, cultural, and linguistic aspects of narrative production.* Norwood, N.J.: Ablex.

Dewaele, Jean-Marc, and Aneta Pavlenko. 2003. Productivity and lexical diversity in native and non-native speech: A study of cross-cultural effects. In *Effects of the second language on the first,* ed. Vivian Cook. Clevedon, England: Multilingual Matters, 120–41.

Gee, James Paul. 1985. The narrativization of experience in the oral style. *Journal of Education* 167:9–35.

Halliday, Michael, and Ruqaiya Hasan. 1976. *Cohesion in English.* New York: Longman.

Hatch, Evelyn. 1992. *Discourse and language education.* Cambridge: Cambridge University Press.

Henkin, Roni. 1998. Narrative styles of Palestinian Bedouin adults and children. *Pragmatics* 8:47–78.

Holmes, Janet. 1998. Narrative structure: Some contrasts between Maori and Pakeha story-telling. *Multilingua* 17:25–57.

Hymes, Dell. 1981. *"In vain I tried to tell you": Studies in Native American ethnopoetics.* Philadelphia: University of Pennsylvania Press.

Jarvis, Scott. 2002. Short texts, best-fitting curves and new measures of lexical diversity. *Language Testing* 19:57–84.

Labov, William. 1972. *Language in the inner city.* Philadelphia: University of Pennsylvania Press.

Labov, William, and Joshua Waletzky. 1967. Narrative analysis: Oral versions of personal experience. In *Essays on the verbal and visual arts: Proceedings of the 1966 annual spring meeting of the American Ethnological Society,* ed. June Helm. Seattle: University of Washington Press, 12–44.

Lafford, Barbara. 1998. Toward a variable "native norm": The development of narrative structure in the acquisition of Spanish as a second language. Paper presented at American Association of Applied Linguistics conference, Seattle, March 20.

Leppänen, Sirpa, and Paula Kalaja. 2002. Autobiographies as constructions of EFL learner identities and experiences. In *Studia Linguistica et Litteraria Septentrionalia. Studies presented to Heikki Nyyssönen,* ed. Elise Kärkkäinen, James Haines, and Timo Lauttamus. Oulu, Finland: Oulu University Press, 189–203.

Maeno, Yoshimi. 1995. Acquisition of oral narrative skills by foreign language learners of Japanese. In *Proceedings of Boston University Conference on Language Development,* vol. 19, ed. Dawn McLaughlin and Susan McEwen. Boston: Cascadilla Press, 359–66.

Mandler, Jean. 1982. Some uses and abuses of a story grammar. *Discourse Processes* 5:305–18.

Matsuyama, Utako. 1983. Can story grammar speak Japanese? *The Reading Teacher* 36:666–69.

McCabe, Allyssa, and Lynn Bliss. 2003. *Patterns of narrative discourse: A multicultural, lifespan approach.* Boston: Allyn and Bacon.

McCarthy, Michael. 1991. *Discourse analysis for language teachers.* Cambridge: Cambridge University Press.

McMahill, Cheiron. 2001. Self-expression, gender, and community: A Japanese feminist English class. In *Multilingualism, second language learning, and gender,* ed. Aneta Pavlenko, Adrian Blackledge, Ingrid Piller, and Marya Teutsch-Dwyer. Berlin: de Gruyter, 307–44.

Minami, Masahiko. 2002. *Culture-specific language styles: The development of oral narrative and literacy.* Clevedon, England: Multilingual Matters.

Mistry, Jayanthi. 1993. Cultural context in the development of children's narratives. In *Cognition and culture: A cross-cultural approach to psychology,* ed. Jeanette Altarriba. Oxford: Elsevier Science, 207–28.

Nistov, Ingvild. 2001. Reference continuation in L2 narratives of Turkish adolescents in Norway. In *Narrative development in a multilingual context,* ed. Ludo Verhoeven and Sven Strömqvist. Amsterdam/Philadelphia: John Benjamins, 51–85.

Ordóñez, Claudia Lucia. 2004. EFL and native Spanish in elite bilingual schools in Colombia: A first look at bilingual adolescent frog stories. *International Journal of Bilingual Education and Bilingualism* 7:449–74.

Pavlenko, Aneta. 2002. Bilingualism and emotions. *Multilingua* 21:45–78.

———. 2005. *Emotions and multilingualism.* Cambridge: Cambridge University Press.

———. In press. Narrative analysis in the study of bi- and multilingualism. In *The Blackwell guide to research methods in bilingualism,* ed. Li Wei and Melissa Moyer. Malden, Mass.: Blackwell.

Pavlenko, Aneta, and Scott Jarvis. 2002. Bidirectional transfer. *Applied Linguistics* 23:190–214.

Pearson, Barbara. 2002. Narrative competence among monolingual and bilingual school children in Miami. In *Language and literacy in bilingual children,* ed. D. Kimbrough Oller and Rebecca Eilers. Clevedon, England: Multilingual Matters, 135–74.

Propp, Vladimir. 1968. *The morphology of the folktale.* Austin: University of Texas Press.

Ries, Nancy. 1997. *Russian talk: Culture and conversation during perestroika.* Ithaca, N.Y.: Cornell University Press.

Riessman, Catherine. 1991. When gender is not enough: Women interviewing women. In *The social construction of gender,* ed. Judith Lorber and Susan Farrell. Newbury Park, Calif.: Sage, 217–36.

Rifkin, Benjamin. 2002. A case study of the acquisition of narration in Russian: At the intersection of foreign language education, applied linguistics, and second language acquisition. *Slavic and East European Journal* 46:465–81.

Rintell, Ellen. 1990. That's incredible: Stories of emotion told by second language learners and native speakers. In *Developing communicative competence in a second language,* ed. Robin Scarcella, Elaine Andersen, and Stephen Krashen. Boston: Heinle & Heinle, 75–94.

Stein, Nancy, and Christine Glenn. 1979. An analysis of story comprehension in elementary schoolchildren. In *New directions in discourse processes,* ed. Roy Freedle. Norwood, N.J.: Ablex, 53–120.

Strömqvist, Sven, and Dennis Day. 1993. On the development of narrative structure in child L1 and adult L2 acquisition. *Applied Psycholinguistics* 14:135–58.

Tannen, Deborah. 1980. A comparative analysis of oral narrative strategies: Athenian Greek and American English. In *The pear stories: Cognitive, cultural, and linguistic aspects of narrative production,* ed. Wallace Chafe. Norwood, N.J.: Ablex, 51–87.

———. 1982. Spoken and written narrative in English and Greek. In *Coherence in spoken and written discourse,* ed. Deborah Tannen. Norwood, N.J.: Ablex, 21–41.

———. 1993. What's in a frame? Surface evidence for underlying expectations. In *Framing in discourse,* ed. Deborah Tannen. Oxford: Oxford University Press, 14–56.

Verhoeven, Ludo, and Sven Strömqvist, eds. 2001. *Narrative development in a multilingual context.* Amsterdam/Philadelphia: John Benjamins.

Viberg, Ake. 2001. Age-related and L2-related features in bilingual narrative development in Sweden. In *Narrative development in a multilingual context,* ed. Ludo Verhoeven and Sven Strömqvist. Amsterdam/Philadelphia: John Benjamins, 87–128.

Wajnryb, Ruth. 2003. *Stories: Narrative activities in the language classroom.* Cambridge: Cambridge University Press.

8

Lexical Inferencing in L1 and L2:
Implications for Vocabulary Instruction and Learning at Advanced Levels

T. SIMA PARIBAKHT AND MARJORIE WESCHE
University of Ottawa

LEXICAL INFERENCING, or how one makes an informed guess about the contextual mean-ing of an unfamiliar word, is a central process in both first language (L1) and second language (L2) comprehension.[1] It frequently serves as the initial step in the acquisi-tion of new word knowledge. "In inferencing, attributes and contexts that are famil-iar are utilized in recognizing what is not familiar" (Carton 1971, 45). More specifi-cally, lexical inferencing involves "making informed guesses as to the meaning of a word, in light of all available linguistic cues in combination with the learner's gen-eral knowledge of the world, her awareness of context and her relevant linguistic knowledge" (Haastrup 1991, 40). Given the importance of lexical inferencing, a pre-cise understanding of this process is needed for theory development and to inform in-struction. The present study compares lexical inferencing by university Farsi-speaking learners of English and English native speakers and considers the implica-tions of this and related research for instruction of advanced language learners.

Lexical inferencing while reading in a second language is particularly important for advanced learners, whose study of language and other disciplines through a sec-ond language depends heavily on understanding written texts—often in contexts in which looking up unfamiliar words in a dictionary or asking someone their meanings is not feasible. Lexical inferencing is an active, creative process of hypothesis-making and testing that—if it produces an appropriate word meaning—enhances the accuracy of text comprehension and interpretation, whereas a wrong inference may result in miscomprehension. Lexical inferencing also may lead to acquisition of word knowledge. Establishing a form/meaning relationship between a written word and an inferred contextual meaning may begin the complex, iterative process of learning new lexical forms, meanings, associations and uses and integrating them into one's existing lexical knowledge. For this reason, for most advanced L2 learners reading for comprehension—a process that depends heavily on lexical inferencing—is the major context for learning less frequent words (Horst, Cobb, and Meara 1998; Huckin and Coady 1999).

Research has demonstrated that lexical inferencing is the most important of sev-eral strategies that L2 readers use to resolve their vocabulary knowledge gaps as they seek to understand written passages (Fraser 1999; Kim 2003; Paribakht and Wesche

1999; Parry 1993, 1997; Schmitt 1997). Inferencing also may be used in combination with information from an informant or dictionary or word retrieval tactics such as repeating a word aloud (de Bot, Paribakht, and Wesche 1997; Fraser 1999; Paribakht and Wesche 1999). Of course, L2 readers ignore many unfamiliar words; they tend to concentrate their efforts on words that are either easy to guess or appear central to text understanding (Fraser 1999; Kim 2003; Paribakht and Wesche 1997). Longitudinal studies of L2 speakers reading English academic textbooks (Kim 2003; Parry 1997) have shown that individual readers attempted to infer meanings for as many as 60 percent of the unfamiliar words they did not ignore;[2] in our 1997 study, although L2 students reading short texts for comprehension ignored up to 50 percent of such words, they attempted inferencing for 80 percent of those they chose to deal with.

In spite of its pervasive use in reading comprehension, lexical inferencing in an L2 frequently fails (Laufer 1997). There are many specific explanations for unsuccessful inferences, including lack of adequate textual cues to support an accurate guess (Dubin and Olshtain 1993; Li 1988; Mondria and Wit-de Boer 1991). However, the relatively high success rate of L1 readers inferring contextually appropriate meanings for dummy words or for unfamiliar technical words suggests that this lack of cues is not the major factor.

L2 lexical inferencing success also is related to L2 proficiency (see Bengeleil and Paribakht 2004 and Haastrup 1991). These studies found that even when adequate cues are available, the ability to use them to construct appropriate meanings for unfamiliar words varies, depending on proficiency level. More specifically, lexical knowledge—itself highly correlated with both reading comprehension and general language proficiency—appears to be the primary key to successful inferencing for reading comprehension. This factor has been recognized in research on the number of words L2 readers need to know to successfully infer appropriate contextual meanings of unknown words; estimates range from 95 percent to 99 percent coverage of words in a given text, with higher estimates corresponding to academic texts (Coady 1997; Hazenberg and Hulstijn 1996; Hirsch and Nation 1992; Laufer 1997).[3] In addition to knowledge of word meanings, other knowledge about a word is important. Research by Qian (1999) demonstrated high correlations between a measure of "vocabulary depth" (as well as breadth) with L2 reading comprehension, and Nassaji (2004) demonstrated a similar relationship between a vocabulary depth measure and L2 inferencing success. Depth of vocabulary knowledge refers to aspects such as a word's syntactic behavior, frequency, and occurrence in specific contexts or register and, perhaps most important, to the multiple networks through which it is associated with other words in the mental lexicon. As Meara (1996, 49) has noted regarding L1 and L2 lexical networks, "in general, L2 words have a smaller number of shared associations than would be the case in an L1 lexicon."

Another possible explanation for unsuccessful lexical inferencing is that L2 readers, who are accustomed to lexical inferencing in their L1, may not know how to use their limited L2 knowledge to full effect in L2 inferencing. For example, they may overrely on cue types they regularly use in L1 inferencing, which may not be as useful in the L2. They may lack confidence in their ability to guess word meanings or may even have been discouraged by L2 instructors from attempting it (Huckin and

Jin 1986). If they do make guesses, they may not adequately evaluate them and accept misguesses. Effective inferencing involves identification of useful textual cues; using relevant knowledge to generate appropriate guesses; and evaluating these guesses in context, using other textual cues and knowledge, which may lead to revision and a new meaning to be tried out.[4] Like other highly contextualized, complex procedures, this process is learned through practice in relevant contexts of use.

The many different *knowledge sources* (KSs) L2 readers can use in lexical inferencing include target language and other knowledge, as well as world knowledge, as these interact with cues found in the L2 text at all levels of linguistic organization—from morphological forms to discourse patterns. In our research we have developed succeeding versions of a descriptive taxonomy of KSs as a means of systematically describing the kinds of knowledge learners use in this process (Bengeleil and Paribakht 2004; de Bot, Paribakht, and Wesche 1997; Paribakht 2005; Paribakht and Wesche 1999). The types of KSs readers use illustrate how knowledge and textual cues interact in inferencing and reflect the nature of word knowledge stored in the mental lexicon. Not surprisingly, learners who vary in L2 proficiency, general and topic knowledge, previous language instruction, and native language also vary in their ability to access and use available textual cues.

Relatively little is known about differences between L1 and L2 inferencing, either in terms of how L1 and L2 speakers differ in their approaches or how a given first language might influence the way a reader would go about inferring the meaning of an unfamiliar word in English. In the present study, we have dealt with these two aspects of L1 and L2 inferencing—one relating to "nativeness" in terms of linguistic and cultural proficiency and the other relating to interlingual "transfer" in inferencing behavior.

The linguistic and cultural proficiency of native speakers of the text language (i.e., those who learned it in early childhood and have maintained it) compared with that of advanced nonnative speakers of a language may influence their respective lexical inferencing behavior and rate of success. Readers faced with unfamiliar words in L1 texts evidently are much more likely to have the lexical and related cultural knowledge required to arrive at contextually appropriate word meanings than are L2 readers of the same texts. Are certain lexical inferencing patterns underlying this success shared by L1 speakers of different languages and different from those of L2 readers? If so, can aspects of "nativeness" be identified that might inform the L2 inferencing process?

Potential L1 transfer effects have to do with how one's internalized knowledge of the native language (in this case Farsi) and its particularities may influence lexical processing in a given L2 (in this case English). Studies of L2 reading provide some examples of L1 influence on L2 lexical inferencing related to L1 syntactic (Nagy, McClure, and Mir 1997) and orthographic features (Wade-Woolley 1999). Thus, we would expect to find systematic cross-lingual patterns when the same readers infer word meanings in Farsi L1 and English L2 texts, as highlighted through comparison with inferencing by English L1 readers. How can such information contribute to our understanding of the lexical inferencing process, and what are the implications for learners from particular language backgrounds who wish to become more successful in inferring appropriate word meanings in a given L2?

One of our research motivations has been to discover ways to improve advanced L2 readers' inferencing ability through instruction and practice. Such readers often are in situations in which they have no recourse to relevant instruction and in which diverse lexical demands make instruction that is based on particular lexical items of doubtful value. These learners need instruction that develops their ability to identify and learn the words they need, including an emphasis on effective lexical inferencing and related retention strategies. Several studies have demonstrated that learners can improve their inferencing success and word learning through training (Fraser 1999; Huckin and Jin 1986; Kim 2003; Parry 1997; Sternberg 1987), but more work in this area is needed. A better understanding of the information available to readers, how successful readers use it, and specific influences on L2 lexical inferencing should help in this endeavor.

Research Question

The following research question guided the study: What similarities and differences are there between Farsi-speaking English learners inferring the meanings of unfamiliar lexical items in their L1 and L2, compared with English native speakers in their L1? More specifically:

- What is their relative likelihood of attempting to infer unfamiliar word meanings?
- How successful are they in inferring meanings of unfamiliar words in context?
- What KSs and patterns of KS use do they use in inferencing?

Participants

We selected twenty Farsi-speaking high intermediate/advanced-level university English as a Foreign Language (EFL) learners (ten male and ten female)—the L1Farsi–L2English speakers—on the basis of their reading comprehension level.[5] The native speaker group comprised twenty English-speaking Canadian university undergraduates.

Instruments and Procedures

We selected fifty English target words according to their likely unfamiliarity to advanced Farsi-speaking EFL learners. They represented four word classes: twenty nouns, sixteen verbs, eight adjectives, and six adverbs (e.g., *retaliation, to elope, proactive, retroactively*). The relative frequencies of the target words were generally similar according to the Collins COBUILD English Language Dictionary (Collins 1995).

We grouped the target words thematically and composed six general interest paragraphs, each presenting seven to ten target words. (See Appendix A for a sample text.) The topics of the passages were "Marriage," "Preserving the Environment," "The Ice Age," "The World's Forgotten Poor," "Big City Dreams," and "Genetic Engineering."

Because the original target words already were familiar to the English speakers, we prepared a second version of each paragraph for the participants in which the target words were replaced by "dummy" words, all of which were morphologically

possible in English. Thus, the words for the English L1 and L1Farsi–L2English readers were the same. In addition, to provide the native speakers and L2 participants
with the same range of knowledge sources at the word level, the dummy words included the same affixes and other morphological cues as the original words (e.g.,
"quallies" for "glaciers," "tovingly" for "intuitively," and "nelking" for "eloping").

For Farsi L1 inferencing, we used a one-page general interest Farsi text on "How
to Make the New Year More Memorable" with twenty-five target words, representing
the same word types (ten nouns, eight verbs, four adjectives, and three adverbs). The
target words were replaced with dummy words, all possible in Farsi, constructed like
those in English to provide inflectional cues matching those of the original L1 words.

The research procedures were essentially the same for the Farsi and English
speakers in both L1 and L2, except that Farsi speakers did the L2 task first, followed
by the L1 task in a single session. Before the individual research sessions, participants were trained in groups in think-aloud procedures. During the individual research sessions, participants again briefly practiced the think-aloud procedures and
then received the L2 texts one at a time, with the target words bolded, all in the same
order. They were asked to read each text once for general comprehension and then
reread it and try to guess the meanings of the unfamiliar target words. They also were
asked to talk aloud about what they were thinking and doing while performing the
task. The research assistant conducting the interviews did not answer any questions
regarding the target words and prompted participants only when necessary. All research sessions were tape-recorded and transcribed.

Analyses

We analyzed the data with respect to

- Whether the participant attempted to infer the meaning of each target word
- How successful the inferencing was (i.e., whether the inferred meaning was
  correct or partially correct or a wrong inference was made)
- Which KSs participants reported using in their inferencing, and if more than
  one, their sequence.

Results

Table 8.1 displays the findings regarding inferencing attempts and success for each
data set.

Table 8.1
Inferencing Attempts and Success: L1 Farsi, L1Farsi–L2English, and L1 English Readers

	Inferences	Success		
Group	Attempts %	Full	Partial	Total
L1 English	99.8	89.3	4.3	93.6
L1Farsi–L2English	79.0	11.0	11.0	22.0
L1 Farsi	99.2	79.0	4.0	83.0

Inferencing Attempts

Farsi-speaking participants reading in English inferred meanings for a high percentage (79 percent) of unfamiliar L2 words, demonstrating strong motivation to fulfill the research task. For L1 reading tasks, all of the Farsi speakers inferred meanings for almost all dummy words, as did English speakers in their L1 texts (99.2 percent and 99.8 percent, respectively).

Success

Participants' inferred meanings for unfamiliar target words were evaluated as "successful" if an appropriate meaning was provided and "partially successful" if an approximate meaning was given. Either an inaccurate inference or no inference was classified as failure. The findings were dramatic: L2 inferencing was far less successful than L1 inferencing. In their respective L1s, the Farsi speakers arrived at appropriate meanings 79 percent of the time and the English speakers did so 89 percent of the time; an additional 4 percent of partially correct inferences occurred in both cases.[6] In contrast, L1 Farsi speakers were able to infer appropriate meanings for only 11 percent of the L2 English words they dealt with and were partially successful for another 11 percent. In other words, they did not arrive at correct inferences 78 percent of the time.

Knowledge Sources Used in Inferencing

In the qualitative data analyses, we identified all KSs used by L1 and L2 readers in inferring unfamiliar target words, and we developed a taxonomy (see table 8.2) by drawing on our previous work.[7] The taxonomy shows that participants used KSs from the text language and their *world knowledge*—a *nonlinguistic* source—in inferencing; in the case of L2 readers, there were occasional references to L1-based sources, namely *L1 collocation*. The *linguistic* KSs reflect many different aspects of *word* knowledge, operating at different levels of text organization. Taken together, the KSs attest to the many different kinds of knowledge and contextual cues involved in lexical processing and text comprehension. (See Appendix B for transcript examples of each KS.)

Farsi readers in L1 and L2 and English L1 readers all drew mainly from the same KSs in inferring meanings for target words—representing *word*, *sentence*, and *discourse* levels of language as well as *nonlinguistic* (*world*) knowledge. Three exceptions to these behaviors were that knowledge of *text style/register* was used only by L1 readers, *L1 collocation* (evidently) was used only in L2 inferencing, and use of *word association* was not reported by Farsi L1 readers.

Patterns of KS Use

The patterns and relative frequencies of use of the ***main categories*** of the taxonomy (word, sentence, discourse, nonlinguistic) by English L1 readers and L1Farsi–L2English and L1 readers are shown in figure 8.1. Within these main categories, KS use reflected shared tendencies across groups, patterns that are traceable to L1 influence (English versus Farsi as a text language), and shared characteristics of native speaker inferencing. Sentence-level knowledge was by far the main KS category used by all participant groups in lexical inferencing, accounting for 73.4 percent

Taxonomy of Knowledge Sources (KSs) Used in Lexical Inferencing (L1 and L2)

I. Linguistic Sources

A. L2-Based Sources

1. Word Level

a. Word Association

Association of the target word with another familiar word or a network of words

b. Word Collocation

Knowledge of words that frequently occur with the target word

c. Word Morphology

Morphological analysis of the target word, based on knowledge of grammatical inflections, stem, and affixes

d. Homonymy

Knowledge of form (orthographic or phonetic) similarity between the target word or a part of it and another word—that is, mistaking the target word for another that resembles it

2. Sentence Level

a. Sentence Meaning

The meaning of part or all of the sentence containing the target word

b. Sentence Grammar

Knowledge of the syntactic properties of the target word, its speech part, and word order constraints

c. Punctuation

Knowledge of rules of punctuation and their significance

3. Discourse Level

a. Discourse Meaning

The perceived general meaning of the text and sentences surrounding the target word (i.e., beyond the immediate sentence that contains the target word)

b. Formal Schemata

Knowledge of the macrostructure of the text, text types and discourse patterns, and organization

c. Text Style and Register

Knowledge of stylistic and register variations in word choice

B. L1-Based Source

L1 Collocation

Knowledge of words in L1 that have collocational relationship with the L1 equivalent of the target word, assuming that the same relationship exists in the target language

II. Nonlinguistic Source

World Knowledge

Nonlinguistic knowledge, including knowledge of the topic of the text and other related background knowledge

(Farsi L2), 48.5 percent (English L1), and 64.6 percent (Farsi L1) of the inferences. This finding suggests that in lexical inferencing, readers tend to focus primarily on the immediate context of the word.

As shown in the bar graph and percentages of figure 8.1, all three groups gave similar importance to discourse-level KSs. Strikingly, English L1 readers used word, discourse, and nonlinguistic KSs almost equally, whereas Farsi speakers tended not to use word cues either in L1 or L2, although they used them more in L2 than in L1. They also tended not to use nonlinguistic (world) knowledge, although they used it more in L1 than in L2.

The patterns of use of *specific* KSs reflect the general utility of some and the special uses of others, as well as differences related to L1 influence, the text language, and native proficiency as seen in the analysis of *main* categories (table 8.2). As table 8.3 shows, *sentence meaning* (SM) is by far the most important single KS in all three data sets; other KSs—such as *punctuation* (P) and text style/register (S)— were used infrequently and by only a few participants in some data sets. We describe the findings with respect to each main category.

Word-level KS use, which is displayed in figure 8.1 and table 8.3, is much lower for Farsi speakers (in both L2 and L1 inferencing) than for English speakers in L1 inferencing. Their relative use of specific word cues also differs, and some but not all the differences appear to reflect an *L1 effect*. Homonymy accounts for much of this difference; its use in the English L1 data (7 percent) contrasts sharply with the L1Farsi–L2English and L1 Farsi data (1 percent in each case). There is a strong similarity between L1Farsi–L2English and English L1 readers' use of *word morphology* cues, which account for 6 percent of both the L1Farsi–L2English readers' overall KS use and that of the English L1 readers. This finding is notable because in L1 inferencing, Farsi speakers almost never used word morphology cues, even though Farsi is a highly inflected language—which suggests a *text language* (English) effect. Another, weaker similarity between L1Farsi–L2English and English L1 word level KS use is that unlike the Farsi L1 data, the L1Farsi–L2English data show occasional use of word association (WA) cues (1 percent), which also are used in English L1 (2 percent) but never by Farsi readers in L1. The other word-level cue, *word* collocation

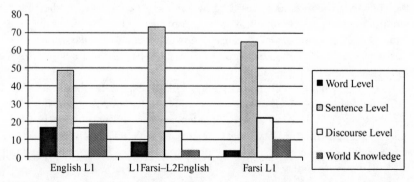

▓ Figure 8.1 Comparative Data for Main Categories of Knowledge Sources (KSs) Used in Lexical Inferencing

▓ Table 8.3
Specific Knowledge Sources (KSs) Used in Lexical Inferencing: Relative Frequencies (%) and Orders of Frequency

L1 English	SM>	WK>	DM>	H >	WM>	SG>	WA=	S=	WC>	FS
	44	19	14	7	6	5	2	2	2	1
L1Farsi–L2English	SM>	DM=	SG>	WM>	WK>	H=	P=	WA=	WC	
	59	14	14	6	4	1	1	1	1	
L1 Farsi	SM>	DM>	SG>	WK>	FS>	S=	WC>	H		
	53	14	11	10	5	3	3	1		

Note: Percentages rounded to nearest digit. Only percentages over 0.5 are reported.

Abbreviations:

Word Level	Sentence Level	Discourse Level	Nonlinguistic
WA = word association	SM = sentence meaning	DM = discourse meaning	WK = world knowledge
WC = word collocation	SG = sentence grammar	FS = formal schemata	
WM= word morphology	P = punctuation	S = text style/register	
H = homonymy			

(WC), has yet another pattern that one might call a ***native speaker effect***. Its highest percentage of use is by Farsi L1 readers (3 percent), and it also is used by English L1 readers (2 percent), whereas Farsi readers in L2 never use it.

As table 8.3 shows, sentence meaning was the most important specific KS for all three conditions; it accounted for 44 percent (English L1), 59 percent (L1Farsi– L2English) and 53 percent (Farsi L1) of reported KS uses respectively, as well as for the prominence of sentence-level KSs. Notably, sentence meaning is used more frequently by Farsi L1 and L2 readers than by English L1 readers, suggesting an ***L1 effect***. Sentence grammar also is important—again particularly for Farsi L1 (11 percent) and L1Farsi–L2English (14 percent) readers, distinguishing them somewhat from English L1 readers (5 percent). Punctuation, the third sentence-level KS, is a minor knowledge source for Farsi speakers (1 percent in both L1 and L2 data sets) and is never used by English L1 speakers. At the sentence level, then, overall and within each category, a pattern is apparent that strongly suggests a Farsi L1 influence on the knowledge sources and cues used by Farsi speakers reading in their L2. The greater use of sentence grammar and punctuation cues by Farsi speakers may reflect a training effect, to some extent, because grammar instruction in Farsi receives considerable emphasis throughout schooling in Iran, and English instruction also often tends to be grammatically based.

Discourse meaning is substantially and similarly used in all three data sets, accounting for 14 percent of KS use in each case. Thus, it is the second most important KS for Farsi L1 and L1Farsi–L2English readers and the third most important KS for English L1 readers. Like sentence meaning, it is a widely useful KS across language groups and in both L1 and L2. Although discourse meaning serves all three groups, both of the other discourse-level KSs found in the data, *formal schemata* and text style/register, are essentially limited to L1 readers; furthermore, their main users are Farsi speakers in L1. Formal schemata cues represent 5 percent of KS use in Farsi L1 and 1 percent in English L1; text style/register cues represent 3 percent of KS use in Farsi L1 and 2 percent in English L1. Both are related to high language proficiency, and contribute to L1 readers' greater ability to engage in top-down processing. In the case of formal schemata use in these data, there also may be a *text genre effect*.

Finally, world knowledge (WK) was the second most important single KS for English L1 speakers, accounting for 19 percent of inferences. It also was used by Farsi L1 readers (10 percent), but it was much less prominent for L1Farsi–L2English readers (4 percent). The fact that it is used more often in L1 inferencing raises the possibility that native language proficiency may promote greater reliance on top-down processing in lexical inferencing.

Discussion and Implications of Findings for Instruction

What insights can we draw from our findings that could inform instruction in reading and vocabulary learning for advanced learners? How should the features of a learner's particular L1 and L2 be taken into account? What can L2 readers themselves do to better comprehend texts containing some unknown words and to gain new word knowledge through reading more effectively?

The most striking characteristic of L2 inferencing by these relatively proficient university students is its low success rate. Why is L2 inferencing by these and other English learners so unsuccessful? We propose three main explanations: insufficient L2 proficiency, lack of relevant content schemata, and less effective L2 inferencing procedures.

Limited L2 Proficiency

Although these Farsi speakers are relatively advanced English users, they appear to lack the lexical knowledge needed to comprehend the text around unfamiliar words well enough to generate and evaluate appropriate contextual meanings. As we have noted, lexical knowledge must be understood not only as the ability to recognize words and identify primary meanings but also as knowledge of the ways they interact with other words in networks of meanings, forms, and functions. L2 readers tend to have less of this deeper knowledge than do L1 readers and thus may overrely on form-based local cues such as sentence grammar or word morphology in inferencing. Although these cues often are useful, they are limited to certain words and by themselves may not provide enough information for meaning construction. As our findings indicate, some KSs available to native speakers—such as stylistic and register constraints on the use of certain words, the formal schemata underlying the organization of texts in given genres, or knowledge of word collocations—often are not available to L2 speakers.

Limited Relevant Content Schemata

L2 readers also may lack relevant cultural and topical knowledge, which could provide useful information for successful inferencing. In L1 inferencing, both Farsi and English speakers frequently used world knowledge, but the Farsi speakers used it much less in inferring meanings for English (L2) words. Native proficiency not only means that readers have high levels of linguistic knowledge but that they also tend to have a deeper understanding of cultural and societal issues and probably greater familiarity with the topics of texts originating in that language. This knowledge will allow them to more easily comprehend content relationships.

Less-Effective Lexical Inferencing Behaviors

These Farsi-speaking readers of English naturally attempt to infer unfamiliar L2 word meanings, but they are far less successful in their L2 (see table 8.1). As we have noted, this difference may be related largely to lower L2 proficiency and background knowledge, but it also is possible that they could be taught to use their limited knowledge more effectively in L2 inferencing. For example, they may give up too quickly because they are unaware of the importance of lexical inferencing in both L2 reading comprehension and vocabulary learning. Even if they know the importance of inferencing, they may not be aware of the range of sources of information available to them. In some cases their lack of success also may be a result of accepting the first meaning that comes to mind, rather than making sure it is appropriate in the larger textual context.

Matching Language and Background Knowledge with Reading Tasks

For text comprehension and lexical inferencing to succeed, L2 readings must be accessible to learners with respect to both language and content. Familiar content will allow successful inferencing of new word meanings in texts that are linguistically somewhat challenging, and more familiar language will allow inferencing and comprehension of occasional words in texts that deal with somewhat less familiar content. The interface between language and content difficulty, which will permit comprehension, is elusive; most important is that language instructors are aware that *simultaneously maximizing difficulty on both dimensions may impede learning of both*. L2 reading comprehension and vocabulary development both require (and help to further develop) topic-related and culturally specific knowledge. Instructors can promote this complex process by preparing learners for written texts that involve unfamiliar content and specialized language. There are many well-known methods, many of which independent readers can learn on their own:

- Generation of *advance organizers* for topical and cultural content—such as guiding questions, attention to titles and illustrations, and explicit learning of new terminology—can help learners activate appropriate schemata for text comprehension.
- Rapid *prereading* of texts to get the gist prepares readers for more careful reading and inferencing and further activates content schemata that may lead to better comprehension and more accurate lexical inferencing.
- Intensive, thematically related reading provides an effective framework for implementing these practices in the classroom and for self-study. First, such reading, whether it is based on personal interest or course-related requirements, tends to engage and motivate learners to understand the texts. Second, themes and related concepts and protagonists gradually become more familiar, promoting more accurate guessing. Third, important theme-related words will

appear more than once—signaling their importance, providing associations
with slightly different contexts, and encouraging deeper processing of form,
meaning, and contextual relationships. Each meaningful exposure will contribute to fuller comprehension and more elaborated word knowledge in the mental lexicon.

Inferencing Strategy Instruction

In our view, instruction in L2 lexical inferencing should be part of advanced L2 reading and vocabulary instruction. Learners first need to be aware of the role and importance of lexical inferencing—in both text comprehension and vocabulary acquisition—as well as its pitfalls. Many learner participants in Bengeleil and Paribakht's
(2004) study reported that they had no formal training and practice in lexical
inferencing and that they found the inferencing task difficult. Inferencing exercises
over an extended time period have proven useful in promoting L2 learners'
inferencing frequency and success (Fraser 1999).

- Learners can practice with short texts related to their interests and needs. Certain words that are important to text comprehension and are likely to be unfamiliar can be underlined, and students, working either alone or collaboratively, can identify all relevant knowledge sources for each word and infer
  appropriate meanings.

- Inferencing for comprehension means that readers must not only identify and
  use KSs to generate guesses; they also must verify these guesses in context to
  confirm that the inferred meanings make sense in the sentence and discourse
  context and that they fit with other kinds of knowledge about the word, such
  as its structure and word class. If not, a partial fit may lead to a new guess.

Taxonomy of Knowledge Sources

The taxonomy of KSs identified in this study can be used as a basis for learner training in lexical inferencing. Through study of the taxonomy and examples and practice
in different kinds of cue uses, learners (and instructors) can gain awareness of the different types of cues available, frequent patterns of their use in the target and native
language, and their particular relevance to given text genres, word classes, and
phrases. For example:

- Low-proficiency L2 learners often use homonymy (similarity of an unfamiliar
  word's sounds or written features to another word in the language) (Holmes
  and Ramos 1997; Huckin and Bloch 1997).[8] Homonymy use tends to indicate
  a word retrieval strategy, as differentiated from meaning construction.
  Learners need to be aware that verification of homonymy-based guesses with
  meaning-based cues is crucial.

- Awareness of differences in L1 inferencing patterns between native speakers
  of two different languages, as well as awareness of how the same speakers infer meanings in an L1 and L2, also may help pinpoint what L2 learners need
  to know to infer word meanings more successfully in an L2. For example,
  Farsi readers in English may benefit from knowing about shared patterns of

KS use by Farsi and English L1 speakers, specific Farsi speaker patterns in both L1 and L2, and patterns related to English language use by both L1 and L2 speakers, as reflected in the findings from the quantitative analyses of this study.

▧ The fact that word-level cues were second to sentence-level (i.e., sentence meaning) cues for English readers in L1, whereas discourse-level cues (primarily discourse meaning) were second in importance for Farsi L2 and L1 readers, may be explained at least partially by differences in Farsi and English orthography, which—even though Farsi is highly inflected—limit the reliability of word-level cues as a source of information for inferring word meanings in Farsi. Vowels generally are not represented in Farsi orthography, so readers are accustomed to relying on the meaning of the context (sentence and discourse) to identify the exact word they are reading and pronounce it accurately when reading aloud. This L1 processing strategy appears to be carried over to L2 lexical processing in that even though more word-level cues are available in English (and often are used by English L1 readers), Farsi-speaking English L2 readers appear to rely more on sentence- and discourse-level meaning in lexical inferencing. This L1 influence should be pointed out to Farsi speakers of English, and they should be made more aware of the range of word-level cues available in English that they can draw on in lexical inferencing.

▧ Word morphology may be learned through instruction. The fact that these Farsi speakers frequently used such cues in English (but not Farsi) probably reflects systematic attention paid to grammatical inflections and word derivations in their English language instruction. Although word collocation is very language-specific, learners can be made aware of its importance and specific frequent cases in English through instruction that emphasizes identification and learning of multiword phrases and collocations. On the other hand, word association—a high-proficiency KS—is learned largely through extensive exposure to a word in various contexts, although semantic web exercises also may help to build learners' lexical networks.

Word Learning

Inferencing success while reading for comprehension, in itself, is not likely to lead to learning a new word, even though successful inferencing indicates that some initial processing has occurred. Retention of newly inferred form-meaning relationships depends on further "processing"; in Hulstijn's (2001, 8) terms, "elaboration on aspects of a word's form, meaning and rehearsal determine retention of new information." This elaboration can take place through repeated encounters with the words in different contexts. Instruction—for example, content-based exercises with selected words from readings—can support such learning (see, for example, Paribakht and Wesche 1997; Wesche and Paribakht 2000; Zimmerman 1994).

Advanced learners and instructors must understand how lexical knowledge is developed gradually over time, through multiple, meaningful encounters with words that allow development and strengthening of mental representations linking word forms, meanings, semantic boundaries, syntactic information, and associations with other words. Word-learning through reading is most effective when students know how to take advantage of it—for example, by knowing when and how to use contextual cues, by being aware of word families and productive affixes for analyzing words into parts, and by knowing when and how to use a dictionary effectively. An inferencing process that includes evaluation of inferences in the context of reading, using other KSs, is more likely to lead to retention, particularly when this internal verification procedure is followed by external verification with another source, such as a dictionary.

Finally, advanced learners need to consciously develop individual strategies for promoting their own learning of the infrequent but important words they need, such as thematic reading, inferencing practice, and retention strategies. Although there are no shortcuts to lexical development, learners themselves eventually can find the strategies that work best for them.

Acknowledgments

Funding by the Social Sciences and Humanities Research Council of Canada made this research possible. We are particularly grateful to our research assistants Shiva Sadeghi, Nazmia Bengeleil, Danielle Higgins, and Helene Lamarche, who conducted the interviews and assisted with the data analysis, and to Julita Kajzer, Karen Jesney, Shahla Shoeibi, and Ali Abasi for their help with different aspects of the project. We also thank Dr. Akbar Mirhassani, who facilitated data collection in Iran, and Doreen Bayliss and Frederic Nolet, who carried out the statistical analyses.

NOTES

1. "Inferencing" is a term coined by Aaron S. Carton (1971) in an early study of how foreign language readers infer meanings of unfamiliar words.
2. In both studies, rates of inferencing varied dramatically among individuals.
3. A word family includes "a base word, its inflected forms and a small number of reasonably regular derived forms" (Nation and Waring 1997, 8). Different meanings of the same form are different words.
4. This internal evaluation or verification of meaning should be distinguished from external verification with a dictionary or an appeal to outside expertise. These alternative ways of finding word meanings also are effective ways to confirm inferred meanings.
5. We determined the participants' reading proficiency by using a reading comprehension test developed at the Second Language Institute of the University of Ottawa. The test comprises two reading comprehension subtests and a multiple-choice cloze. Participants had sixty minutes to complete the test.
6. The lower success rate for Farsi L1 readers may reflect a fatigue factor, given that their research sessions included extra activities ending with the L1 inferencing task and were about 1½ hours longer than those of English L1 speakers.
7. Each successive version of our taxonomy of knowledge sources incorporates new sources related to the present data set. Thus, this "L1 and L2" taxonomy includes "text style and register," which is not found in the previous version in Paribakht (2005).
8. Guesses based on similar L1 words also may occur in cognate languages but were not found in these data.

REFERENCES

Bengeleil, Nazmia F., and T. Sima Paribakht. 2004. L2 reading proficiency and lexical inferencing by university EFL learners. *Canadian Modern Language Review* 6:225–49.

Carton, Aaron S. 1971. Inferencing: A process in using and learning language. In *The psychology of second language learning,* ed. Paul Pimsleur and Terence Quinn. Cambridge: Cambridge University Press, 45–58.

Coady, James. 1997. L2 vocabulary acquisition: A synthesis of the research. In *Second language vocabulary acquisition,* ed. James Coady and Tom Huckin. Cambridge: Cambridge University Press, 273–90.

Collins COBUILD English Language Dictionary, 2nd ed. 1995. London: Harper Collins.

de Bot, Kees, T. Sima Paribakht, and Marjorie Wesche. 1997. Toward a lexical processing model for the study of second language vocabulary acquisition: Evidence from ESL reading. *Studies in Second Language Acquisition* 19:309–29.

Dubin, Fraida, and Elite Olshtain. 1993. Predicting word meanings from contextual clues: Evidence from L1 readers. In *Second language reading and vocabulary learning,* ed. Tom Huckin, Margot Haynes, and James Coady. Norwood, N.J.: Ablex, 181–202.

Fraser, Carol A. 1999. Lexical processing strategy use and vocabulary learning through reading. *Studies in Second Language Acquisition* 21:225-41.

Haastrup, Kirsten 1991. *Lexical inferencing procedures or talking about words.* Tübingen, Germany: Gunter Narr.

Hazenberg, Suzanne, and Jan Hulstijn. 1996. Defining a minimal receptive second-language vocabulary for non-native university students: An empirical investigation. *Applied Linguistics* 17:145–63.

Hirsch, David, and Paul Nation. 1992. What vocabulary size is needed to read unsimplified texts for pleasure? *Reading in a Foreign Language* 8:689–96.

Holmes, John, and Rosinda G. Ramos. 1997. False friends and reckless guessers: Observing cognate recognition strategies. In *Second language reading and vocabulary learning,* ed. Tom Huckin, Margot Haynes, and James Coady. Norwood, N.J.: Ablex, 86–108.

Horst, Marlise, Tom Cobb, and Paul Meara. 1998. Beyond *A Clockwork Orange*: Acquiring second language vocabulary through reading. *Reading in a Foreign Language* 11:207–23.

Huckin, Tom N., and James Coady. 1999. Incidental vocabulary acquisition in a second language: A review. *Studies in Second Language Acquisition* 21:181–93.

Huckin, Tom, and Joel Bloch. 1997. Strategies for learning word meaning in context: A cognitive model. In *Second language reading and vocabulary learning,* ed. Tom Huckin, Margot Haynes, and James Coady. Norwood, N.J.: Ablex, 153–78.

Huckin, Tom N., and Zhendong Jin. 1986. Inferring word-meaning from context: A study in second language acquisition. In *Proceedings of the third eastern states conference on linguistics,* ed. Fred Marshall, Ann Miler, and Zheng-Sheng Zhang. Columbus: Ohio State University Press, 271–80.

Hulstijn, Jan H. 2001. Intentional and incidental second-language vocabulary learning: A reappraisal of elaboration, rehearsal and automaticity. In *Cognition and second language instruction,* ed. Peter Robinson. Cambridge: Cambridge University Press, 256–84.

Kim, Heuwon. 2003. *Vocabulary comprehension of advanced ESL learners in academic reading: A collective case study.* Master's thesis, University of Ottawa.

Laufer, Batia. 1997. The lexical plight in second language reading. In *Second language vocabulary acquisition: A rationale for pedagogy,* ed. James Coady and Tom Huckin. Cambridge: Cambridge University Press, 20–34.

Li, Xiaolong. 1988. Effects of contextual cues on inferring and remembering meanings of new words. *Applied Linguistics* 9:302–13.

Meara, Paul. 1996. The dimensions of lexical competence. In *Performance and competence in second language acquisition,* ed. Gillian Brown, Kirsten Malmkjaer, and John Williams. Cambridge: Cambridge University Press, 35–53.

Mondria, Jan-Arien, and Marijke Wit-de Boer. 1991. The effects of contextual richness on the guessability and the retention of words in a foreign language. *Applied Linguistics* 12:249–67.

Nagy, William E., Erica F. McClure, and Monteserrat Mir. 1997. Linguistic transfer and the use of context by Spanish-English bilinguals. *Applied Psycholinguistics* 18:431–52.

Nassaji, Hossein. 2004. The relationship between depth of vocabulary knowledge and L2 learners' lexical inferencing strategy use and success. *Canadian Modern Language Review* 61:107–34.

Nation, Paul, and Robert Waring. 1997. Vocabulary size, text coverage and word lifts. In *Vocabulary: Description, acquisition, and pedagogy*, ed. Norbert Schmitt and Michael McCarthy. Cambridge: Cambridge University Press, 6–10.

Paribakht, T. Sima. 2005. The influence of first language lexicalization on second language lexical inferencing: A study of Farsi-speaking learners of English as a foreign language. *Language Learning* 55:701–48.

Paribakht, T. Sima, and Marjorie Wesche. 1997. Vocabulary enhancement activities and reading for meaning in second language vocabulary acquisition. In *Second language vocabulary acquisition: A rationale for pedagogy*, ed. James Coady and Tom Huckin. Cambridge: Cambridge University Press, 174–200.

———. 1999. Reading and "incidental" L2 vocabulary acquisition: An introspective study of lexical inferencing. *Studies in Second Language Acquisition* 21:195–224.

Parry, Kate. 1993. Too many words: Learning the vocabulary of an academic subject. In *Second language reading and vocabulary learning*, ed. Tom Huckin, Margot Haynes, and James Coady. Norwood, N.J.: Ablex, 109–27.

———. 1997. Vocabulary and comprehension: Two portraits. In *Second language vocabulary acquisition*, ed. James Coady and Tom Huckin. Cambridge: Cambridge University Press, 55–68.

Qian, David D. 1999. Assessing the roles of depth and breadth of vocabulary knowledge in ESL reading comprehension. *Canadian Modern Language Review* 56:282–307.

Schmitt, Norbert. 1997. Vocabulary learning strategies. In *Vocabulary: Description, acquisition and pedagogy*, ed. Norbert Schmitt and Michael McCarthy. Cambridge: Cambridge University Press, 199–227.

Sternberg, Robert J. 1987. Most vocabulary is learned from context. In *The nature of vocabulary acquisition*, ed. Margaret G. McKeown and Mary E. Curtis. Hillsdale, N.J.: Erlbaum, 89–105.

Wade-Woolley, Lesly. 1999. First language influences on second language word reading: All roads lead to Rome. *Language Learning* 49:447–71.

Wesche, Marjorie, and T. Sima Paribakht. 2000. Reading-based exercises in second language vocabulary learning: An introspective study. *Modern Language Journal* 84:196–213.

Zimmerman, Cheryl B. 1994. *Self-selected reading and interactive vocabulary instruction: Knowledge and perceptions of word-learning among L2 learners*. Ph.D. diss., University of Southern California, Los Angeles.

Appendix A

The Ice Age

If you could visit the North America of ten thousand years ago, you probably would not recognize it at all. No cities or freeways graced the landscape. The millions of people who now inhabit the continent were absent. In fact, the landscape would probably have appeared rather **bleak**. Portions of what is now called the United States and much of what is now called Canada were covered by **glaciers**. To say that the ice mass was very big would be a dramatic **understatement**. It would be more precise to describe it as **overwhelmingly** vast, covering hundreds of thousands of square kilometers. The climate across North America was considerably colder than it is now. Influenced by the cold ice to the north, rain, **sleet**, and snow poured down continually. As the ice advanced southward, trees disappeared and wide valleys were carved from the plains. There was life on the continent, however. In the shadow of the great mass of ice, larger animals **stalked** smaller ones for food, and hardy grasses struggled to survive. Despite the harsh environment, a balance was reached. Eventually, the ice slowly retreated over many thousands of years, leaving behind a **devastated** landscape. However, it also left behind all the elements necessary for new life. The melting ice released sediment, which formed a thick **layer** of fertile soil. Trees grew again as the cold gradually released its grip on the land. Eventually people settled where once there had only been ice, and North America began to take the shape that we now know. When we consider these ancient events **chronologically,** we are reminded that the surroundings that are so familiar to us, and indeed, the history of nations, mean little when considered in the perspective of geological time.

Appendix B
Knowledge Sources (KSs) in Lexical Inferencing: Examples from Transcripts of English and Farsi Native Speakers Reading English Texts

English L1 data; Target word: roshies (masterpiece); word collocation, sentence meaning

P: Obviously, everybody . . . . galleries where great (works) are displayed or attending concerts . . . . artists. Great (works) is just a standard phrase in English, so, that's why I assumed *roshies* are probably (works), pieces of art,

I: So then, previous words helped you guess?

P: Oh yes, the art galleries, when you are in the art galleries, museums, they say it is great (works), great pieces of art, something like that.

English L1 data; Target word: plish (sleet); word association, sentence grammar

P: The next being *influenced . . . continually.* I just assumed by association with rain and snow, this would be (sleet), or (slush). It's another noun.

Farsi L2 data; Target word: genocide; word meaning

P: I think it means . . . . If we parsed it, it'd mean (to kill a generation).

I: How would you parse it?

P: *geno* means gene and generation, and *cide* means to kill. So **[genocide]** should probably mean (to kill a generation).

Farsi L2 data; Target word: stalked; sentence meaning

P: I think **[stalked]** means to (hunt) because here it comes between *larger animals* and *smaller animals.*

Farsi L2 data; Target word: bleak; discourse meaning

P: The only guess that I can make, for example, meaning (grim, pale . . . . desolate)

I: What helped you to make such a guess?

P: The sentence just before it reads *the millions of people who . . . . the continent were absent*, the words *were absent . . . .* and *have appeared rather bleak*, it seems as if it must be (desolate).

English L1 data; Target word: vishel (layer); sentence grammar, world knowledge

P: The next line would be *the melting . . . soil.* I assumed that to be (layer), just by the structure of the sentence, *thick* being the adjective describing something. So I thought that would be (layer). And soil is formation of (layers).

English L1 data; Target word: senclorated (sophisticated); discourse meaning, text style / register

P: What pops into my head is (sophisticated) people. I'm not sure why. I mean, after reading the entire paragraph, we are talking a lot about rich people and luxuries, going into shops and buying expensive clothes and what not. (Sophisticated) seems to be an appropriate word there.

Transcription Conventions

P = participant, I = interviewer

Normal font = translation of utterances from Farsi to English

Bold face = target words

Italics = words/phrases read from the target text

[ ] = words spoken in English by Farsi speakers

( ) = the inferred meaning(s)

. . . . = pause

. . . = missing text

9

From Sports to the EU Economy:

Integrating Curricula through Genre-Based Content Courses

SUSANNE RINNER AND ASTRID WEIGERT

Georgetown University

BEYOND THE INITIAL LANGUAGE COURSES, foreign language (FL) departments generally offer a broad array of courses with diverse content areas. The intention is to attract and satisfy students' interests and to draw on the breadth and depth of the faculty's research areas and expertise. Although variation in course offerings certainly is desirable, it also raises questions. In particular, second language acquisition (SLA) researchers and scholars in FL departments have begun to call attention to the need to conceptualize programs as articulated entities, rather than as an aggregation of separate courses—a need that is more pronounced if students are to attain advanced levels of FL ability along with acquiring the literary-cultural content that characterizes the educational goals of departments (among many other sources, we mention Benesch 1996; Berwick 1989; Brown 1995; Byrnes 1998, 2005; Kern 2000; Lange 1997; Swaffar 1998; Swaffar and Arens 2005).

Rather than treating the entire expansive and complex subject of constructing an integrated curriculum and doing so from the top down, we have chosen a targeted, bottom-up approach. Specifically, we are interested in addressing how departments might begin to organize their diverse content courses—the so-called upper-level advanced courses—by finding commonalities among them with regard to their language acquisitional goals. Not only would such an approach lead to greater clarity about the goals and nature of language acquisition in advanced courses—in itself a desirable outcome—it also would begin to provide broad criteria for sequencing of content courses, which is a critical step toward the larger goal of creating articulated curricula within FL departments.

Accordingly, in this chapter we focus on the following questions:

- What makes a collegiate FL course an "advanced" course? We answer that question by taking a cognitive-linguistic approach that is textually oriented.

- How can one gauge the cognitive and linguistic demands and goals of diverse courses within a program to specify their acquisitional goals and, by extension, ensure continuous language development within a curricular context? We propose a literacy and genre orientation for that critical task.

▓ Finally, what benefits would arise from a coordinated approach to creation and sequencing of advanced, upper-level courses within a program for teaching and learning languages? We suggest that FL departments might thereby affirm their particular educational contributions within contemporary higher education.

We approach this set of questions from two separate but interrelated perspectives—one focusing on institutional/departmental aspects and one focusing on faculty and student needs. Both perspectives are informed by our involvement with curriculum renewal, course development, and pedagogical decision making in our home department, the German Department at Georgetown University (GUGD) (for details on the department's curriculum, "Developing Multiple Literacies," see www3.georgetown.edu/departments/german/programs/curriculum). We are satisfied that the department's overall curricular proposal for integrating content and language acquisition by taking a social-semiotic perspective throughout the four years of undergraduate collegiate instruction has proven to be highly beneficial for faculty members and students. Nevertheless, further clarity is required, especially regarding the diverse upper-level courses the department regularly offers.[1] Although our concerns are grounded in our particular experience, we maintain that their link to larger theoretical issues in SLA and insights from educational practice reveals broader implications beyond our own setting.

The Need for Coordinating Advanced Courses: An Institutional/Departmental Perspective

On an institutional/departmental level, program articulation and coordination in most FL departments is assured in the so-called language sequence—typically the language requirement of an institution—by the presence of a language program director or language coordinator (LPD/C). As others have stated repeatedly (e.g., Byrnes 1998; Swaffar and Arens 2005), what is lacking is a well-motivated link between these language courses and the more advanced courses. The "bridge courses" that now are features of many FL departments represent an attempt to handle the difficult transition—if not the divide—between the language sequence and content courses at the single course level. By its very nature, however, the goal of linking content and language acquisition cannot be accomplished in a single course.

In response, the GUGD project in curriculum renewal has created an encompassing conceptual framework for an entire undergraduate curriculum that explicitly integrates all levels of instruction, from the very beginning (level I) to the most advanced level (level V), to ensure continuous and continued language and content acquisition. It has done so by choosing a textually oriented and genre-based approach to curriculum construction that is translated into genre-based pedagogical tasks at all instructional levels.

Even within this beneficial framework for integrating content and language, however, the department recognizes a need for greater specificity for its level IV and V courses than is currently the case. Part of the difficulty stems from the fact that the SLA field is only now beginning to develop workable definitions of the characteristics of advanced learners, as well as theoretical models for the intellectual, cognitive, and linguistic goals of these learners (aside from the contributions in this volume, see also the papers in Byrnes and Maxim 2004 and Byrnes 2006). Because an agreed-upon framework for what constitutes an "advanced-level" course from the standpoint of language learning remains elusive, content foci, as they manifest themselves in different courses, continue to characterize what counts as instruction.

Lack of coordination at the advanced level also can be traced to reasons that go beyond the dearth of SLA statements about the nature of advanced learning. First, faculty members who teach advanced-level courses traditionally base their course design and materials selection on the erroneous premise that language acquisition has already been completed in the lower-level courses, thereby freeing them to devote themselves solely to content. Second, these teachers retain that fundamental misjudgment because of the persistent notion that content can be addressed validly separately from language and that language as a system of meaning-making exists, in some abstract fashion, outside of and independent from content considerations. (For research challenging this position, see Byrnes 1998; James 1989; Kern 2000, 2002; Swaffar 1991, 1998; Swaffar and Arens 2005.) Finally, FL departments traditionally have imbued the faculty's content courses with a strong aura of "ownership" and research-derived intellectual merit. Not surprisingly, separate or—as we might now say—uncoordinated course development has been positively associated with notions of academic freedom.

Course Coordination: A Faculty and Student Perspective

Coordinating upper-level content courses is not merely a structural and programmatic issue. It also and crucially is a pedagogical concern that requires close collaboration among faculty members in the following areas: choice of topics; overall design of courses; selection of appropriate materials; and, most important, preferred pedagogical approaches that attend to continued language development alongside acquisition of content. To make that goal possible, faculty members first and foremost must acknowledge the need to address language acquisitional issues on all levels of instruction and then find ways to integrate these issues in a well-motivated fashion into each course, including upper-level courses.

The necessary collaboration comes with undeniable costs in time commitments. At the same time, individual faculty members and entire departments stand to benefit because resulting exchanges should decrease the burden of the intellectually challenging task of developing courses and materials—often a formidable, if unspoken, impediment to curriculum renewal. Beyond that, they will reap the benefit of shared pedagogical expertise that can change the culture of an entire department (Byrnes 2001) and, most important, the educational environment for students.

Indeed, fostering continued enhancement of students' literacy in the foreign language, regardless of the content area they choose to study as advanced learners, is crucial. If adult advanced instructed FL learners require more than expanded vocabulary lists or more detailed grammar instruction that insists on accuracy, as recent SLA research suggests (Swaffar 2004; Swaffar and Arens 2005), best practices for constructing curricula, designing courses, and choosing materials that address the specific needs of advanced learners and the multiple connections between content and language must be identified and promulgated.

Byrnes (2002) lays out some broad characteristics of pedagogical interventions that would benefit learners in the challenging task of acquiring a FL to upper levels: a cognitive focus on the learner; a pedagogy of modeling, coaching, and scaffolding; explicit, genre-based teaching; and a genre-derived and task-based pedagogy. In this chapter we explore further what this approach might mean for closer coordination of what are commonly referred to as advanced content courses.

Proposing a Theoretical Framework

As we have noted, our home department has adopted a social-semiotic perspective that recognizes the interdependence of knowledge creation, the development of cognitive skills, and language development—a stance that is largely inspired by the work of Halliday (e.g., 1993) and Vygotsky (1978). This perspective allows FL departments both to conceptualize their programs in terms of a continuous link between content and language and to seek out ways in which that link can be articulated at some level of detail—particularly at the advanced level, where content is diverse and language acquisitional issues remain remarkably underspecified.

For the present discussion of the limitations and needs of FL programs, we find the constructs of literacy and genre particularly useful. Specifically, we draw on Gee's (1998) socioculturally based definition of literacy, with its distinction between primary and secondary discourses. To Gee, primary discourses evolve around the familiar and personal environment, whereas secondary discourses involve institutions beyond the family. Gee defines literacy as "control of secondary uses of language," meaning the ability to participate appropriately in public discourses (Gee 1998, 56). To us, this distinction provides an initial step toward addressing the sequencing demands any FL curriculum must meet.

More recent discussions of literacy in the SLA literature (Byrnes 2005; Kern 2004; Schleppegrell 2004; Swaffar 2004; Swaffar and Arens 2005) consider specific linguistic, cognitive, and sociocultural characteristics of texts and propose to analyze them in terms of the reciprocal relations of readers, writers, texts, culture, and language use (Bakhtin 1986) and, by extension, language learning. These considerations rely on a wide range of cognitive abilities, explicit knowledge of written and spoken language, cultural knowledge, and—most important for our argument—knowledge of genre.

The notion of genre builds on the following relations. Each discourse community develops its own ways of "getting things done" with language by developing particular genres. As Martin (1997, 13) states, "genre represents the system of staged goal-oriented social processes through which social subjects in a given culture live their lives." Understood as a social as well as a textual practice, the construct of genre therefore enables researchers and educators to explore and pedagogically build on the cultural specificity of language and the situatedness of its textual expression (see particularly Martin 1993, 1997, 2000). In short, a genre-based approach to language teaching facilitates a focus on "rhetorical structures as well as syntactical and lexical choices as they relate to specific communicative purposes" (Crane, Liamkina, and Ryshina-Pankova 2004, 161).

Maxim (2004) links the construct of genre to the design of advanced-level courses when he points out that the public and formal genres typically are associated with advanced language use. To recognize that connection, a genre-based approach to course design and material selection would introduce advanced learners to genres used in secondary discourses—in the professions, in various institutions, and in the general conduct of public life. This approach will allow learners gradually to acquire the characteristic forms of language use of these discourse communities and, as opportunities permit, become confident and competent participants in these communities themselves. Most important for our discussion of curricular coherence and integration is that genre-based pedagogies can integrate different themes within a particular course but also create coherence and comparability among a variety of upper-level courses with their own respective content foci.

Finally, for faculty members trained in literature, a genre focus has the advantage of being more familiar than the prevalent input-interaction paradigm of much SLA-inspired communicative language teaching because of the longstanding use of genre in literary analysis. As a consequence, faculty members with diverse research interests and areas of expertise, both in literary-cultural studies and in SLA, can use genre to negotiate a shared approach to teaching that, ideally, results in articulation of comparable pedagogical goals in terms of language acquisition despite different content foci. In such a proposal, the notions of literacy and genre would serve as connectors among the individualized content courses at the advanced level and as anchors for collaboration among faculty members teaching advanced-level content courses.

As an example of such a collaborative alignment, we jointly articulated language-learning goals for two courses with very different content foci by means of genre: a business-culture course and a cultural studies course. By selecting one particular genre shared by both discourse communities—the newspaper interview—we were able to identify and emphasize within both courses comparable cognitive and linguistic features that relate to development of advanced literacy, use these genre-based foci as ways of structuring learning units within the courses, and, finally, develop appropriate pedagogies for them.

The desired horizontal link between diverse advanced courses through the construct of genre can be established if one chooses genres that are used in a variety of discourse communities and then repeats them across different content courses. Such a narrowing of options from among the seemingly endless number of genres of secondary discourses initially might appear to be undesirable. It can become an advantage, however, inasmuch as it can create both horizontal and vertical articulation: Students who are enrolled in different content courses at a particular point of their study nevertheless would be comparably prepared to handle the next instructional level, with its array of content courses.

Among obvious candidates for such linkages, Schleppegrell (2004, especially 77–112) emphasizes analytical genres for advanced learners and, among those, focuses on the genre of the expository essay. Byrnes and Sprang (2004) discuss the genre of the public speech; Hyland (2000) analyzes a variety of academic genres, such as the abstract and the scientific letter; Swaffar (2004) explores the potential of the précis; and Weigert (2004) points to the book review as a genre that is particularly well suited to foster advanced-level literacy.

The Integrative Power of the Published Interview Genre
We are now ready to explore how the published interview might yield structural and programmatic benefits, help to specify the nature of advancedness, and aid development of a pedagogy toward advanced language learning.

The Published Interview as a Curricular Anchor
The occurrence of the published interview in a large variety of content areas, from politics to literature—and in our specific case from economics to sports—makes it a productive genre for integrating a broad range of content courses. More important, the interactions between interview participants are highly marked for key features of discourse, in terms of what systemic-functional linguistics refers to as field, or the subject matter under discussion; tenor, or the relations established between the conversational partners; and mode, or the kinds of textual practices that enact them (Halliday 1994). These interrelations, furthermore, show both a considerable range of what is being expressed and tight interdependence among the categories. Thus, they exemplify well how language does not merely reflect reality but construes it (Halliday 1994, xiii–xxxv). For example, the interactions between interviewer and interviewee can range from amicable to confrontational, even belligerent, as reflected in features of language at all levels of the language system—from vocabulary to syntax to discourse-level phenomena. Similarly, register phenomena show considerable range and variation, from relatively informal conversational style that is nonetheless suited for public settings to quite formal and distanced forms of expression.

That openness of the genre is a plus because repeated focus on the genre in a variety of courses can be used to enable students to explore increasingly sophisticated links between meaning and form so that, ultimately, students may gain a voice and identity of their own. As they work with the interview genre they will uncover the genre's intricate linkage between content, personal interaction, and specific choices with regard to language form that add layers of meaning to what otherwise might appear to be a straightforward conversation. As Byrnes, Crane, and Sprang (2002) point out, students may be familiar with the genre and can draw on some background knowledge. However, "their familiarity is different from a knowledge grounded in explicit reflection on the nature of these text structures" (Byrnes, Crane, and Sprang 2002, 30). Analyzing interviews therefore enhances students' abilities to notice and reflect on nuances in meaning-making by, for instance, focusing on implications of specific word choices, recognizing the metaphoric or ironic use of language, and tracing the often significant difference between explicit wording and inferable meaning.

Interviews also exemplify the phenomena of heteroglossia and multivoicedness that Bakhtin has made the center of his philosophy of language and that Wertsch (2006), with his notion of generalized collective dialogue, explicitly links to advanced FL capabilities. Analyzing the diverse intratextual and intertextual connections of a particular utterance in terms of a larger cultural collective dialogue that resonates in the language used by the individual participants and marks them as members of particular groups is an ability that is required for a high level of expertise in a language, both in language interpretation (listening and reading) and in language production (writing and speaking).

Finally, the interview genre is particularly prevalent in the German visual and print media, ranging from the boulevard press to journalism that is directed at the educated elite. Thus, it presents great topical variety as well as various instantiations of the continuum from personal to public discourses—a feature that can foster language development within a particular thematic unit, within a course, and, ultimately, across instructional levels.

Exploring Features of the Published Interview for Advanced Learning

As we have indicated, a helpful framework for the analysis of textual features in any genre is provided by systemic-functional linguistics, which differentiates between a text's field, tenor, and mode (Halliday 1994). In the following, we address all three categories, with an emphasis on *tenor* because it may be the most distinctive feature of interviews.

With regard to *field*, interviews do not cover a content area in its entirety; they select a few salient issues. In our examples, the business interview is located within the larger discussion of challenges facing the European Union (EU) economy; the interview with the soccer coach occurs in the context of pervasive complaints about the dismal state of German soccer. To understand the subtopics chosen, students engaging in textual work with interviews must already possess some background knowledge on the theme under investigation or be given the opportunity to acquire it.

The definition of *tenor* explicitly mentions the *roles and statuses* of participants—aspects that prove highly relevant for the analysis of the genre's interactional aspect. In the vast majority of cases, interviewees are high-ranking officials, widely acknowledged experts on a specific topic, or people of public interest. The fact that they have been asked to participate in an interview on a specific topic underscores their importance. At the same time, the interviewee's high status also advances the status of a newspaper or magazine within a country's media landscape. Finally, decisions on interview participants also reflect a newspaper's target audience inasmuch as they highly predispose the content areas to be addressed.

A salient point in the analysis of the category of *tenor* is the overtly asymmetric form of interaction in an interview. Thus, one of the distinct genre features is the privileged position of the interviewer, who determines the topic, opens and concludes the interview, and decides on the interview's course and length. There also is a certain covert asymmetry, however, that works in favor of the interviewee, who typically is the authority on a subject. These two contradictory asymmetries enable a fluid and changing enactment of the role relationships between interviewer and interviewee throughout the course of the interview—a fact that can create interesting sites of contestation that will be marked through deployment of diverse interpersonal resources. These resources range from relatively overt strategies of conversation management—such as the interviewee asking questions of the interviewer or responding only in short answers and terse language—to covert strategies of avoiding a topic, evading a question, and even explicitly changing it.

Considering the potentially "underprivileged" position of high-ranking officials/experts in the interactional dynamic of the genre interview, one might inquire why they agree to interviews at all. Aside from a general expectation that public figures must make themselves available for the kind of public discourse with which an open society conducts its business, the answer may lie in the opportunity it affords these experts to present themselves to the public in an "authentic" and "unfiltered" way that straddles and interweaves their personal-conversational and public-professional personas. Because of that feature, learners can begin to discern sophisticated forms of voicing and identity construction through language that pertain to the interaction between the interviewee and the interviewer and always have a trajectory toward the intended audience—whether a live audience in a studio or at a public event or an imagined audience in the form of an intended readership.

Printed interviews also show particular characteristics of *mode*. First, they typically are edited, both in terms of length and language use—a process that often targets what the editors perceive to be infelicities of oral language. Not surprisingly, then, interviewees often stipulate the right of final approval of the print version to ensure that their intended meanings are, in fact, retained; at other times, one can observe slight changes in the meanings themselves. For that reason, the printed interview offers a valuable window on issues of language choice, particularly if a video or audio as well as a printed version of the interview exist. As numerous authors are beginning to indicate (e.g., Byrnes 2002), the notion of language choice, as contrasted with rule application, may turn out to be one of the defining characteristics of advanced levels of language learning. Thus, television interviews—especially interviews on live TV—manifest the close interrelation of the visual and auditory aspects of meaning creation and meaning interpretation in any language use. Printed interviews manifest how texts create their own contexts, through coherence and cohesion markers and through construction of frames of reference that make choices about what needs to be stated explicitly and what can be assumed to be shared knowledge (for the effect of such world knowledge on lexical inferencing, see chapter 8, this volume).

We have identified the reader as the third participant in the interview. Consideration of the readership probably influences, at least implicitly, the strategies and language choices made by both the interviewer and the interviewee at the time of their oral interaction. The reader enters into the interaction explicitly, however, through the medium of the printed text. Presumably, a newspaper or journal publishes the interview for the information, benefit, and edification of the readership. What, then, one might ask, attracts readers to this genre? Again, features of language use play a prominent role. For the reader too, interviews seem to offer the opportunity for authentic, seemingly unfiltered access to the opinions of officials/experts on current issues in a field. Readers can imagine hearing/reading the information "straight from the source," as it were, in dialogic interaction with themselves.

The reader not only "observes" as a third party, however, but enters into the inherent dialogicality of the communicative event—a fact that is prominently featured in the question-and-answer structure of an interview. Here readers can draw both content and sociopragmatic inferences from that very dynamic. For example, they can note the possible overlap between questions asked by the interviewer and questions they themselves might have posed to the interviewee. This overlap creates forms of identification and social affirmation of values and beliefs that not only explain the genre's appeal to a native readership but also highlight its suitability for FL instruction, where a literacy and genre orientation identifies language acquisition to advanced levels as the acquisition of genre-based positioning toward the values and beliefs of the L2 culture (Byrnes 2007).

Finally, another favorable aspect of the genre is its inherently attractive feature of affording a glimpse, however limited, into the interviewee's personality. The interviewee's reaction to the interviewer's questions, the formality or informality of the interviewee's language, and the occasional inclusion of laughter or anecdotes all provide a personal touch to the genre.

Given the foregoing considerations of the two kinds of benefits a genre approach provides—namely, a programmatic benefit alongside a linguistic and language acquisitional benefit—we have created a template for analysis of printed interviews that is structured according to the criteria of field, tenor, and mode. Although such a template shows a neat separation between the three categories, the linguistic reality, of course, is that all three are intimately interrelated: There is no content without language and no interaction without textual language that manifests it. At the same time, a focus on generic features should make this template applicable to interview texts in any content area. In the following sections, analysis of two specific interview texts— one from a business course and one from a cultural studies course—demonstrates this applicability. (Table 9.1 shows a template we have developed for the analysis of printed interviews.)

▓ Table 9.1
Template for Analysis of Printed Interviews

I. Analyzing visual aspects of text
  1. Layout, inclusion of photos
  2. Overall length
  3. Q&A breakdown
  4. Subtitles

II. Analyzing **Field***: Content*
  1. Identifying theme and topics covered in interview text
  2. Determining situatedness and relevance of topics within overall theme

III. Analyzing **Tenor***: Relationship between participants*
  1. General analysis of dialogic pattern of questions/answers/comments
      A.   Question types, comments by interviewer
      —Open/closed questions; rephrased questions; posing more than one question at a
        time; use of rhetorical questions

      —Comment instead of question
   B. Nature of answers/comments by interviewee
      —Direct answers
      —Expanding comments
      —Question to interviewer
      —Length/expansiveness

2. Close analysis of strategies used by interviewer *on the basis of specific language choices at the word, sentence, and turn level*
   A. Identification of communicative intentions of specific communicative turns
      —Seeking information, highlighting details, insisting, accepting, commenting, agreeing/disagreeing/provoking, hypothesizing, confronting with opposing view, changing topics
   B. Identification of interviewer stance
      —Topic management
         —Topic maintenance and continuity
         —Topic shift
      —Presentation of personal stance toward topic through expression of judgment, beliefs, values

3. Close analysis of strategies used by interviewee *on the basis of specific language choices at the word, sentence, and turn level*
   A. Identification of communicative intentions of specific communicative turns
      —Informing, agreeing, clarifying, repositioning, evading, stonewalling, concealing, distorting, withholding information
   B. Identification of interviewee stance
      —Topic management
         —Responsiveness to interviewer through question response and/or topic shift
         —Nonresponsiveness to interviewer through question evasion and/or topic shift
         —Presentation of personal stance toward topic through expression of judgment, beliefs, values
         —Presentation of interviewee persona, private or public
         —Personal narrative passages (e.g., anecdotes)
         —Creation of authority

4. Analysis of reader's response to interview
   A. Content issues
      —Confirm/disconfirm old information
      —Summarize new information
      —Identify possible additional topics/questions
   B. Tenor issues
      —Response to persona of interviewer
      —Response to persona of interviewee

IV. Analyzing **Mode:** *Language use*
1. Field-related language: Create topic-based semantic fields
2. Tenor-related language: Language used in interaction

Horizontal Integration across Two Courses through One Genre

In this section we analyze textual examples of printed interviews according to the aforementioned template to demonstrate how a genre approach might answer questions about the nature of advancedness in terms of cognitive and linguistic demands and to establish comparable acquisitional goals across courses in different content areas. To contextualize these examples we first provide a brief overview of the respective courses.

Course #1: "The Culture of Soccer" (course developed by Susanne Rinner)

This course explores the significance of soccer as a sport in Germany, Europe, and the world and its cultural, historical, economical, political, and social implications. The course is divided into three units, with topics and materials grouped so that students can focus on genre-specific language use within each topic: The first unit, on soccer in Germany, focuses on the genre of the newspaper report; the second unit, on the representation of soccer in literature and film, focuses on the genre of the book and film review; and the third unit, on soccer in the world, emphasizes the genre of the interview.

The *printed interview* on the topic of soccer involves interviews not only with players and coaches right after soccer games to comment on successes and shortcomings of a particular match but also with managers, referees, and, most important, fans from all walks of life who discuss the significance of soccer more generally. Such a diverse group of participants indicates that soccer truly is the sport with which Germany and Germans identify most. It also shows that such talk about soccer extends beyond sports proper to negotiation of a complex array of topics. Judging from the number of interviews printed in newspapers such as *Die Zeit* and political newsmagazines such as *Der Spiegel,* the interview is the preferred genre for treating the topic.

The sample text is an interview with Otto Rehhagel, formerly a German soccer player in the national league and currently a coach for the Greek national team. In terms of field, the interview focuses on the current dismal state of German soccer and attempts to identify possible remedies. More specifically, the interviewer is interested in soliciting Rehhagel's assessment of his own career and ascertaining whether Rehhagel is willing to leave Greece to work with the German national team.

In terms of overall tenor, the interview reveals a certain urgency to finding a solution to a pressing problem: Germany is hosting the World Cup in 2006, and German fans have high expectations of their national team despite its recent poor performance. This sense of urgency is expressed early on, through the subtitle's use of the word "urgent" (*dringend*) to describe the interview and through commentary accompanying the interview text. There are even higher stakes associated with the desire for victory, however. The interview is conducted and published on the fiftieth anniversary of Germany's unexpected soccer World Cup victory in 1954. This victory was widely interpreted as an important milestone in the self-healing of West Germany after the end of World War II. This context, which the accompanying commentary foregrounds, frames the tenor of the dialogue between the interviewer and Mr. Rehhagel and shapes the reception of the interview.

Although the interview is called a conversation (*Gespräch*) in the subtitle, a constantly shifting relation of power between interviewer and interviewee is at work. On one hand, Mr. Rehhagel is in a position of authority because the interviewer expects him to propose workable solutions for improving the quality of German soccer. The subtitle accompanying Mr. Rehhagel's photo reads "this is the image of a winner," alluding to Rehhagel's successful career as a player and coach and emphasizing his position to speak knowledgeably about soccer. On the other hand, the interviewer possesses significant knowledge on the topic himself, enabling him to fill his role as interviewer with competence: He asks directed questions that reveal in-depth familiarity with Mr. Rehhagel's career and supplements them with carefully chosen follow-up questions. Showing considerable variety, the interviewer's own questioning routines are located along a continuum that includes genuine questions for which he seeks information; display questions, whose primary purpose is to give the interviewee the opportunity to voice an opinion on a topic that is deemed to be of interest to the audience in a kind of "staged ignorance"; and questions that mark contested space between the conversational partners.

Beyond the complex role relationship—which inherently marks all interviews—however, the relationship between the interviewer and Mr. Rehhagel is subject to another dynamic. Customary deference toward the authority of the coach aside, the interviewer marks Mr. Rehhagel as an outsider because he left Germany to work in Greece with the Greek national team. This labeling occurs through the use of "we" as referring to German fans, German soccer teams, and the German national team in a way that excludes Mr. Rehhagel. In other words, marking for exclusion occurs at the intersection of field and tenor. It continues with the interviewer initiating a discussion of the number of foreign players on German teams—a controversial issue that reveals much about broader identity questions in present-day Germany. Word choices that are associated with the discourse of globalization tie the world of sports to the world of commerce and thus emphasize the nexus of economic, cultural, and political considerations in soccer. In addition, the mode of the interview is marked by heavily metaphorical language use that can be described within semantic fields; for example, the metaphor of illness and healing is used to talk about the current dismal state of German soccer. The topic thereby is elevated much beyond its narrow significance for sports.

Ultimately, constructing a relationship marked by the opposition insider/we–outsider/you challenges Rehhagel's presumed authoritative position: The interviewer pushes him to disclose his availability for coaching the German team if he were approached to do so. In avoiding a direct answer by pointing to existing obligations with the Greek team and the hypothetical nature of such a question, Rehhagel's answers convey a quality of evasion and defensiveness. This stance is apparent even though the interviewer portrays such a potential return as the height of Rehhagel's career: He could repeat the miracle of 1954 by supporting the German team in its effort to win the World Cup in 2006.

Course #2: "German Business Culture" (course developed by Astrid Weigert)

The second course falls under the general category of business language and culture courses. It is structured according to a theme and genre link: The first unit, on international mergers, focuses on the genre of the book review; the second unit, on the labor movement, focuses on the genre of the public speech; and the third unit, on current challenges in the EU economy, emphasizes the genre of the published interview. The interview we analyze and discuss below is part of this last unit.

In terms of field, the interview's content focus deals with three specific areas: Europe's goal to become the world's largest industrial power, the transfer of jobs to new EU member states in Eastern Europe, and the industrial sectors with the highest growth potential. In terms of tenor, the interviewee is a highly respected and experienced German career public servant, Günter Verheugen, who at the time of the interview was the EU Commissioner Designate for Industry—a high position in the EU hierarchy. The interviewer is indicated solely by the name of the weekly newsmagazine in which the interview is published—namely the left-leaning *Der Spiegel,* which is known for its combative and aggressive interviewing style. Indeed, *Der Spiegel* is true to its reputation in this interview: The interaction is characterized by challenges and provocations on the interviewer's part and by a steadfast attempt on the part of the interviewee to remain calm and professional, not allowing himself to be drawn into a discussion of his personal views rather than his public professional views.

The first few exchanges in the interview illustrate this point. The *Der Spiegel* interviewer begins not by exchanging pleasantries or congratulating Verheugen on his imminent new position. Instead, the interviewer challenges Verheugen from the start. In the first question the interviewer suggests that because of internal personnel wrangling in the EU Commission, Verheugen might not even get to take on the position for which he has been designated, asking provocatively whether Verheugen fears for his job. This inquiry is the first attempt of many throughout the interview in which the interviewer tries to provoke the interviewee into making a personal statement. Verheugen, however, rejects the provocation by responding that he will simply not comment on this personnel issue.

Just a few exchanges later, the interviewer raises the ante by challenging Verheugen's qualification for his new position as EU Commissioner for Industry. Again, Verheugen refuses to be drawn into a personal argument about his qualifications; instead, he points out that his long record of public service speaks for itself. Several times more *Der Spiegel* intentionally phrases its questions to provoke a personal answer, but each time Verheugen refuses to "take the bait." At times his strategy is not to refer to or repeat extreme word choices used by the interviewer (e.g., the term "megalomania" in a question about the Commission's goal to catch up with U.S. productivity numbers). At other times Verheugen ignores personally pointed questions, such as, "What would you say to someone who . . .?" and sticks with a purely political answer.

In terms of mode or language use in a specific situation, the field-related language can be mapped into semantic fields that cover the three topic areas of the interview. The language used in the interactional exchanges depends heavily on the use of flavoring particles that help set the tone and reveal judgments, beliefs, and values of the interview participants. This is particularly true for provocative questions posed by the interviewer. An example is the question in which the interviewee's qualifications are challenged. Here, the German "*überhaupt*" (at all) renders the provocation almost impertinent: "As a trained foreign policy expert, are you *at all* the right man for industry issues?" The interviewee, for his part, relies heavily on the use of formulaic phrases that have a distancing flavor—a strategy that allows him to avoid stating any personal opinions. An example of such a formulaic phrase is "May I remind you that . . . ." Verheugen also uses impersonal constructions such as "there is" (*es gibt*) or "it seems to me" (*mir scheint*) quite frequently, which allows him to avoid the use of the personal pronoun "I." Such lexical choices in answering a particular question are a prominent strategy with which Verheugen deflects questions on his personal views. He makes his replies as Verheugen the Commissioner, not as Verheugen the private person.

Conclusion

Achieving advanced-level competencies requires long-term attention to balanced language development, which in turn requires a coherent curricular progression within a department's course offerings. This coherence is particularly necessary for advanced-level content courses in which students are expected to acquire complex forms of literacy in a range of content areas. An emphasis on genre as a way to operationalize a developing literacy and on selecting particularly productive genres for linking diverse content areas is a conceptual tool for a first level of integration of otherwise separate content courses in FL departments. By concentrating on a single genre in different content courses, students can reach the level of metalinguistic awareness about the intricate two-way relation between language form and meaning and, in time, the reflected and situated language use that characterizes advanced levels of language ability. As a conceptual anchor, genre also can provide a much-needed basis for establishing comparability in the difficulty level of different content courses. In this fashion, the cognitive and linguistic challenges for two different content courses—a business course and a cultural studies course—are not only specified, they also are located within a curricular progression. Returning to the question of benefits that can accrue for individual faculty members and departments, our own experience suggests that such an approach can play a crucial role in presenting language study to the entire academic community as a substantive contribution to the general education goals of any college program, while presenting a viable foundation for overcoming the internal programmatic split that characterizes many of them. Such newfound bases for integration and coherence should enable departments to help their students attain high levels of literacy not only in a second language but also in their native language—part of their educational preparation for thriving in a multilingual and multicultural world. ▧

NOTE

1. Course offerings in the Department of German at Georgetown University (GUGD) include the following advanced-level courses: "Mystery, Madness, Murder"; "Liebe, Lust und Leidenschaft";

"Berlin Stories"; "Germany in Europe"; "Grim(m) Fairytales"; "The German Language"; "From the Reformation to Freud"; "Language in the Media"; "Realizations of Identity"; "Business in Germany"; "Turn of the Century Vienna"; "German Cinema"; "German Business Culture"; and "The Culture of Soccer."

REFERENCES

Interviews

Was Hänschen nicht lernt. Was müssen wir besser machen, Herr Rehhagel? Ein dringendes Gespräch über den Fußballstandort Deutschland. *Die Zeit,* 1 July 2004, Leben, 49.

Probleme beim Vollzug. Interview with Günter Verheugen, EU-Commissioner Designate for Industry. *Der Spiegel* 43, 18 October 2004; available at www.spiegel.de/spiegel/0,1518,324499,00.html.

Secondary Literature

Bakhtin, M. M. 1986. The problem of speech genres. In *Speech genres and other late essays,* ed. Caryl Emerson and Michael Holquist. Austin: University of Texas Press, 60–102.

Benesch, Sarah. 1996. Needs analysis and curriculum development in EAP: An example of a critical approach. *TESOL Quarterly* 30:723–38.

Berwick, Richard. 1989. Needs assessment in language programming: From theory to practice. In *The second language curriculum,* ed. Robert Keith Johnson. Cambridge: Cambridge University Press, 48–62.

Brown, James Dean. 1995. *The elements of language curriculum. A systematic approach to program development.* Boston: Heinle & Heinle.

Byrnes, Heidi. 1998. Constructing curricula in collegiate foreign language departments. In *Learning foreign and second languages: Perspectives in research and scholarship,* ed. Heidi Byrnes. New York: MLA, 262–95.

———. 2001. Reconsidering graduate students' education as teachers: It takes a department! *Modern Language Journal* 85:512–30.

———. 2002. Toward academic-level foreign language abilities: Reconsidering foundational assumptions, expanding pedagogical options. In *From advanced to distinguished: Developing professional-level language proficiency,* ed. Betty Lou Leaver and Boris Shekhtman. Cambridge: Cambridge University Press, 34–58.

———. 2005. Content-based foreign language instruction. In *Mind and context in adult second language acquisition: Methods, theory, and practice,* ed. Cristina Sanz. Washington, D.C.: Georgetown University Press, 282–302.

———, ed. 2006. *Advanced language learning: The contribution of Halliday and Vygotsky.* London: Continuum.

———. 2007. Language acquisition and language learning. In *Introduction to scholarship in modern languages and literatures,* ed. David Nicholls. New York: MLA.

Byrnes, Heidi, and Hiram H. Maxim, eds. 2004. *Advanced foreign language learning: A challenge to college programs.* Boston: Heinle Thomson.

Byrnes, Heidi, and Katherine A. Sprang. 2004. Fostering advanced L2 literacy: A genre-based, cognitive approach. In *Advanced foreign language learning: A challenge to college programs,* ed. Heidi Byrnes and Hiram H. Maxim. Boston: Heinle Thomson, 74–85.

Byrnes, Heidi, Cori Crane, and Katherine A. Sprang. 2002. Non-native teachers teaching at the advanced level: Challenges and opportunities. *ADFL Bulletin* 33:3.25–34.

Crane, Cori, Olga Liamkina, and Marianna Ryshina-Pankova. 2004. Fostering advanced level language abilities in foreign language graduate programs: Applications of genre theory. In *Advanced foreign language learning: A challenge to college programs,* ed. Heidi Byrnes and Hiram H. Maxim. Boston: Heinle Thomson, 150–77.

Gee, James Paul. 1998. What is literacy? In *Negotiating academic literacies: Teaching and learning across languages and cultures,* ed. Vivian Zamel and Ruth Spack. Mahwah, N.J.: Erlbaum, 51–59.

Halliday, M. A. K. 1993. Towards a language-based theory of learning. *Linguistics and Education* 5:93–116.

————. 1994. *An introduction to functional grammar,* 2nd ed. London: Edward Arnold.

Hyland, Ken. 2000. *Disciplinary discourses: Social interactions in academic writing.* New York: Longman.

James, Dorothy. 1989. Re-shaping the "college-level" curriculum: Problems and possibilities. In *Shaping the future. Challenges and opportunities,* ed. Helen S. Lepke. Middlebury, Vt.: Northeast Conference on the Teaching of Foreign Languages, 79–110.

Kern, Richard. 2000. *Literacy and language teaching.* Oxford: Oxford University Press.

————. 2002. Reconciling the language-literature split through literacy. *ADFL Bulletin* 33:3.20–24.

————. 2004. Literacy and advanced foreign language learning: Rethinking the curriculum. In *Advanced foreign language learning: A challenge to college programs,* ed. Heidi Byrnes and Hiram H. Maxim. Boston: Heinle Thomson, 2–18.

Lange, Dale L. 1997. Models of articulation: Struggles and successes. *ADFL Bulletin* 28:2, 31–42.

Martin, James R. 1993. Genre and literacy—modeling context in educational linguistics. *Annual Review of Applied Linguistics* 13:141–72.

————. 1997. Analysing genre: Functional parameters. In *Genre and institutions: Social processes in the workplace and school,* ed. Frances Christie and James R. Martin. London: Continuum, 3–39.

————. 2000. Design and practice: Enacting functional linguistics. *Annual Review of Applied Linguistics* 20:116–26.

Maxim, Hiram H. 2004. Expanding visions for collegiate advanced foreign language learning. In *Advanced foreign language learning: A challenge to college programs,* ed. Heidi Byrnes and Hiram H. Maxim. Boston: Heinle Thomson, 178–93.

Schleppegrell, Mary J. 2004. *The language of schooling. A functional linguistics perspective.* Mahwah, N.J.: Erlbaum.

Swaffar, Janet K. 1991. Articulating learning in high school and college programs: Holistic theory in the foreign language curriculum. In *Challenges in the 1990s for college foreign language programs,* ed. Sally Sieloff Magnan. Boston: Heinle & Heinle, 27–54.

————. 1998. Major changes: The Standards Project and the new foreign language curriculum. *ADFL Bulletin* 30:1, 34–37.

————. 2004. A template for advanced learner tasks: Staging genre reading and cultural literacy through the précis. In *Advanced foreign language learning: A challenge to college programs,* ed. Heidi Byrnes and Hiram H. Maxim. Boston: Heinle Thomson, 19–45.

Swaffar, Janet, and Katherine Arens. 2005. *Remapping the foreign language curriculum: An approach through multiple literacies.* New York: MLA.

Vygotsky, Lev. 1978. *Mind in society. The development of higher psychological processes,* ed. Michael Cole, Vera John-Steiner, Sylvia Scribner, and Ellen Souberman. Cambridge, Mass.: Harvard University Press.

Weigert, Astrid. 2004. What's business got to do with it? The unexplored potential of business language courses for advanced foreign language learning. In *Advanced foreign language learning: A challenge to college programs,* ed. Heidi Byrnes and Hiram H. Maxim. Boston: Heinle Thomson, 131–50.

Wertsch, James V. 2006. Generalized collective dialogue and advanced foreign language capacities. In *Advanced language learning: The contribution of Halliday and Vygotsky,* ed. Heidi Byrnes. London: Continuum.

10

Hedging and Boosting in Advanced-Level L2 Legal Writing:
The Effect of Instruction and Feedback

REBEKHA ABBUHL
California State University at Long Beach

ONE OF THE MOST COMMON TASKS writers face, whether in the field of law or elsewhere, is to present an argument in a persuasive fashion. In this task, the writer must present a cogent explanation of the argument that is not only supported with evidence that readers will find convincing but is presented in language that they will find credible. In the U.S. academic and professional context, the latter requirement generally entails indicating, through various textual and linguistic means, that the claims made are open to discussion and debate—for example, by recognizing the audience's potentially opposing views or, more subtly, by finding ways of engaging the audience in the writer's line of argumentation.

One crucial way of accomplishing this goal is through various devices that, in their totality, are referred to as markers of epistemic modality. Key among these markers are hedges and boosters. Briefly defined, *hedges* are words and phrases that signal the writer's lack of full commitment to a particular claim that, itself, may be a subtle rhetorical device aimed at persuasion. These hedges generally include modals (e.g., *may, might, should, can*), adverbs (e.g., *almost, possibly, usually*), adjectives (*likely, possible*), verbs (e.g., *seem, appear, indicate*), nouns (e.g., *possibility, assumption, tendency*), and even phrases (such as references to limiting conditions or the writer's lack of knowledge) that are used to weaken or strategically attenuate the strength of a particular statement. These hedges stand in contrast to *boosters* (also known as emphatics) that mark the writer's commitment to a particular statement (e.g., *must, certainly, obviously, it is without doubt*) (Hyland 1998).

Using these signals appropriately is crucial in legal writing, particularly in writing legal memoranda (Langton 2002). Because these documents involve making predictions about the future (i.e., the most likely outcome of the case) based on available evidence, the writers (most likely junior members of a law firm) must present their claims to the readers (most likely senior members) with caution and anticipate possible objections to their lines of reasoning. A legal writer's failure to abide by these discipline-specific writing conventions can negatively impact the reader's perception of the writer's text. For example, when claims are presented too forcefully (e.g., "It is without doubt that Urbania will win the lawsuit" instead of, for example, "Based on the available evidence, Urbania will most likely win the lawsuit"), the reader may dismiss the text as arrogant or unworthy of careful reading and analysis (Crismore and Vande Kopple 1997). Overly "boosted" statements also "leave no room for dialogue and [are] inherently face-threatening to others. They indicate that the arguments need no feedback and relegate the reader to a passive role" (Hyland 1995, 35; see also Allison 1995a, 1995b).

Competent use of epistemic modality to signal nuanced levels of commitment to the value of a proposition is notoriously problematic, especially for nonnative speakers (NNS)—even those at the advanced level of proficiency (Bloor and Bloor 1991; Hinkel 1997; Holmes 1982, 1988; Hyland 1996; Hyland and Milton 1997; Karkkainen 1992; Langton 2002; McEnery and Kifle 2002; Milton and Hyland 1996; Nikula 1993, 1997). Because the linguistic devices that can be used to signal commitment and detachment to a particular claim are nearly limitless (Lewin 2005), L2 writers may have mastered only a subset of these devices, leaving them with fewer choices than their more proficient L1 counterparts. Furthermore, having been enculturated and educated in languacultures and disciplines that may have different norms concerning appropriate use of epistemic modality, L2 learners (and disciplinary neophytes in general) may not be aware of discipline-specific conventions that guide the "hedging" choices writers make. In some cultures/disciplines, for example, the writer is expected to adopt an authoritative stance, showing the reader that a particular argument has been well researched and contemplated. Here, hedging could have the undesired effect of indicating that the writer is not confident in his or her assertions (perhaps because of lack of knowledge) and thus would compromise the persuasiveness of the text (e.g., Kreutz and Harres 1997 on German academic writing). Researchers also have suggested that L2 writers' difficulty with hedges in English is related to the traditional lack of attention these devices receive in second language classrooms (Holmes 1988; Milton 2001). Milton (2001), for example, notes that in Hong Kong instruction on hedging devices often is limited to presenting students with decontextualized lists of modals and sentence connectors, and students are not made sufficiently aware of their use in actual discourse. Similarly, Wishnoff (2000, 123) comments that many writing classrooms do not address hedges adequately; writing textbooks and instructors take the stance that "writing research articles in English requires direct, linear arguments . . . [that] are weakened by *any* personal references or hedges."

Given these factors, L2 learners may lack not only a full "hedging repertoire" from which to choose but also the sociocultural and disciplinary knowledge that would guide their choices. The result of this situation, researchers have found, is that L2 writers producing English texts tend to "underhedge" their texts, producing writing that is significantly more forceful in its claims than that produced by more expert L1 writers. Milton and Hyland (1996) and Hyland and Milton (1997), for example, note that their Hong Kong English-language learners used more boosters than did a comparison group of native speakers of English—a finding that also has been reported in studies of Finnish learners of English (Karkkainen 1992; Nikula 1993, 1997), Russian learners of English (Wärnsby 1999), Arab learners of English

(Scarcella and Brunak 1981), Chinese learners of English (Allison 1995a; Hu, Brown, and Brown 1982), Australian learners of Indonesian (Hassall 2003), and even novice L1 writers (Hewings and Hewings 2002; Longo 1994).

Only one study, however, appears to have examined the effect of instruction on the use of hedging by L2 writers (Wishnoff 2000). Wishnoff compared two groups of English as a Foreign Language (EFL) graduate students (an experimental group that received instruction on qualifying claims in scientific writing and a control group that did not) and calculated the total number of hedges produced per 1,000 words on a pretest and posttest. Wishnoff reports that the experimental group produced significantly more hedges on the posttest than they did on the pretest, as well as significantly more hedges on the posttest than did the control group. Although the quantitative analysis of the number of hedges used was not supplemented with information about the overall *quality* of the writing (for example, holistic scores), Wishnoff argues that the instructional activities had helped the students *notice* hedging devices in their own and in published samples of writing.

Thus, Wishnoff's (2000) study seems to suggest that pedagogic intervention that targets specific L2 writing concerns has the potential to help L2 writers *notice* subtle linguistic and pragmalinguistic features of the L2 and *produce* writing that is more consistent with the discourse norms of their particular disciplinary community. Unfortunately, in the field of legal education L2 writers generally do not receive this kind of specialized writing instruction because legal writing courses that are designed specifically to meet the needs of L2 writers are the exception rather than the rule (Craig Hoffman, personal communication, September 2005). Although this lacuna may result in part from budgeting concerns and institutional constraints, it also may reflect the widespread view that advanced-level L2 writers are best served by being placed in content courses with native speakers of the target language. The expectation is that they will be able to *intuit* the conventions and norms of their particular discipline through the lectures they listen to, the articles they read, and the interactions they have with professors and other students (e.g., Hansen 2000; Spack 1988). By contrast, other researchers have argued that a more interventionist approach may be necessary to help advanced-level L2 writers notice and bridge the remaining gaps between their interlanguage and the target language and that writing instruction designed specifically for L2 learners in the disciplines also may be necessary (e.g., Allison et al. 1998; Bruce 2002; Swales 1990). Given the scarcity of empirical studies on the issue, the study I discuss in this chapter sought to address the following research question: Do advanced-level L2 legal students make significant changes in their use of hedging devices after receiving individualized feedback over the course of three months relative to a group of L2 legal students in the same program who do not receive this kind of feedback?

Participants and Instructional Setting

Participants for the study were drawn from two classes of international law students studying full-time at Georgetown University Law Center as part of a master's program in law. The two classes were United States Legal Discourse (USLD) and English for Lawyers (EL). The USLD course, which was developed in fall 2003, was designed to familiarize its 120 students with the conventions of U.S. legal discourse. The professor who taught the course, a former lawyer with both a J.D. and a Ph.D. in theoretical linguistics, used an interactive approach to teach common law analysis. Speakers from prominent law firms and international organizations also gave supplemental lectures on the topic, which involved New York and federal laws as they applied to a sovereign debt instrument of a fictitious country, Urbania. In the course, students were familiarized with the format and purpose of the legal memorandum, and their attention was drawn to the importance of considering the needs and opinions of their particular audience. The particular *linguistic* means of doing so, however, were beyond the scope of the class.

The EL class was an optional, non–grade-assigning, zero-credit course offered to USLD students as a means of receiving extra instruction and feedback on their writing from L2 writing specialists. This class of nineteen students, taught by a linguist with a background in L2 writing and discourse analysis, met once a week for two hours. In the first hour the professor provided a group lesson on a range of writing skills, including organization, coherence, paraphrasing, supporting an argument, and rhetorical conventions in U.S. legal writing, as well as the structure and purpose of the office legal memorandum. The students' attention also was brought to the *linguistic* means of achieving these skills. For example, concerning the use of hedging devices, one class period was devoted to discussing the role of modals (e.g., *will, can, should, might*) in creating a nuanced legal argument (e.g., recognizing opposing points of view and acknowledging potential weaknesses in an argument). To this end, a worksheet that provided examples of contextually appropriate and inappropriate uses of modals was distributed to the students; the students discussed these examples in small groups before entering into a whole-class discussion with the instructor. The purpose of this session was to draw the students' attention to these devices— which students may have had a solid control of *linguistically* but may have lacked a full awareness of *pragmalinguistically*.

In the second hour the students typically met in small groups with the five teaching assistants (the Writing TAs), who gave the students individualized feedback on their weekly writing assignments, as well as on their rough drafts of legal memoranda for the USLD course.[1] For the feedback session itself, the students would e-mail their writing assignments to their Writing TA two days prior to the meeting; the Writing TA would then highlight lexicogrammatical errors (without providing explicit correction) and provide both marginal and end comments on issues of global and local organization, as well as contextually inappropriate use of hedging devices. Each student then reviewed the highlighted concerns and comments, making revisions and noting questions to ask the Writing TA during the meeting. During the actual meeting, the Writing TA and student discussed these problematic aspects of the memorandum.

Thus, the participants in the study consisted of two groups of students. The first group comprised the nineteen students in the EL course (the EL group); the second group was a random sample of nineteen USLD students who were not enrolled in the EL course (the USLD group).[2] Like all international students admitted to the law school, participants had received a paper-based Test of English as a Foreign

Language (TOEFL) score of 600 or higher (or a computer-based TOEFL score of 250 or higher), placing them at advanced levels of proficiency in English. To ensure that the two groups were roughly equivalent in terms of proficiency, the first assignment the students submitted (a short overview of a case they had read) was evaluated holistically on a scale of 1 (poor) to 6 (excellent). According to this measure, the EL group (M = 3.21, SD = 0.98) and the USLD group (M = 3.32, SD = 1.00) were not significantly different [$t(36)$ = –0.33, n.s]. In terms of the native languages as well, the two groups were roughly equivalent with regard to the distribution of Indo-European and Asian languages.

Materials

As part of the coursework in the USLD class, all students were required to write two drafts of a legal memorandum—a genre in which writers are expected to summarize the facts of a case and predict its most likely outcome. The first draft of the memorandum was submitted toward the beginning of the semester; the final draft was due at the end.

Procedures

Because all thirty-eight students in the study were enrolled in the USLD class, they received comments on their legal argumentation (and only on the legal argumentation) in the first draft of their memorandum from one of the USLD class's fifteen teaching assistants (the Law TAs). These assistants were trained by the faculty member who taught the USLD class to comment on the papers; in addition, the faculty member reviewed all of the comments before they were returned to the USLD students. The EL students in the study also received weekly feedback from the Writing TAs and instruction that had as its primary focus the *linguistic* means of creating a persuasive legal argument. The Writing TAs provided comments to the students both via e-mail (prior to the meeting so the students could review the comments) and orally during the meeting itself.

Data Coding

Concerning identification of hedges and boosters, the focus was restricted to more explicit instances of epistemic modality—that is, linguistic features that have been identified in previous studies as overt markers of hedging and boosting (e.g., Hyland 1998). Thus, the main lexical items that were singled out for analysis and quantification were modal auxiliaries, modal adjectives, modal adverbs, and references to limiting conditions (e.g., lack of information on a particular topic). This focus can serve as only a rough approximation of the writers' use of hedging and boosting devices, however, because, as I have noted, the number of devices that can be used to signal commitment and detachment is nearly limitless; they include, among many others, passivization (e.g., *it is thought* rather than *I think*), "scare" quotes (e.g., *this "fact"* versus *this fact*), quantifiers, tense marking, omission and word choice. In fact, although hedging has received considerable attention in the literature, no agreed-upon definition of epistemic modality has emerged (Markkanen and Schröder 1997; Narrog 2005), and no consensus has been reached about the relationship between the quantity of hedges in a particular piece of writing and the overall quality of the writing. Note also that certain words that can be considered hedges (e.g., *may*) may not always serve as hedges—*may*, for example, also can serve as a marker of permission (e.g., *you may leave*).

To determine the degree of hedging and boosting in the students' writing, the present study used a measure of "epistemic modality density": the number of hedges and boosters per T-units (see Hyland 1995, 1996, 1998). T-units—independent clauses with all accompanying dependent clauses (Hunt 1965)—were chosen as the main production unit for analysis because of the relatively high frequency of run-on sentences in the legal memoranda. The number of T-units was counted by hand, using criteria adapted from Polio, Fleck, and Leder (1998). The T-unit count for 25 percent of the memoranda was calculated by two raters working independently; the Pearson product-moment correlation coefficient was .98. The T-unit count for the remaining memoranda was performed by the researcher alone.

Hedges were identified in context. In this process, two raters—the researcher and an assistant—coded 25 percent of the memoranda independently. Pearson product-moment correlation coefficients were calculated ($r = .87$ for hedges, $r = .92$ for boosters). The researcher and her assistant discussed and resolved all discrepancies, and the researcher alone coded remaining data.

Results

To ascertain whether there were significant differences between the EL and USLD groups on Draft 1 of the legal memoranda with respect to their use of hedges and boosters, the mean hedging and boosting density values were calculated and compared using Mann Whitney U tests (see table 10.1). According to these tests, there were no significant differences between the EL and USLD groups on Draft 1 with respect to the use of either hedges or boosters. This finding provides additional support for the claim that the two groups were roughly equivalent at the beginning of the semester.

The Mann Whitney U test also was used to determine whether significant differences existed between the EL and USLD groups on Draft 2 of the memorandum (see table 10.2). The results indicate that the EL group used significantly more hedges and significantly fewer boosters on Draft 2 than did the USLD group.

To determine whether there were significant differences in the use of hedges and boosters across the two drafts of each group, the Wilcoxon Signed Ranks test was used. The results reveal that for the EL group, Draft 2 contained significantly more

▓ Table 10.1
Mann Whitney U Test for EL and USLD Draft 1 Hedges and Boosters

All measures per T-units	EL ($n = 19$)		USLD ($n = 19$)		
	M	SD	M	SD	U
Hedges	.42	.12	.35	.13	124
Boosters	.22	.08	.24	.10	165

$df = 36$, *sig. $p \leq .05$, **sig. $p \leq .01$ (two-tailed)

▓ Table 10.2
Mann Whitney U Test for EL and USLD Draft 2 Hedges and Boosters

	EL		USLD		
All measures per T-units	M	SD	M	SD	U
Hedges	.48	.14	.32	.13	75**
Boosters	.17	.06	.26	.11	86**

$df = 36$, *sig. $p \leq .05$, **sig. $p \leq .01$ (two-tailed)

hedges than Draft 1 and significantly fewer boosters (see table 10.3). By comparison, the USLD group showed no significant differences in the use of hedges and boosters between Draft 1 and Draft 2 (see table 10.4).

In summary, although there were no differences between the EL and USLD groups at the beginning of the semester (i.e., on Draft 1) in terms of epistemic modality, significant differences emerged by the end of the three-month course (i.e., on Draft 2). Specifically, the EL group's second drafts contained significantly more hedges per T-unit than did the second drafts of the USLD group; in addition, the amount of hedging on the EL group's second drafts was significantly greater than on their first drafts. The EL group also produced significantly fewer boosters on Draft 2 than did the USLD group, as well as significantly fewer boosters than on EL Draft 1. No significant differences were evident in the use of epistemic modality for the USLD group.

To examine the students' overall quality of writing on their legal memoranda, an analytic rubric was used to assess five aspects of the students' writing: grammar, lexicon (word choice), global organization, local organization (organization at the sentence level and connection between ideas), and argumentation (supporting an argument with facts of law from previous cases, as is required in common law systems such as that of the United States). Analyses reveal that the EL and USLD groups did not differ significantly on any measure assessed by the analytic rubric on Draft 1 of the legal memorandum (a .05 alpha probability level was required to claim that differences between groups were significant). By Draft 2, however, significant differences had emerged: The EL group significantly outperformed the USLD group on two of the five measures (local organization and argumentation). Concerning intragroup differences, the EL group received significantly higher scores on Draft 2 than on Draft 1 for all five measures assessed, whereas the USLD group received

▓ Table 10.3
Wilcoxon Signed Ranks Test for EL Drafts 1 and 2 Hedges and Boosters

	Draft 1		Draft 2		
All measures per T-units	M	SD	M	SD	Z
Hedges	.42	.12	.48	.14	−2.09*
Boosters	.22	.08	.17	.06	−2.66**

$df = 18$, *sig. $p \leq .05$, **sig. $p \leq .01$, (two-tailed)

Table 10.4
Wilcoxon Signed Ranks Test for USLD Drafts 1 and 2 Hedges and Boosters

All measures per T-units	Draft 1		Draft 2		
	M	SD	M	SD	Z
Hedges	.35	.13	.32	.13	−.85
Boosters	.24	.10	.26	.11	−.56

$df = 18$, *sig. $p \leq .05$, **sig. $p \leq .01$ (two-tailed)

significantly higher scores on Draft 2 than on Draft 1 for two of the five measures (global organization and argumentation) (Abbuhl 2005).

Discussion and Conclusion

The question of how to best assist L2 students in acquiring discipline-specific literacy remains controversial. Some L1 and L2 researchers have argued that students implicitly learn the discursive practices of a particular community through their exposure to those practices in their classes (for example, readings and lectures). On this view, students do not require explicit instruction or feedback to acquire discipline-specific literacy practices (for examples from the L1 literature, see Berkenkotter and Huckin 1993; Freedman 1993). This argument has played out in similar terms in the L2 writing literature; Spack (1988, 29), for example, has argued that "the teaching of writing in the disciplines should be left to the teachers of those disciplines" because L2 writing teachers generally lack the necessary disciplinary knowledge to conduct classes that would be of any significant benefit to students writing in those disciplines. On this view, content courses are adequate for enculturating students into the discipline-specific practices of the community, and writing courses are needed only insofar as they provide general academic skills that can transfer to a wide variety of different disciplines.

Other researchers, however, though recognizing the challenges of providing writing classes to students within the disciplines, have criticized the view that students do not require explicit instruction or feedback to acquire discipline-specific literary practices. In particular, they have argued that this view ignores the unique needs and characteristics of L2 writers and that L2 writing teachers *can* play a significant role in helping nonnative students acquire discipline-specific literacy practices. Concerning the former point, researchers have argued that because L2 writers are unique not only linguistically but also culturally (e.g., Connor 2002; Grabe and Kaplan 1989) and different languacultures tend to privilege different rhetorical systems, L2 students often hold very different values on how ideas should be organized, how texts should be structured, how to use source materials, what the nature of the relationship between the writer and reader is, and so on. In content courses in which L2 students often find themselves, however, the rhetorical systems they are expected to learn often are not made explicit. Nonnative students, like their native-speaking peers, are expected to *intuit* the rhetorical systems through their readings, lectures, writing assignments, and interactions with other students and professors. In this approach, students are expected to discover appropriate forms in the process of writing itself, gleaning this knowledge from unanalysed samples of expert writing, from the growing experience of repetition, and from suggestions in the margins of their drafts. This deflects attention from language and presupposes a knowledge of genre outcomes. While well-intentioned, this is a procedure which principally advantages middle class L1 students who, immersed in the values of the cultural mainstream, share the teacher's familiarity with key genres. . . . L2 learners commonly do not have access to this cultural resource and so lack knowledge of the typical patterns and possibilities of variation within the texts that possess cultural capital (Hyland 2003, 19).

Thus, although an inductive approach may be appropriate for (at least some) native speakers of the language, nonnative speakers are at a considerable disadvantage when they are placed in courses in which they are expected to intuit culturally bound (and often tacit) notions of academic and discipline-specific literacy.

For this reason, some researchers have argued that L2 writing teachers have a potentially significant role to play. Although L2 writing teachers and researchers are cognizant of the challenges that nonspecialist teachers may face, they maintain that L2 writing teachers can make discipline-specific literacy practices explicit, helping nonnative writers notice differences in the rhetorical strategies that are preferred in the L1 and L2 and, ultimately, facilitating the acquisition of the L2 strategies (e.g., Allison et al. 1998; Braine 1988, 1995; Bruce 2002).

This argument also finds support in the literature on second language acquisition. Several studies have claimed that simple exposure to the target language and opportunities to produce that language are not sufficient for bridging the linguistic and, in many cases, rhetorical or discoursal gaps between the learner's interlanguage and the target language. These gaps, many of which may not be perceptually salient (such as the use of hedges and boosters), are not likely to be bridged unless the L2 learners' attention is *specifically directed to* them—for example, through provision of negative feedback or instruction (e.g., Doughty and Varela 1998; Doughty and Williams 1998; Long and Robinson 1998).

With this argument in mind, it is worthwhile to compare the two groups that participated in this study. On one hand there are the USLD students—students who were enrolled in the content-based USLD course, which was designed to introduce students from civil law traditions to the common law system employed in the United States. In this course, students received extensive exposure to the disciplinary conventions of the U.S. legal discourse community from the professor and guest lecturers, readings, and writing assignments. The only feedback they received was one set of comments on the content (legal argumentation) of their memoranda. Although the USLD group evidenced some significant improvements in their writing (comparing their Draft 1 with their Draft 2) over the course of the semester (notably in global organization and argumentation—"the two most genre specific (and socially constructed) areas of the scoring rubric" [Archibald 2001, 165]), the group that received extra feedback and instruction, the EL group, experienced greater gains. Not only did this EL group—the ones who received weekly instruction and feedback that was designed to focus their attention on the linguistic and pragmalinguistic underpinnings of a successful legal argument—receive significantly higher scores on each of the five aspects of their writing assessed by the analytic rubric (grammar, lexicon, global organization, local organization, and argumentation) when their Draft 2 was compared with Draft 1, they also had significantly higher scores for local organization and argumentation in comparison with the USLD group on Draft 2. In addition, the EL group used significantly more hedges in their legal memoranda. Given the importance of hedges in both academic and legal writing—as Hyland (1995, 39) notes, "hedging represents a major 'rhetorical gap' that L2 students have to cross before they can gain membership of a discourse community and pursue their chosen careers"—and given the fact that the EL group was the only group in this study to evidence change in the use of hedges, subtle aspects of discipline-specific language use apparently may require a more interventionist approach if they are to be acquired by L2 writers. In other words, without explicit instruction and feedback, advanced L2 learners in the disciplines may not notice or have the full ability to bridge this gap.

This conclusion must remain tentative, however, for several reasons. As is often the case in studies of intact classrooms, no control group could be studied. Because the pool of students from which the study participants were selected had invested considerable time and money into their courses and expected, as part of their education, to receive feedback, creating a control group that would be denied that feedback was not feasible. In addition, because the study was conducted over a three-month period and examined two drafts of the same piece of writing, we do not know whether the gains the EL group experienced would have transferred to a new piece of writing. Longitudinal studies would be valuable in determining whether the extra feedback and instruction led to long-term gains.

Furthermore, given that the differences between advanced L2 writers and expert L1 writers often are subtle and not easily captured by rough-grained measures, such as holistic (or even analytic) rubrics, greater use should be made of finer-grained measures, such as those that examine advanced L2 writers' use of epistemic modality. In this vein, quantitative analyses of epistemic modality, such as those used in this study, should be supplemented with analyses of the *types* of hedging and boosting devices used, as well as corpus-based studies comparing hedging frequencies and patterns of use between expert L1 writers and advanced L2 writers.

Despite these limitations, however, the findings reported here may be relevant to the debate on assisting L2 writers in the disciplines and to legal educators struggling to decide whether additional, systematic writing instruction is useful or necessary for international legal writing students. The results of this study suggest not only that more studies are warranted in this area but also that providing specialized legal writing instruction for international students in a regular, systematic fashion should be the rule rather than the exception.

NOTES

1. Although the Writing TAs had not completed any formal training in law or legal writing, they collaborated closely (along with the instructor of the course) with the USLD professor—attending the USLD class, reading all of the assigned readings required of the USLD students, and analyzing

examples of legal memoranda for their discoursal and rhetorical features. In addition, the Writing TAs had completed a course on second language writing (taught by the instructor of the EL class), which provided them with specific guidelines for providing feedback to second language writers (such as the use of underlining to highlight an error that the student would then correct, rather than providing explicit correction).

2. The fact that these students *self-selected* to participate in this extra writing course raises the question of whether they possessed greater motivation than the USLD students who had not elected to participate in this course. To control for this possibility, an exit questionnaire that focused on the students' motivation was administered to the EL and USLD classes. Analysis of the questionnaire results reveals that there were no significant differences between the two groups in terms of their motivation. (See Abbuhl 2005 for more details.)

REFERENCES

Abbuhl, Rebekha (2005). *The effect of feedback and instruction on writing quality: Legal writing and advanced L2 learners.* Unpublished Ph.D. diss., Georgetown University.

Allison, Desmond. 1995a. Assertions and alternatives: Helping ESL undergraduates extend their choices in academic writing. *Journal of Second Language Writing* 4:1–15.

———. 1995b. Modifying meanings: Modality and argumentation in students' written answers to a legal problem. *Hong Kong Papers in Linguistics and Language Teaching* 18:59–72.

Allison, Desmond, Linda Cooley, Jo Lewkowicz, and David Nunan. 1998. Dissertation writing in action: The development of a dissertation writing support program for ESL graduate research students. *English for Specific Purposes* 17:199–217.

Archibald, Alasdair. 2001. Targeting L2 writing proficiencies: Instruction and areas of change in students' writing over time. *International Journal of English Studies* 1:153–74.

Berkenkotter, Carol, and Thomas N. Huckin. 1993. Rethinking genre from a sociocognitive perspective. *Written Communication* 10:475–509.

Bloor, Meriel, and Thomas Bloor. 1991. Cultural expectations and socio-pragmatic failure in academic writing. In *Socio-cultural issues in English for academic purposes,* ed. Penny Adams, Brian Heaton, and Peter Howarth. London: MacMillan, 1–12.

Braine, George. 1988. Two commentaries on Ruth Spack's "Initiating ESL students into the academic discourse community: How far should we go?" *TESOL Quarterly* 22:700–702.

———. 1995. Writing in the natural sciences and engineering. In *Academic writing in a second language: Essays on research and pedagogy,* ed. Diane Belcher and George Braine. Norwood, N.J.: Ablex, 113–34.

Bruce, Nigel. 2002. Dovetailing language and content: Teaching balanced argument in legal problem answer writing. *English for Specific Purposes* 21:321–45.

Connor, Ulla. 2002. New directions in contrastive rhetoric. *TESOL Quarterly* 36:493–510.

Crismore, Avon, and William J. Vande Kopple. 1997. The effects of hedges and gender on the attitudes of readers in the United States toward material in a science textbook. In *Culture and styles of academic discourse,* ed. Anna Duszak. Berlin: de Gruyter, 223–47.

Doughty, Catherine, and Elizabeth Varela. 1998. Communicative focus on form. In *Focus on form in classroom second language acquisition,* ed. Catherine Doughty and Jessica Williams. Cambridge: Cambridge University Press, 114–38.

Doughty, Catherine, and Jessica Williams. 1998. Pedagogical choices in focus on form. In *Focus on form in classroom second language acquisition,* ed. Catherine Doughty and Jessica Williams. Cambridge: Cambridge University Press, 197–261.

Freedman, Aviva. 1993. Show and tell? The role of explicit teaching in the learning of new genres. *Research in the Teaching of English* 27:222–51.

Grabe, William, and Robert B. Kaplan. 1989. Writing in a second language: Contrastive rhetoric. In *Richness in writing: Empowering ESL students,* ed. Donna M. Johnson and Duane H. Roen. New York: Longman, 263–83.

Hansen, Jette G. 2000. Interactional conflicts among audience, purpose, and content knowledge in the acquisition of academic literacy in an EAP course. *Written Communication* 17:27–52.

Hassall, Tim. 2003. Modifying requests in a second language. *International Review of Applied Linguistics* 39:259–83.

Hewings, Martin, and Anne Hewings. 2002. "It is interesting to note that . . .": A comparative study of anticipatory 'it' in student and published writing. *English for Specific Purposes* 21:367–83.

Hinkel, Eli. 1997. Indirectness in L1 and L2 academic writing. *Journal of Pragmatics* 27:361–86.

Holmes, Janet. 1982. Expressing doubt and certainty in English. *RELC Journal* 13:2.9–28.

———. 1988. Doubt and certainty in ESL textbooks. *Applied Linguistics* 9:20–44.

Hu, Zhuang-Lin, Dorothy F. Brown, and L. B. Brown. 1982. Some linguistic differences in the written English of Chinese and Australian students. *Language Learning and Communication* 1:39–49.

Hunt, Kellogg W. 1965. *Grammatical structures written at three grade levels.* Champaign, Ill.: National Council of Teachers of English.

Hyland, Ken. 1995. The author in the text: Hedging scientific writing. *Hong Kong Papers in Linguistics and Language Teaching* 18:33–42.

———. 1996. Nurturing hedges in the ESP curriculum. *System* 24:477–90.

———. 1998. *Hedging in scientific research articles.* Amsterdam/Philadelphia: John Benjamins.

———. 2003. Genre-based pedagogies: A social response to process. *Journal of Second Language Writing* 12:17–29.

Hyland, Ken, and Milton, John. 1997. Qualification and certainty in L1 and L2 students' writing. *Journal of Second Language Writing* 6:183–205.

Karkkainen, Elise. 1992. Modality as a strategy in interaction: Epistemic modality in the language of native and non-native speakers of English. *Pragmatics and Language Learning* 3:197–216.

Kreutz, Heinz, and Annette Harres. 1997. Some observations on the distribution and function of hedging in German academic writing. In *Cultures and styles of academic discourse,* ed. Anna Duszak. Berlin: de Gruyter, 181–201.

Langton, Nicola M. 2002. Hedging argument in legal writing. *Perspectives: Working Papers in English and Communication* 14:16–51.

Lewin, Beverly A. 2005. Hedging: An exploratory study of authors' and readers' identification of 'toning down' in scientific texts. *Journal of English for Academic Purposes* 4:163–78.

Long, Michael H., and Peter Robinson. 1998. Focus on form: Theory, research and practice. In *Focus on form in classroom second language acquisition,* ed. Catherine Doughty and Jessica Williams. Cambridge: Cambridge University Press, 15–41.

Longo, Bernadette. 1994. Current research in technical communication: The role of metadiscourse in persuasion. *Technical Communication* 41:348–52.

Markkanen, Raija, and Hartmut Schröder. 1997. Hedging: A challenge for pragmatics and discourse analysis. In *Hedging and discourse: Approaches to the analysis of a pragmatic phenomenon in academic texts,* ed. Raija Markkanen and Hartmut Schröder. Berlin: de Gruyter, 3–18.

McEnery, Tony, and Nazareth A. Kifle. 2002. Epistemic modality in argumentative essays of second-language writers. In *Academic discourse,* ed. John Flowerdew. London: Longman, Pearson Education, 182–95.

Milton, John. 2001. *Elements of written interlanguage: A computational and corpus-based study of institutional influences on the acquisition of English by Hong Kong Chinese students.* Hong Kong: Language Centre, Hong Kong University of Science and Technology.

Milton, John, and Ken Hyland. 1996. Assertions in students' academic essays: A comparison of English NS and NNS student writers. Available at http://hdl.handle.net/1783.1/1045.

Narrog, Heiko. 2005. On defining modality again. *Language Sciences* 27:165–92.

Nikula, Tarja. 1993. The use of lexical certainty modifiers by non-native (Finnish) and native speakers of English. In *Pragmatics and language learning,* vol. 4, ed. Lawrence F. Bouton and Yamuna Kachru. Urbana: Division of English as an International Language, University of Illinois at Urbana-Champaign, 126–42.

———. 1997. Interlanguage view on hedging. In *Hedging and discourse: Approaches to the analysis of a pragmatic phenomenon in academic texts,* ed. Raija Markkanen and Hartmut Schröder. Berlin: de Gruyter, 188–207.

Polio, Charlene, Catherine Fleck, and Nevin Leder. 1998. "If I only had more time": ESL learners' changes in linguistic accuracy on essay revisions. *Journal of Second Language Writing* 7:43–68.

Scarcella, Robin, and Joanna Brunak. 1981. On speaking politely in a second language. *International Journal of the Sociology of Language* 27:59–75.

Spack, Ruth. 1988. Initiating ESL students into the academic discourse community: How far should we go? *TESOL Quarterly* 22:29–51.

Swales, John M. 1990. *Genre analysis: English in academic and research settings.* Cambridge: Cambridge University Press.

Wärnsby, Anna. 1999. The use of modal expressions in English by native speakers of Russian. *The Department of English in Lund: Working Papers in Linguistics* 1:2–17; available at www.englund.lu.se/images/stories/pdf-files/workingpapers/vol01/Anna2.pdf.

Wishnoff, Jennifer R. 2000. Hedging your bets: L2 learners' acquisition of pragmatic devices in academic writing and computer-mediated discourse. *Second Language Studies* 19:119–48.

The Role of Assessment in Advanced Learning

11

Assessing Advanced Foreign Language Learning and Learners:

From Measurement Constructs to Educational Uses

JOHN M. NORRIS
University of Hawai'i at Manoa

WHY WORRY ABOUT ASSESSMENT in advanced foreign language education? As the title of this volume indicates, assessment is—or should be—one of the main concerns in educating for advanced foreign language (FL) capacities. In addition to defining exactly what constitutes "advancedness," developing a curriculum that captures the complexities of the construct, and delivering instruction that helps learners to get there, we need to put careful thought into the role of assessment within this ambitious agenda. Of course, that is exactly the assertion to expect from a researcher who works in language assessment and who would benefit from increased attention to it. In critical response, some educators—especially those who have witnessed FL instructional innovations over the past three decades—should be asking at this point, "But why worry about assessment?" Is assessment really an essential piece of the advanced learning puzzle? Or, truth be told, is it just a politically astute add-on that reflects an unfortunately vigorous trend toward testing and accountability in education—what Shavelson and Huang (2003, 10) have called a "frenzy to assess"?

Indeed, for many of us in language education, the term *assessment* conjures images of large-scale federal- or state-mandated testing for the purpose of holding teachers, schools, and, ultimately, students accountable for abstract expectations such as "sustained improvement." For others, assessment implies a means for more-or-less objectively generating students' course grades to meet the bureaucratic demands of educational institutions. Still others think of assessment as a necessary evil for motivating students to study and learn. From each of these perspectives, assessment is understood as a requisite if peripheral educational process—the impetus for which generally occurs outside our primary concerns with language teaching and learning. Likewise, the methods of assessment are presumed to be someone else's responsibility: Assessments are delivered by governmental authorities, or they are developed by testing experts and disseminated through our professional organizations, or they arrive neatly packaged at the end of each chapter in the textbook. So what is there really to worry about in assessment, beyond staying alert so that students don't copy from each other or making sure to select the appropriate answer key before we grade their test responses?

The short (and correct!) answer is that there is much to worry about and that now is a particularly important time to do so. In this chapter, I suggest (not surprisingly) that assessment is a key piece of the advanced learning puzzle. In addition (perhaps surprisingly), I argue that we do not need to develop more and better language tests—or, at least, that approaching the problem as a "how-to-develop-good-language-tests" question is misguided, at best. Furthermore, I contend that we have not given assessment proper attention to date in FL education—that we need to worry about it for much more fundamental reasons than those provided by the educational accountability movement and that if we do not worry about it, assessment practice will undermine or even derail the advanced learning agenda.

As we embark on broad-based discussions about what educating for advanced FL capacities requires, assessment poses a daunting challenge for FL educators and language testers alike, but it also offers a valuable opportunity. We are all challenged by the basic facts (see Cheng and Watanabe 2004; Norris and Pfeiffer 2003; Shohamy 2001): Assessment will occur in language classrooms and programs, whether it is designed in support of teaching and learning or mandated to hold education accountable; teachers will "teach to the test," and students will "learn to the test"; and assessment therefore will define the scope of language education in classrooms and programs, as well as the perceived value of language learning in higher education and society. Because assessment practices can and do play such a powerful, even deterministic, role, we face the challenge of ensuring that the kinds of assessments we develop in advanced FL education and the ways in which we use them actually promote rather than delimit language teaching and learning. As we begin to engage in innovative thinking about the constructs, curriculum, and pedagogy of "advancedness," we also have the opportunity to get assessment right from the get-go. If we take an equally serious look at the variety of roles to be played by assessment, we may find that conceiving of assessments as integral (rather than peripheral) to our educational efforts likewise will inspire us to innovate with assessment designs, hand-in-hand with curriculum and instruction. As a result, we may be able to revise our assessment practices so that they contribute more than just an accountability monitoring function and, ideally, so that they enable valuable advanced learning to take place. Along the way, if we manage to get it right, we may even engender improvements in assessment practice beyond the advanced FL domain.

In this chapter I articulate further why we should worry about assessing advanced language learners and learning and present a means for organizing our concerns into a systematic response. I first outline the role(s) played by assessment in the advanced language agenda, highlighting its current status in related discussions and providing several concrete examples that typify major problems. I then suggest that current problems, which reflect historic trends, will be resolved only through a fundamental shift in our thinking about assessment—from a focus on "how" to a focus on "why"—and introduce a mechanism for organizing change. Building from this foundation, I explore two major "whys" for assessment in the advanced language learning agenda: assessment as a measurement tool in research on language learning and assessment of learners as an essential educative component in language programs. For each, I outline the potential contributions to be made and the major challenges that must be faced, provide related examples from my own research in the advanced language arena, and point to demands for assessment that we will need to meet to ensure that the project of educating for advanced language capacities will succeed. In closing, I offer a few suggestions to the foreign language education community about where to go from here.

What Is the Current Role of Assessment in Advanced Foreign Language Education?

A useful starting point may be to consider the place that assessment currently occupies in discussions of advanced FL education. Although a comprehensive synthesis of this relationship is beyond the scope of this chapter, a quick glance into some of the relevant literature highlights the extent to which assessment has been considered an important component in the advanced agenda. It also points to gaps, similar to concerns with assessment throughout FL education, and provides a foundation for exploring how assessment might (perhaps must) play an integral role if we are to achieve the goal of effectively educating for advanced capacities.

Although available FL educational literature on the topic of "advancedness" is scarce, two book-length collections dealing exclusively with the topic have been published (Byrnes and Maxim 2004; Leaver and Shekhtman 2002). These books provide a litmus test of what seems to be on the minds of those concerned with advanced FL education, principally in the context of U.S. higher education; these books bring together researchers and practitioners who are at the forefront of work in the advanced FL domain. On the basis of the substantive content covered in these two books, assessment does not seem much on the minds of these authors (or at least it did not as they were writing for these cutting-edge publications). Of twenty-two chapters covered in the two books, none addresses assessment as the principal topic; nor does assessment figure as one of the main areas of concern. Although broad topics such as curriculum, pedagogy, technology, and the nature of "advanced" proficiency—as well as narrower topics such as study abroad, immersion, genres, literacy, and heritage learners—all receive treatment as primary topics of interest in one or more chapters, assessment does not. When assessment is mentioned, in a few of the chapters, the authors either address it as a technocratic afterthought to whatever other main topic they are exploring (e.g., how to assess heritage learners) or assume as a default the ubiquitous Interagency Language Roundtable (ILR)/American Council on the Teaching of Foreign Languages (ACTFL) Proficiency Guidelines and associated testing procedures. The authors only allude to, but nowhere explore in depth, the programmatic roles to be played by assessment, its essential relationship to curriculum and instruction, or its potential negative as well as positive consequences on teaching and learning.

I am not suggesting that the content in these books is not of value; on the contrary, the assembled chapters provide perhaps the best coverage to date of theory and practice in the advanced FL domain. To the credit of the editors of the two volumes, they had the foresight to address several years ago what is becoming an increasingly important discussion within the FL education community. For precisely this reason, however, the fact that assessment did not receive more serious attention in these books—both of which rightly portray the problems of advanced FL education as problems best understood at the educational program level—is revealing. Thus, although Byrnes and Maxim (2004) is subtitled "A challenge to college programs," and Leaver and Shekhtman (2002) "aims to fill the gap and assist those developing language programs" (back cover), neither treats assessment as a main programmatic concern. This concern, by the way, has been identified by educators for some time as a key piece of the program puzzle (e.g., Popham 2004; Stiggins 1988; Wiggins 1998). My worry, then, is that otherwise well-intentioned FL educators are relegating assessment to backseat status in the drive toward advanced language programs; in doing so, I predict that they will incur considerable difficulties in achieving their educational goals (as the examples below suggest).

Of course, the status of assessment as an "afterthought" (or an appeal to the "default") in these advanced FL educational discussions reflects a historical lack of attention to assessment in the broader FL domain. As Norris (2004) details, assessment has not received anywhere near the degree of attention that language curriculum and instructional methods have, in the research literature, professional development standards, or FL teaching methods textbooks. For example, as shown in figure 11.1, in a review of articles published between 1984 and 2002 in five representative journals I found that only between 5 percent and 14 percent of all articles focused on foreign language assessment, between 4 percent and 8 percent focused on college FL assessment, and the majority of these reported on only one type of assessment—namely, tests based on the ACTFL (1986, 1999) Proficiency Guidelines. Furthermore, I found that in every one of the five journals, the average annual number of articles that reported FL assessment research actually decreased substantially in the period from 1984 to 1993 compared with those from 1994 to 2002. As readers will correctly surmise, this discrepancy was related directly to the larger proportion of articles

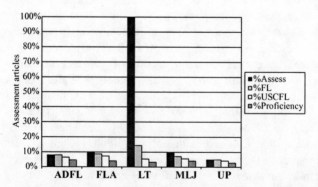

Figure 11.1 Percentage and Type of FL Assessment Articles in Five Journals, 1984–2002
Note: ADFL = *ADFL Bulletin*; FLA = *Foreign Language Annals*; LT = *Language Testing*; MLJ = *Modern Language Journal*; UP = *Die Unterrichtspraxis*; %Assess = percentage of assessment-focused articles; %FL = percentage of total non-English FL assessment articles; %USCFL = percentage of assessment articles related to U.S. college foreign language context; %Proficiency = percentage of articles related to assessment based on ACTFL Proficiency Guidelines.

published in conjunction with the initial dissemination of the ACTFL Proficiency Guidelines and associated testing techniques (i.e., the Oral Proficiency Interview and variants) during the 1980s and early 1990s.

This kind of gap led Spolsky (2000) to conclude that FL educators historically have downplayed the importance of assessment in language teaching and that FL assessment has not contributed much over the past century to the advance of language testing theory and practice. Of course, the reverse also seems true, in that language testers have been occupied principally with large-scale English-language testing at the expense of attention to other domains—in figure 11.1, the proportion of articles on topics other than FL assessment in the *Language Testing* journal is suggestive of this difference. Only very recently, in response to these gaps, has consistent concern been voiced from within the U.S. FL education community, as assessment has begun to appear in overviews of the basic needs of FL programs (e.g., Bernhardt 2002; Lariviere 2002; Phillips 2003). Indeed, the fact that assessment skills were included at all in the ACTFL (2002) *Program Standards for the Preparation of Foreign Language Teachers* is testament at least to a nascent awareness of its increasing importance in the professional domain. At the same time, the assessment content of these standards, like assessment coverage in prominent FL professional development texts (e.g., Omaggio-Hadley 2001), remains decidedly narrow, with preeminent attention paid to the development of educators' abilities to use the ACTFL Proficiency Guidelines.

As I have discussed in detail elsewhere (Norris 1997, 2001a, 2004), this dependence on one type of assessment is a symptom of a larger gap in FL education. The reason existing proficiency measures have been adopted so readily, for a variety of unintended as well as a few intended uses, is that FL assessment has been and continues to be perceived and portrayed as a simple "how-to" problem that entails using good tests. Why bother to invest more thinking in assessment if the proficiency movement has already provided us with "validated" measures of language ability? Unfortunately, what has been missing in FL research, as well as in the professional development of FL educators, is systematic attention to the variety of ways in which assessments actually are (or can be) used, the implications that these distinct uses have for unique assessment designs, and the underlying interrelationships between assessments and the other components of language education. Because of this gap, assessment is just as likely to cause problems for educators as to contribute to educational effectiveness, as the following examples illustrate.

Several cases of recent assessment practice in advanced language education settings provide further insights into the kinds of problems that ensue when assessment is not taken seriously from the outset of instructional design. For example, Moir and Nation (2002) report on a study of supplemental vocabulary instruction in which advanced learners in an intensive English program were asked to keep vocabulary notebooks. The notebooks were rationalized as a means for individualizing vocabulary acquisition, based on the needs of the students as they progressed into increasingly divergent areas of interest—a characteristic commonly attested for advanced language learners. Students were asked to identify and record thirty new and personally meaningful words at the beginning of each week, regularly review the words throughout the week, and acquire the meanings of the words by the end of the week.

Despite much to recommend the instructional intent of this exercise, assessment practice intervened and contributed to a lack of instructional effectiveness. To ensure that students were keeping the notebooks and ostensibly acquiring new words, a recall test was introduced at the end of each week. In large part because of this test, apparently, learners adopted strategies that detracted from the desired learning outcome (as revealed through case studies). First, they selected words that were not particularly suitable for their needs but were amenable to memorization. Second, they did not study the words throughout the week; instead, they sought to memorize the word meanings, generally the night before the test. As a result, most of the students performed well on the tests but promptly forgot the new vocabulary.

In this case of advanced learners and instruction that was tailored to their diverging needs, assessment practice introduced an unanticipated dynamic into what learners actually did, leading to a negative outcome in terms of instructional effectiveness. Because assessment was not designed explicitly to support instructional intent, the potential benefit of the vocabulary notebooks was seriously undermined, and assessment apparently led learners to engage in behaviors that have been found to be particularly *ineffective* for vocabulary acquisition (i.e., memorization; see Gu Yongqi 2004).

In a second example, Starkey and Osler (2001) investigated the instructional emphases in an online course for advanced adult learners of French. Within a teaching methodology that subscribes to the *Common European Framework of Reference* (Council of Europe 2001), they sought to clarify the extent to which not only language development but also multicultural values, such as antiracism and human rights, were taught in line with the intended outcomes of the course. In particular, they examined students' writing tasks and teachers' assessment and feedback processes as key sources of evidence. They found that teacher assessments of student writing focused largely on language features (e.g., in the form of error correction) rather than on the sociocultural learning objectives of the course. In addition, when teachers did (infrequently) address culture-related points in student writing, their feedback actually reinforced a stereotypical view of cultures within the French-speaking world, rather than an awareness of the pluricultural and plurilingual values emphasized in the *Common European Framework of Reference*. Again, assessment practices that were not carefully designed in articulation with the instructional emphases of a course seem to have worked against its intended learning outcomes.

Within advanced language learning, where a division between content and language instruction becomes increasingly blurred (e.g., Byrnes and Maxim 2004), the role of assessment in supporting (or detracting from) the full range of learning objectives will demand much more explicit attention. These two examples (and others—e.g., Norris and Pfeiffer 2003) point to the kinds of problems that arise when the educational role assessment itself plays is not taken seriously, along with the effect of curricular scope and sequence, instructional techniques, and pedagogic materials.

Similarly, research on "advancedness" also pays insufficient attention to the extent to which assessment determines study outcomes. Indicative in this regard are the ways in which the term "advanced" itself has been operationalized in the form of measurement tools and the constructs they target. Thus, in studies of "advanced" FL learning (e.g., Bartning 2000; Bongaerts 1999; Cobb 2003; Freed, Segalowitz, and Dewey 2004; Geeslin 2003; Kotz and Elston-Guttler 2003; Liskin-Gasparro 1998, 2000; Montrul and Slabakova 2003; von Stutterheim 2003), the following kinds of measures (among others) have been adopted as indicators of "advancedness":

- Between 4.5 and 6 years of preuniversity French instruction
- A rating of level C1 or C2 on the *Common European Framework of Reference* scales
- Graduate student status in Spanish
- An Advanced rating on the ACTFL Oral Proficiency Interview (OPI)
- A Superior rating on the ACTFL OPI
- Enrollment in an advanced grammar course
- More than two years of college FL instruction
- at least thirty-seven out of fifty points on the Modern Language Association (MLA) Spanish grammar test
- A 2+ (or a 3, or a 4) on the ILR oral proficiency scales
- An accent that is indistinguishable from that of native speakers.

Clearly, in a research domain that is seeking to relate specific educational causes with learning effects and generalize about instructional effectiveness, such a variety of measurement operationalizations for "advancedness" will lead to little more than findings that defy comparison and interpretation.

How Can We Take the Intended Uses of Assessment Seriously?

The kinds of problems I discuss above are indicative of the ways in which assessment is being treated within work at the forefront of advanced FL education. Incipient though it may be, at least in the adult learner context of focus here, education of advanced FL learners already has begun to adopt the patterns of assessment that have marked the broader FL community for some time, perhaps because few alternatives have been presented. By focusing on technocratic concerns about how to assess "advancedness," when they focus on assessment at all, language educators and researchers alike continue to miss the point that good assessment calls for more than creation of accurate testing tools. The uses to which those tools are put will determine their worth, and serious consideration of those uses has been largely lacking. Because educating for advanced FL capacities only recently has generated wide-scale and carefully considered attention, however, a fundamental reconsideration of language assessment might coincide with and build on this new focus.

If the goal of changing FL assessment practice is to be realized, on what basis might it proceed? How can we rethink our preoccupation with the "how-to" question that has driven assessment to date, by and large? Beginning in the early 1990s I initiated what has now become a long-term endeavor to investigate and respond to this basic problem in language assessment. In retrospect, it may not be a coincidence that the driving focus of my response to the problem came initially from a perusal of the literature on literacy assessment, given that our understandings of literacy and language development seem to be increasingly intertwined (particularly in discussions of "advancedness"—e.g., Byrnes and Maxim 2004). The key to improving language assessment, I thought at the time, was to take seriously the uses to which it was put—a sentiment captured by literacy researchers Hill and Perry (1994): "How we go about assessing literacy skills depends crucially on *why* we are doing it. Our reasons for assessing students are manifold" (254; emphasis added). As I eventually articulated in a variety of places (Norris 1996, 1997, 2000, 2002, 2004), I suggested that a careful and comprehensive understanding of *why* we assess must drive all other design and procedural considerations regarding *how* we assess. If we want assessment to contribute to language education programs and processes, first we need to figure out in exactly what ways it is supposed to do so, and we need to develop and implement assessments accordingly.

As a heuristic for determining the "why" of language assessments, I devised a model and process of "specifying intended uses" for assessment, depicted in figure 11.2 (from Norris 2000). Although some experts might like to think that we already know why we use assessments, I have argued that we need to understand assessment's intended uses at much greater depth than the traditional "received view"—that is, the categories provided by language testers and educational measurement experts. I do not think simply stating that an assessment is needed "for placement purposes" or for "determining language proficiency" is sufficient. Instead, we need to consider the underlying social and educational value of assessments as part of our practice. To engage in assessments that will accomplish something worthwhile, we need to specify exactly what they will be used to do and why, by addressing the following kinds of questions for every instance in which assessments are to be used: First, who will use the assessment to make interpretations about language learners? Second, what information will the users need from the assessment, to make these interpretations with accuracy and consistency? Third, what decisions or other actions will be informed by these interpretations? Finally, what will be accomplished by

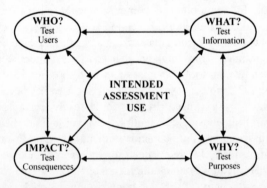

▓ Figure 11.2 Specification of Intended Uses for Assessment
Source: Norris (2000). Reprinted with permission from the English Teaching Forum, U.S. Department of State.

using the assessment in this way, in terms of consequences for learners and others with a stake in the assessment event?

By applying this framework and achieving consensus on the intended uses for assessments, the community of advanced FL educators (as well as individual practitioners) will be in a much better position to design assessments that can contribute to improved educational programs and outcomes. Furthermore, such an explicit treatment of the intended value of assessments provides an essential basis for evaluating, understanding, and ensuring the quality of assessment instruments and procedures once they are put into practice (see details in Norris 2004).

So, why do we need to use assessments in educating for advanced FL capacities? What roles should assessment be playing to advance this educational agenda? Based on current discussions, and in light of historical roles for assessment in FL education, I suggest that two main and overarching purposes should be distinguished. On one hand, assessment is essential for helping us to *understand* advanced FL learning within educational settings. More specifically, following the Norris (2000) framework, assessment should be used (a) by language education researchers and consumers of that research (b) for consistent measurement of language learning variables (c) to inform trustworthy interpretations about what actually happens and what works best in language instruction and (d) improve advanced FL teaching and learning. In other words, assessment must meet the demands of rigorous educational research by operationalizing consistent and replicable measures that provide for valid interpretations about variables of interest in advanced FL education. If assessment cannot meet this demand—and it probably does not at this time—research on instructional effectiveness in advanced FL education, as well as in other L2 domains, will fail to advance our knowledge about teaching/learning of languages (see Norris and Ortega 2003).

On the other hand—and in contrast, importantly, from research measurement purposes—assessment also is a fundamental practice in FL education programs, in that it *enables* advanced learning to occur. That is, assessment is used (a) by a variety of program stakeholders, particularly teachers and learners, (b) to gather immediately meaningful and local information about FL learners' knowledge/skills/abilities/dispositions (c) to inform decisions and actions in language classrooms and programs and (d) improve teaching and learning. In other words, assessment is—or should be—part and parcel of advanced language education programs, in that it interacts with curriculum, instruction, materials, and other program features to enable (or inhibit!) what teachers and learners actually do and accomplish. Without good assessments that are designed to fulfill well-articulated educative uses by actual teachers and learners in actual programs, the likelihood is high that assessment practices will either simply not contribute to or, worse, undermine advanced FL educational efforts.

Notice that point (d) above is identical for the research measurement and the educative functions of assessment; the consequence of using assessment should be an improvement in FL teaching and learning in both cases. Of course, the types of improvements and the means for achieving them are distinct; educative assessments emphasize the immediate needs of educational practitioners in making decisions that affect student learning (local, instantaneous improvements), and research measures respond to the needs of entire research domains for consistent and replicable operationalizations of important constructs (global, gradual improvements). Likewise, within each of these overarching "whys" for assessment there are many possible and particular cases to be made for its intended use in relation to advanced FL education. By way of overview and illustration, in the following two sections, I flesh out these two distinct roles for assessment and provide examples of each within the advanced FL education domain.

Why Worry about Assessment in *Research* on Advanced Language Education?

Assessment plays a key role in helping educational researchers understand language learning and the variables that are related to it. Ideally, assessment—in the form of well-defined and carefully operationalized measures—should lead to clear identification of the targets of advanced FL learning. That is, in research we need measures to inform us about what is learned (the dependent variable) and the degree to which it is learned, by linking observable language behaviors with phenomena that theories about learning at advanced levels predict will occur. For example, we need measures that tell us about vocabulary size and depth, native-like fluency and phonology, sociopragmatic sensitivity, discourse competency, syntactic complexity, and any number of other outcomes of advanced FL learning. Assessment also should tell us about how advanced learning takes place, by providing trustworthy measures of variables that theoretically contribute to or limit language learning (the independent and moderating variables). We need measures that tell us about, for example individual learner variables such as aptitude, motivation, memory, and L1 literacy; learning process variables such as metacognition, attention, awareness, noticing, and automatization; instructional process variables such as focus-on-form, explicit/implicit processes, teacher/peer feedback, and task complexity/variation; and contextual variables that account for myriad features of the learning environment.

When assessments are designed with such uses in mind, they provide evidence researchers need to understand how advanced FL instruction works and what kinds of learning result. Appropriate measures should enable researchers and their audiences to communicate in a commonly understood metric; to trust each metric as a consistent indicator for the specific variable of interest (and no more or less than that variable); and to accumulate, compare, and generalize findings across different research projects and sites. Indeed, these features of mutual intelligibility, specificity, consistency, and generalizability constitute the qualities that are emphasized in assessments used for research purposes. Unfortunately, individual L2 researchers often create idiosyncratic assessment instruments for each new study, without much regard for how others have measured the same variable. Alternately, they may simply adopt existing assessments, without considering the extent to which the variable that actually gets measured is the one that needs to be measured to provide the exact information required for a given study. Furthermore, evidence (e.g., reliability estimates) seldom is provided for why an assessment should be trusted as a consistent indicator of a given variable, and interpretations about multiple variables often are made on the basis of a single and inadequate assessment (e.g., interpretations about instructional processes, learning processes, and learning outcomes that are all based on a single test of learning outcomes). As a result of these and related practices, assessment probably is the weakest link in L2 educational research, and it obscures what we think we know about "what works" in L2 instruction because assessments are not designed with intended research uses and associated qualities in mind (see details in Norris and Ortega 2003). In the advanced domain, then, we should worry about assessment because, more than any other *research* practice, it will help or hinder our understanding of the nature of advanced FL learning and the instructional processes that contribute to it.

By way of example, I summarize a subset of the research measures I sought to implement in line with the foregoing considerations, from an earlier study into the nature of advanced FL proficiency. In Norris (1996) I investigated some of the claims made in the ACTFL (1986) Proficiency Guidelines by analyzing the oral performance data of forty-four FL learners on the German Speaking Test (Center for Applied Linguistics 1995)—a Simulated Oral Proficiency Interview that is rated according to the ACTFL Guidelines. My concern was that the interpretations that were being made about individual FL learners, on the basis of descriptors at each of the ACTFL proficiency levels, were not necessarily warranted. In other words, where the proficiency descriptors depicted a hierarchical progression from level to level in terms of a variety of language features (e.g., lexis, syntax, morphology, pragmatics, pronunciation, fluency), I wanted to find out whether such interpretations rang true for learners who were rated at the corresponding proficiency levels (from Novice-High, the lowest, to Superior, the highest). More specific to notions of "advancedness," I sought to clarify which performance features, among the variety spelled out in the proficiency descriptors, actually distinguished advanced-proficiency from other German FL speakers.

Rather than simply accepting the proficiency characterizations about what a learner's German speech *ought to be like* at a given level—a very common practice—I needed a means for measuring what a learner's German speech was *actually like*, and I needed assessments that would meet the qualities outlined above for research uses. In terms of intended use, then, I sought to use assessments to determine characteristics of FL German that would distinguish "advanced" from "non-advanced" German speakers. I posited the audience for this assessment to be researchers working in FL education in the United States who needed an empirical and trustworthy means for understanding a variety of phenomena in learners' speaking performances. Outcomes of the assessment were to be used for communicating and generalizing about the actual nature of advanced-level (and other) German speech, in comparison with the asserted qualities found in the proficiency descriptors. My hope was that use of this type of assessment would lead to a greatly improved and more detailed understanding of learners' speaking abilities and further that the scope of interpretations that were (and were not) warranted on the basis of ACTFL Guidelines ratings would be clarified.

To fulfill these intended uses, I identified a range of assessment procedures that would provide direct measures of several targeted language phenomena. As detailed in Norris (1996), these measures involved coding of German Speaking Test data for features of fluency, accuracy, syntactic complexity, and lexical sophistication (among many others; see also Norris 1997, 2001b). I selected these measures because they provided exact metrics for the variables of interest, they could be implemented with high degrees of reliability (as reported in Norris 1996), and they could be readily understood and used by other researchers for comparison with related language performance data. So what did I find out about the differences between "advanced" and other levels of German FL speech?

Figures 11.3 through 11.6 provide graphic summaries of the main findings for some of the measures used (note that although the individual graphs are presented in a standard format to facilitate understanding, they reflect a variety of measurement scales, so they should not be compared beyond the general patterns portrayed). Figure 11.3 presents results from three measures of the fluency of learners' German speech. For each of the three measures—speech rate, phonation time, and number of extended pauses—the patterns of average performance differences across the range

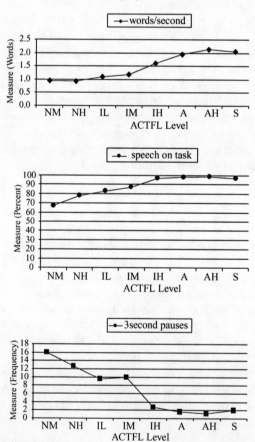

Figure 11.3 Fluency Measures (speech rate, phonation time, and extended pauses), by Proficiency Level

of proficiency levels were quite similar. Thus, fluency phenomena seemed to characterize increases in proficiency level from Novice-High (NH) up to Intermediate-High or Advanced (IH or A); then a "leveling off" was evident, however, in that no major differences were found above the Advanced proficiency level. Figure 11.4 shows that a similar finding emerged from the measurement of accuracy with three fixed rules of German word order—separation, inversion, and verb-end movement—in that considerable change occurred up to the IH/A proficiency level, but there was little differentiation in accuracy among the higher proficiency performances, including Advanced-High and Superior (AH and S).

Fluency and syntactic accuracy features, then, distinguish well between the levels up to IH/A but not at all among the higher-proficiency German users. Several other measures, however, did indicate that performance differences were evident between those upper proficiency levels—that is, that "advanced" and "really advanced" were not producing the same quality of German speech. Figure 11.5 shows that three measures of lexical sophistication—use of non-German words, German lexical range, and German lexical originality—all replicated the initial pattern found for fluency and accuracy, in the form of increases from NH to IH followed by a leveling off. In addition, however, these measures indicated that another major performance difference was located at the juncture between Advanced-High and Superior. In other words, the "really advanced" Superior proficiency speakers distinguished themselves from all other levels in terms of higher degrees of lexical sophistication (on all corresponding measures).

An even more interesting picture emerged through the use of syntactic complexity measures, as shown in figure 11.6. First, as with the lexical sophistication measures, an initial syntactic complexity measure of the average length of utterances (mltu) indicated, again, a major difference up to the IH proficiency level, a leveling through AH, and another increase at the Superior level. When utterances were broken down into single clauses, however, the measure of subordinate clause length (mlsc) did not replicate this pattern: The measure remained relatively stable from IH through S proficiency performances. If clause length was not increasing at the S level, what was the cause of utterance length increases? Only through use of a third measure—a subordination ratio (ctu)—did the answer become clear. Thus, I found that the higher Superior-level measures of utterance length were, in fact, attributable

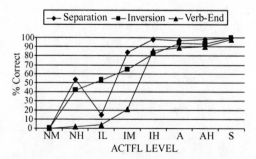

Figure 11.4 Syntactic Accuracy Measures for Three German Word Order Rules, by Proficiency Level

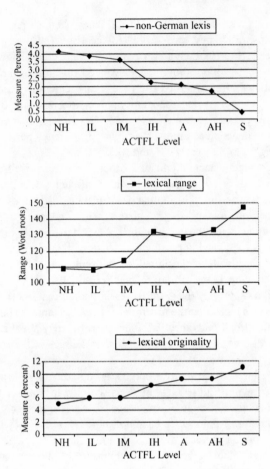

Figure 11.5 Lexical Sophistication Measures (non-German lexis, lexical range, lexical originality), by Proficiency Level

to an increase in the number of subordinate clauses that appeared in each utterance, rather than in the use of longer clauses.

To summarize, although fluency and accuracy measures reflected performance differences among the lower proficiency levels, they did not provide further distinctions among the higher-level (advanced) German users, despite interpretations to this effect that might be implied by ACTFL Guidelines descriptors at those levels (see details in Norris 1996, 1997). Other measures—of syntactic complexity and lexical sophistication—did further differentiate performances of very advanced German users from all others, however, suggesting that a complex constellation of language features best characterizes "advancedness." Of course, I am not suggesting that these findings offer a definitive analysis of the nature of "advanced" or "really advanced" FL proficiency. I do think, however, that these kinds of measures can begin to provide a much more detailed picture of just what "advanced" FL speaking performance

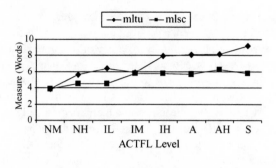

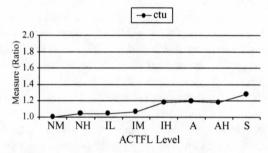

Figure 11.6 Syntactic Complexity Measures (T-Unit and subordinate clause length, ratio of clauses per T-Unit), by Proficiency Level

may consist of and that this picture is more exacting than that found in holistic proficiency scales. Perhaps more important, use of these kinds of measures also allows for exact replication in other studies of other learners, for the purpose of drawing comparisons and for generalizing about our understanding of the complex nature of advanced language learning. Likewise, this process of articulating measures with intended uses can and should be applied to any of the "advanced" learning variables; where it is, resulting assessments will help researchers generate consistency in their communication of new knowledge about advanced learning.

Why Worry about *Educative* Uses for Assessment?

Turning now to assessment's educative roles, as introduced above, assessment also should enable advanced language learning to occur in actual classrooms and programs, by providing FL practitioners and other stakeholders with useful information about language learners. In an immediate, practical sense, assessments designed for particular uses by local users (with local constraints in mind) can facilitate the practice of teaching considerably. Certainly, we need assessments to help us make decisions about individual learners and the educational routes that make the most sense for them, including selection of learners for advanced classes or programs, placement of learners into courses that best match their needs, advancement of learners through a curricular sequence, and certification of learner abilities on program completion.

Beyond these obvious decision-making uses, however, we also need assessment information to provide us with feedback about our educational efforts. For example, at the classroom level we use assessments to clarify the expected learning and performance outcomes of a lesson or course, diagnose learner needs vis-à-vis those outcomes, focus learners on prioritized learning values and reinforce effective study habits, gather information about what is and is not working in our materials, and, generally, improve what we do as teachers and learners on a daily basis. At the language program level, we also need to assess learners to determine that advanced learning is occurring as expected, identify expectations that are not being met and why, provide information to teachers and curriculum developers that is well-articulated with particular features of instruction, and, broadly, evaluate advanced programs for the purpose of ensuring their educational value.

At the societal level, too, there are educative functions for assessment, although they are seldom considered as we go about designing and using FL assessments. For example, locally designed assessments that reflect the true character of a curriculum may provide a means for resisting externally mandated testing that does not; the assessments we use certainly will encourage the public to perceive the value of FL education in terms of what we choose (and do not choose) to assess; the effectiveness of our advanced educational efforts will be judged via assessments, whether well or poorly designed to reflect those efforts; and public policy about language education will be based in part on assessment of particular learning outcomes, which also will determine what and how we teach.

Ideally, assessments designed with these varied educative uses in mind should directly enhance what we do in the name of advanced FL teaching and learning. As such, the qualities of assessment designs that demand prioritization include the utility of information for actual assessment users (i.e., not just for those who are technically sophisticated!); its relevance in helping to resolve the educational problems at hand; clarity for all stakeholders about the selected assessment methods and how they are used; and the consequences (positive, we hope) that ensue from assessment use. In fact, assessment can play a transformative role in FL education if we design it with these qualities in mind; it also can play an inhibiting role, however, if we allow it to do so. If we do not consider carefully the intended educative uses for assessment and if we do not anticipate the consequences for teaching and learning that will result from assessment, we run the risk that assessment will be done *to* teachers and learners (rather than *by* and *for* us), will not be aligned with our curriculum and instruction, will undermine and delimit the intended range of learning values in our programs, and will reinforce social engineering rather than enhance individual potential. In the advanced domain, then, we should worry about assessment because, more than any other *educational* practice, it will enable or inhibit valued and advanced language learning.

Several examples of assessments have been developed explicitly in response to these kinds of educative uses in advanced FL settings. The following assessments were designed in the context of an innovative German FL program at Georgetown University, the express purpose of which is to foster advanced levels of literate language abilities among its adult learners. At an early stage in curricular innovations, I interacted with the educators in this program to help bring assessment practices in line with their values and goals. As an essential starting point, we first developed program-wide specifications of intended uses for assessment, wherein consensus was negotiated for all instances of assessment at classroom and program levels, ranging from the mundane daily quiz to the large-scale semester final exam (Norris 2004). Important outcomes of this process included a set of guiding principles for assessment throughout the program; an actual reduction in the number of assessment instances called for because the educators realized that some existing practices were not particularly necessary; and prioritization of a handful of assessments in need of immediate (re)design to meet important information needs and to reflect new program values.

Among these initial development priorities, two examples may be most interesting for the advanced discussion here. First, we quickly realized that the existing placement exam, which had been in use for three decades, was no longer relevant for locating students within the new curricular sequence (indeed, surveys of students and faculty indicated exactly that). Furthermore, a major challenge was presented to program decision makers—in light of the unique content, literacy, and genre focus that characterized the new curriculum and courses—regarding how best to place the wide variety of incoming students, many of whom had considerable language learning experiences and abilities already, though not necessarily of the sort targeted within the program. After considerable deliberation, we decided to develop a new exam that was based on the major indicator of learner progress throughout the literacy-oriented curriculum—that is, the ability to process authentic German-language *texts* in aural and written modes. The resulting assessment instruments included apparently traditional language testing formats: listening and reading comprehension tests and a C-Test (a variant of the cloze test used in German university settings for assessing foreign students). Unique to our designs, however, and in response to our local intended uses, each test was composed of a series of *texts* that had been carefully selected by curriculum experts to reflect the kinds of textual processing abilities expected at each of the sequential program levels, up to the very highest level (fourth year) of undergraduate instruction. As a consequence of this distinctly curriculum-based design, placements to date have proceeded with high degrees of accuracy, including even incoming students who are located directly into the most advanced courses (see details in Norris 2004, 2006).

A second major intended use for assessment called for information about the extent to which learners were developing prioritized language-use abilities to expected degrees at each curricular level. The purpose of gathering this information was to provide feedback to curriculum developers and teachers regarding expectations that were and were not being met, so that they could revise instruction accordingly. Again, we gave initial priority to the types of language use that most directly reflected curricular values and trajectories—in this case, the ability to perform extended writing tasks within the literate adult genres that characterized the emphasis of each curricular level. To meet this demand, teachers at each curricular level engaged in extensive development efforts, the outcome of which was creation of "prototypical performance tasks" for use at the end of each instructional level. These tasks have been carefully designed and revised to elicit learners' abilities to meet specific curricular expectations, and learner performances continue to be collected and analyzed in detail at the end of each year for the purpose of ongoing program improvement.

One interesting (positive) effect of taking this particular assessment seriously was the revelation that, despite their efforts to that point, the local educators had not yet specified in sufficient detail exactly what their expectations for learning were at each curricular level, nor how well those expectations were articulated from one level to the next. As a result, much more explicit attention was paid to creation of detailed learning expectations, not only for the types of writing performances targeted in this assessment but also for other areas of language development (see Byrnes 2002).

Clearly, each of these examples of intended assessment use resulted in dramatically different assessment designs, as did the other uses for assessment that the program called for. Also worth noting is that these assessment uses could not have been met adequately through existing assessment practices, either from within the program or through unexamined adoption of "off-the-shelf" language tests. Of principal import here, however, is the finding that by taking the educative roles for assessment seriously, FL educators were able to design and implement assessments that provided immediately useful and locally meaningful outcomes. Furthermore, these outcomes and related consequences have been effectively integrated into sustained programmatic thinking (Norris and Pfeiffer 2003), the result of which should be improved development of advanced language learners.

Conclusion: Improving Assessment in Advanced Language Education

Given the wide variety of intended research and educative uses for FL assessment and the diversity of assessment designs they imply, how are we to respond? What steps can we take to reshape our assessment work so that it contributes to (rather than inhibits) effective teaching and learning? In conclusion, I offer six basic suggestions to the foreign language education community and those who work closely with them. These suggestions are intended to help educators shift their thinking and practice from the current focus on "how-to" aspects of assessment to a more systematic treatment of assessment as a purposeful process in both research and education. My hope is that these suggestions will be relevant for educators and researchers who are embarking on creation of innovative programs that seek to develop advanced FL capacities; by taking the role(s) of assessment seriously at the beginning stages of such a development agenda (rather than as an afterthought), educators and researchers will be much better positioned to understand and support effective educational practice. Based on historical trends (see summaries in Norris 2004; Norris and Ortega 2003), by contrast, if we do not change how we conceive of and engage in assessment, in both its research and educative roles, innovations are unlikely to do much to "advance" the cause of advanced FL learning or learners.

1. Treat assessment as an integral part of advanced language education programs, along with curriculum and instruction; realize that these three program

elements all interact to determine the outcomes of instructed learning and therefore should receive balanced and simultaneous attention as programs are developed and implemented.

2. Treat assessment as an integral part of advanced language learning research programs; encourage collaboration among researchers within the advanced FL domain so that assessment measures can be articulated with the ways in which they will be interpreted by other researchers and by consumers of research.

3. Develop FL educators' (teachers', administrators', researchers') abilities in assessment. Local educators are in the best position to respond with sensitivity to local needs and exigencies of assessment, and they will be held responsible for assessment consequences (good and bad); as such, educators should be equipped to identify intended uses for assessment, to develop instruments and procedures accordingly, to evaluate and improve upon them, and to interpret and disseminate assessment outcomes.

4. Consider the impact of assessment practices at all levels of FL education on the goal of educating for advanced FL capacities; how we assess in the early stages of education will play a role in determining what and how students learn in later stages of education.

5. Do not rely on the language testing community to provide off-the-shelf answers to the question of "how to assess advanced FL learning"; instead, seek out language testers who are willing to take seriously the "why" of assessment in advanced FL education, and work with them to design assessments that are usable by intended users, provide trustworthy evidence about learners and learning, inform appropriate decisions and actions, and result in improved teaching and learning.

6. Discuss and disseminate assessment practices, findings, and knowledge at all levels of the advanced FL education domain, including classrooms, programs, school systems, and research or professional communities; in particular, advocate for attention to assessment in public venues, including journals and conferences.

To the extent that we are able to incorporate these kinds of changes into our assessment practices, we will position ourselves to better understand, as well as enable, education for advanced foreign language capacities.

Acknowledgments

This chapter is a revised version of a plenary address delivered at the 2005 Georgetown University Roundtable on Languages and Linguistics (GURT). I thank Heidi Byrnes and the GURT organizers for inviting my participation. I also appreciate critical feedback on my plenary address provided by Lourdes Ortega, although any inadequacies are mine alone.

REFERENCES

American Council on the Teaching of Foreign Languages (ACTFL). 1986. *ACTFL Proficiency Guidelines*. Yonkers, N.Y.: ACTFL.

————. 1999. *ACTFL Proficiency Guidelines—speaking, revised.* Yonkers, N.Y.: ACTFL.

————. 2002. *Program standards for the preparation of foreign language teachers.* Yonkers, N.Y.: ACTFL.

Bartning, Inge. 2000. Gender agreement in L2 French: Pre-advanced vs. advanced learners. *Studia Linguistica* 54:225–37.

Bernhardt, Elizabeth. 2002. A language center director responds. *Modern Language Journal* 86:246–48.

Bongaerts, Theo. 1999. Ultimate attainment in L2 pronunciation: The case of very advanced late learners. In *Second language acquisition and the critical period hypothesis,* ed. David Birdsong. Mahwah, N.J.: Erlbaum, 133–60.

Byrnes, Heidi. 2002. The role of task and task-based assessment in a content-oriented collegiate foreign language curriculum. *Language Testing* 19:419–37.

Byrnes, Heidi, and Hiram H. Maxim, eds. 2004. *Advanced foreign language learning: A challenge to college programs.* Boston: Heinle Thomson.

Center for Applied Linguistics. 1995. *German Speaking Test.* Washington, D.C.: Center for Applied Linguistics.

Cheng, Liying, and Yoshinori Watanabe, eds. 2004. *Washback in language testing.* Mahwah, N.J.: Erlbaum.

Cobb, Tom. 2003. Analyzing late interlanguage with learner corpora: Quebec replications of three European studies. *Canadian Modern Language Review* 59:393–423.

Council of Europe. 2001. *Common European framework of reference for languages: Learning, teaching, assessment.* Cambridge: Cambridge University Press.

Freed, Barbara, Norman Segalowitz, and Dan P. Dewey. 2004. Context of learning and second language fluency in French: Comparing regular classroom, study abroad, and intensive domestic immersion programs. *Studies in Second Language Acquisition* 26:275–301.

Geeslin, Kimberly. 2003. A comparison of copula choice: Native Spanish speakers and advanced learners. *Language Learning* 53:703–64.

Gu Yongqi, Peter. 2004. *Vocabulary learning strategies in the Chinese EFL context.* Singapore: Marshall Cavendish Academic.

Hill, Clifford, and Kate Perry. 1994. Assessing English language and literacy around the world. In *From testing to assessment: English as an international language,* ed. Clifford Hill and Kate Perry. New York: Longman, 253–71.

Kotz, Sonja A., and Kerrie Elston-Guttler. 2003. The role of proficiency on processing categorical and associative information in the L2 as revealed by reaction times and event-related brain potentials. *Journal of Neurolinguistics* 17:215–35.

Lariviere, Richard W. 2002. Language curricula in universities: What and how. *Modern Language Journal* 86:244–46.

Leaver, Betty L., and Boris Shekhtman, eds. 2002. *Developing professional-level language proficiency.* Cambridge: Cambridge University Press.

Liskin-Gasparro, Judith. 1998. Linguistic development in an immersion context: How advanced learners of Spanish perceive SLA. *Modern Language Journal* 82:159–76.

————. 2000. The use of tense-aspect morphology in Spanish oral narratives: Exploring the perceptions of advanced learners. *Hispania* 83:830–44.

Moir, Jo, and Paul Nation. 2002. Learners' use of strategies for effective vocabulary learning. *Prospect* 17:13–35.

Montrul, Silvina, and Roumyana Slabakova. 2003. Competence similarities between native and near-native speakers: An investigation of the preterite-imperfect contrast in Spanish. *Studies in Second Language Acquisition* 25:351–98.

Norris, John M. 1996. A validation study of the ACTFL Guidelines and the German Speaking Test. Unpublished master's thesis, University of Hawaii.

————. 1997. The German Speaking Test: Utility and caveats. *Die Unterrichtspraxis* 30:148–58.

————. 2000. Purposeful language assessment. *English Teaching Forum* 38:18–23.

————. 2001a. Concerns with computer-adaptive oral proficiency assessment. *Language Learning & Technology* 5:99–105.

————. 2001b. Use of address terms on the German Speaking Test. In *Pragmatics in language teaching,* ed. Kenneth Rose and Gabriele Kasper. Cambridge: Cambridge University Press, 248–82.

————. 2002. Interpretations, intended uses, and designs in task-based language assessment: Introduction to the special issue. *Language Testing* 19:337–46.

————. 2004. *Validity evaluation in foreign language assessment.* Unpublished Ph.D. diss., University of Hawaii.

————. 2006. Development and evaluation of a curriculum-based German C-test for placement purposes. In *Der C-Test: Theoretische Grundlagen und praktische Anwendungen,* vol. 5, ed. Rüdiger Grotjahn. New York: Peter Lang, 45–83.

Norris, John M., and Lourdes Ortega. 2003. Defining and measuring SLA. In *Handbook of second language acquisition,* ed. Catherine Doughty and Michael H. Long. Malden, Mass.: Blackwell, 716–61.

Norris, John M., and Peter C. Pfeiffer. 2003. Exploring the use and usefulness of ACTFL Guidelines oral proficiency ratings in college foreign language departments. *Foreign Language Annals* 36:572–81.

Omaggio-Hadley, Alice C. 2001. *Teaching language in context,* 3rd ed. Boston: Heinle & Heinle.

Phillips, June K. 2003. Implications of language education policies for language study in schools and universities. *Modern Language Journal* 87:579–86.

Popham, William J. 2004. Curriculum, instruction, and assessment: Amiable allies or phony friends. *Teachers College Record* 106:417–28.

Shavelson, Richard, and Leta Huang, 2003. Responding responsibly to the frenzy to assess learning in higher education. *Change* 35:10–19.

Shohamy, Elana. 2001. *The power of tests: A critical perspective on the uses of language tests.* New York: Pearson.

Spolsky, Bernard. 2000. Language testing in the *Modern Language Journal. Modern Language Journal* 84:536–52.

Starkey, Hugh, and Audrey Osler. 2001. Language learning and antiracism: Some pedagogical challenges. *Curriculum Journal* 12:313–44.

Stiggins, Richard J. 1988. Revitalizing classroom assessment: The highest instructional priority. *Phi Delta Kappan* 69:363–68.

Stutterheim, Christiane von. 2003. Linguistic structure and information organisation: The case of very advanced learners. *EUROSLA Yearbook* 3:183–207.

Wiggins, Grant. 1998. Educative assessment: Designing assessments to inform and improve student performance. San Francisco: Jossey-Bass.

12

Rethinking Assessment for Advanced Language Proficiency

ELANA SHOHAMY

Tel Aviv University

AS THE THEME OF THIS VOLUME indicates, research on advanced language learning is now capturing the attention of language professionals. Among several research sites in the United States that are dedicated to language learning at this level is the Center for Advanced Language Proficiency (CALPER) at Pennsylvania State University. CALPER's agenda for investigating the nature of advancedness and development toward advanced levels of ability includes a corpus project, a concept project, a metaphor project, and a project to investigate project learning. Each of these focused inquiries seeks to provide theoretical and practical insights that are intended to inform a project that is focused on rethinking advanced language proficiency (ALP) from the perspective of assessment. This chapter arose from and is directed to that effort. In it I discuss how the language profession might rethink assessment for ALP with regard to the construct of advancedness, incorporation of critical features of ALP into assessment procedures, and implications for educational practice.

Relating the "What" to the "How"

Language testing often is described in terms of two components. The component that focuses on the "what" refers to the construct that needs to be assessed, also known as "the trait" or "the construct"; the component that pertains to the "how"—known also as "the method"—addresses specific procedures and methods that can be used to assess the "what" (Shohamy 1998a, 1998b). These two components also are the organizing principles for this chapter. The trait of ALP serves as the foundation for the development of specific assessment procedures; discussion of ALP is followed by methods that I regard as appropriate for assessing the construct of ALP.

Traditionally, ALP has been defined by tangent disciplines that are external to language testing, such as linguistics, applied linguistics, second language acquisition, and language teaching. These disciplines provide essential elements that language testers need to consider in the process of test development. The "how," on the other hand, is derived mostly from the dynamic field of language testing (LT) itself, which, over the years, has developed a broad body of theories, research, and practices about a variety of assessment procedures suited for testing language.

A look at developments in LT since the 1960s reveals that LT theories and practices have always been closely related to definitions of language proficiency. Matching the "how" of testing with the "what" of language uncovers several periods in the development of LT, each instantiating different notions of language knowledge and the specific measurement procedures that go with them. Thus, discrete-point testing regarded language as consisting of lexical and structural items, and language tests presented isolated items in objective testing procedures; in the integrative era, language tests tapped integrated and discoursal language; in the communicative era, tests aimed to replicate interactions among language users by using authentic oral and written texts; and in performance testing, language users were expected to perform tasks in well-defined, real-life contexts.

In a departure from simple correspondences, alternative assessment was a way of responding to the realization that language knowledge is a complex phenomenon that no single procedure can be expected to capture and that therefore requires multiple assessment procedures. In an additional step, the term *multiplism* recognizes that in each assessment phase one can select from among a variety of assessment options (Shohamy 1998a).

Although the "what" to "how" trajectory for the development of tests is intuitively plausible, extensive work in the past decade points to a less overt but highly influential dynamic in the opposite direction: the power of tests to shape definitions of language (Shohamy 2001). Hence, contemporary assessment research has a special obligation to examine the close relationship between methods and traits and to uncover how language tests potentially constrict definitions of language (the "what") to "testable" content—a tendency that disregards the complexity of the construct. Such vigilance is called for particularly in the largely uncharted territory of the "what" of advancedness and the "how" of assessing ALP. In other words, as language testers seek to develop designs, methods, and procedures of assessment (the "how") for ALP, they must be mindful of emerging insights regarding the trait itself: in terms of its complexity, its multiple facets, its dimensions, and its characteristic features. Overlooking those aspects for the sake of practicality and "testability" could result not only in invalid tests or other assessment procedures but, more seriously, false decisions based on tests.

Accordingly, I begin my considerations by arguing for the need to redefine assessment for ALP in a way that recognizes different proficiency levels. I then address specific dimensions that reflect current thinking about the trait of ALP. On that basis I return to assessment and propose some principles for types and methods of assessment that would be suitable for assessing ALP.

On the Need to Redefine ALP

By and large, LT has not differentiated within its theories and methods among different proficiency levels; it has applied similar assessment methods across the board. In that regard it contrasts with foreign language (FL) teaching, which traditionally has structured and organized itself according to proficiency levels (e.g., beginning, intermediate, and advanced). For example, the Oral Proficiency Interview (OPI), with its different phases, is regarded as an appropriate assessment tool for *all*

FL learners regardless of proficiency level. As a result, LT has been free to focus extensively on the specific components of language that needed to be tested, such as grammar, vocabulary, pragmatics, discourse, and content. Proficiency levels entered the discussion only through different types of proficiency scales, mostly in the organization of *rating scales, guidelines, benchmarks,* and *rubrics.*

Anchored historically in definitions provided by U.S. government agencies such as the Foreign Service Institute, the Defense Language Institute, and the Peace Corps, proficiency scales are associated particularly closely with development of the OPI as the major assessment tool for actual language performance. Examination of actual and direct speech, away from discrete-point testing, pointed to a need to value performance-oriented qualities of learner language. At the same time, the U.S. government agencies that developed the oral interview also were looking for criteria that would accord with regarding language development as a progression and a hierarchy of development, similar to the way FL classes were structured and taught: The learner progresses along the second/foreign language continuum from novice (minimal amount of language) through "some language" to "some more" language and through "advanced" to a "professional" level. At that stage much language is required, and the learner can use it broadly in a variety of functions, for a variety of purposes and contexts, on the way to commanding it fully at the "native speaker" level—the correct and true goal. Different terms describe this progress. For example, the Council of Europe proficiency scales differentiate between *Breakthrough* level (A1), *Waystage* (A2), and a mastery level (C2) (North 2000; Morrow 2004), with specific criteria describing the skills associated with each level. The Association of Language Testers of Europe (ALTE) has translated these specifications into similar descriptions that are part of scales (North 1995, 2000).

Despite wide use in the United States and Europe, such descriptions of proficiency levels are the subject of considerable criticism. The first critique pertains to their exclusive focus on language as an isolated entity, unrelated to other abilities and forms of knowledge that learners bring to the language learning and interaction scene—among them knowledge in the first language (L1), content, context, motivation, and knowledge of language and languages besides the language being learned or assessed. In other words, L2 learning is not the same thing as L1 learning, nor is the L1 and the knowledge expressed in and through it inherently an intrusion, even though most L2 instructional and assessment contexts take that position. Near-exclusive concentration on the second/foreign language that disavows all other knowledge projects an artificial way of learning anything, especially learning another language.

A second fundamental criticism pertains to the presumed hierarchical nature of L2 learning, as though it followed a prescribed and controlled linear order. The following questions arise: Do hierarchies represent the reality of the process of L2 learning? Do all learners proceed along the same route? Is a particular level in fact higher than the previous level, as stipulated by the guidelines? Do these levels potentially represent deep-seated ideologies rather than the reality of language development, both in instructed L2 learning and in language acquired at the workplace? These questions deserve serious attention inasmuch as little convincing evidence exists for the claim that L2 learning actually works in a clean, linear, and homogeneous order of progression that is similar for all learners.

Nevertheless, the proficiency descriptions have deeply influenced the views of language learning that schools and universities have adopted in the past two decades. Use of the ACTFL proficiency scales in the United States for curricular and instructional frameworks is pervasive. The *Common European Framework* (CEF) seems to take on a similarly powerful position in educational decision making in most nations in Europe (Morrow 2004). Fulcher (2004) notes that over time, the guidelines have created a "false" truth for teachers and bureaucrats, with no evidence of their validity. More troubling, the guidelines gradually will serve as "prescriptions" that dictate proficiency levels in a way that is detached from reality. Instead of *defining* levels of language proficiency they have become the institutionalized "it" of language: "The main danger is that they [teachers] are beginning to believe that the scales in the CEF represent an acquisitional hierarchy, rather than a common perception. They begin to believe that the language of the descriptors actually relates to the sequence of how and what learners learn" (Fulcher 2004, 260).

That such concerns are by no means unjustified or geographically confined is evident from the fact that similar proficiency scales have been adopted in Australia, Canada, Hong Kong, and Israel. All share the notion of a classification, progression, and hierarchy of language proficiency according to predefined levels that themselves are assigned on the basis of elicited language samples such as the OPI; semi-direct tests such as the Simulated Oral Proficiency Interview (SOPI); or, in some European contexts, a portfolio and/or self assessment procedures (see also chapter 11 in this volume).

A third and related critique, therefore, is that these descriptors cannot draw on a solid research base that might support their definitions of language. That state of affairs is even more troubling with regard to the increasingly urgent need to define ALP. If hierarchical and linear conceptions of language and language learning seem ill-equipped to describe beginning and intermediate levels of language performance, it is doubtful that they can capture the wide array of traits that test takers need to possess to function as advanced language users. According to emerging understandings of ALP, these traits include cognitive abilities, content knowledge, context awareness, input processing capacities, interactive abilities, and multilingual performance options.

The last criticism I mention relates to the notion that most guidelines are detached from contextual variables such as the purpose of the assessment, the particular uses of the language, the context in which the language has been learned, the age of the learners, the learning conditions, the specific languages learned and assessed, and especially the multiple functions of different languages in different contexts. In other words, in contrast with prevailing notions of "one size fits all," ALP in one context, in a given language, with given learners, may not be generalizable to other domains. Further doubts are being raised about whether such broad and generic descriptions are relevant and valid for different language learning contexts and uses, such as foreign language learning, second language learning, immersion programs, bilingual programs, immigration contexts, indigenous languages, specific grade levels, instructed learning, content-based instruction, tertiary education, and elementary and high schools, as well as for capturing the variety of language needs that characterize different workplaces.

The foregoing criticisms indicate that the profession must reconsider its construct for what knowing a language at different levels of proficiency means. Inasmuch as the guidelines presuppose a hierarchy of both development and performance; adhere to generic descriptions; and, at least implicitly, claim to be universally applicable, they are unsuited for what we now know about the contextualized nature of language and language performance in multilingual environments. Inasmuch as these shortcomings—at times fundamental deficiencies—become particularly obvious at advanced levels of language ability, the profession has a near-unique opportunity to begin anew to find different ways of organizing language and language development beyond hierarchies and to consider the relation between meaning-making and formal features of language. For language testers, the additional challenge and opportunity is to develop tests that accord with new insights that are gradually gaining currency and to reconsider the relation between new approaches to testing and curricular and instructional decision making at the advanced level.

In the following section of this chapter I propose appropriate strategies for language assessment that are grounded in the new "what" of ALP. I subsequently offer proposals for methods of assessing the construct—the "how"—in light of expanded notions of ALP.

Proposals for Assessing ALP
Because specifying what is to be tested is fundamental to designing any test, I begin with some of the dimensions of the construct of ALP, based on current thinking in the field. These features, as well as others I do not address in this chapter, indicate a complex and rich construct for ALP and, by extension, for assessment strategies.

Language as a Complex, Flexible, and Personal System
When we approach language and languages in broader terms, we can see that ALP is a complex and rich construct with various components. First, the resources of the semiotic system language do not have defined and clear boundaries because languages do not stand by themselves; they are products of the people who use them and interact and negotiate through and with them. Language use is open, creative, free, dynamic, energetic, personal, and constantly evolving. As a consequence, the product of language use also is flexible and open and reflects the lack of fixed boundaries for interactions and negotiations. The results are mixes and hybrids and endless varieties in terms of accents, lexicon, and syntax, to name only the most obvious.

Variation in language and language use is well manifested in "personal languages" (Shohamy 2006). Even when people use the term *advanced* and regard their language proficiency as such, each person's "advancedness" varies in terms of a personal style—which reflects a kind of personal and public persona—as well as in terms of choices being made, for example with regard to content, words, and intonations.

Language as a Means for Content/Knowledge Creation

At all times and on all instructional levels but especially on the advanced level, language is a means for expressing and interpreting rich and meaningful content through interactions and negotiations (Byrnes 2002a, 2002b). At the latest at the ALP level, that semiotic tool-like function of language in support of the paramount goal of making meanings must receive pedagogical and conceptual primacy, and language form becomes secondary: Language is a means for content and knowledge, for interpretation, ideas, and concepts. In other words, although in most language classes and courses—particularly at beginning and intermediate levels—language itself might appear to be the goal and target of instruction, such a subversion of the real priorities in language cannot be sustained at the advanced levels. Indeed, in a kind of washback effect, the obvious priority of meaning at advanced levels leads to questioning the existence of *language* classes as we commonly know them.

To some extent, content-based classes attempt to assert the priority of content and meaning from the beginning, with language and languages serving as medium and tool rather than as the goal of instruction. As Byrnes (2005) has pointed out, however, most programs that claim a content-based instructional approach retain a conflicted stance toward the relation between content and language and do not necessarily follow through on their best convictions. For example, Cushing Weigle and Jensen (1997) describe a range of content-based programs that differ in their primary focus and in the relative importance of language versus content. Among them are theme-based programs, in which language is organized around a single topic or theme; in these programs, language instruction and acquisition are the primary focus, and the content serves as a vehicle for learning the language. At the other end of the spectrum are programs that give equal weight to content and language and programs that give priority to content, with little attention to language. Typically, a stronger focus on content characterizes more advanced levels of instruction. Byrnes (2002a) reports, however, on a university program that has deliberately chosen to integrate content and language acquisition throughout the undergraduate learning experience, from the beginning of instruction to ALP. In that case, ALP no longer is uniquely defined by its content focus, and the relation between general knowledge and language knowledge requires clarification throughout language instruction. At least two consequences of this reconsideration stand out: first, the need to rectify the intellectual devaluing of learners that often accompanies beginning levels of instruction, and second, imagining learner engagement with content at all instructional levels.

Given that charge, it is interesting to inquire about the origins of the separation of content and language. One answer lies in the structuralist preference of linguistics in the middle of the twentieth century—a formalist bias that universal grammar, all protestations notwithstanding, only served to affirm through powerful theorizing that focused on syntax. A second answer, however, points to roots in a nation-state ideology in which *language* proficiency in the "national" prestigious language became a symbol for group membership. The FL teaching profession in all parts of the world adopted this approach and created a field of study that made language the educational target in its own right. It also created a pool of teachers for whom the major requirement was to be proficient in the language they taught. Ironically, that preference ultimately stood the value of learning a second language on its head because native speakers—that is, those born into the language—were accorded the most authoritative status, including the right to teach it in schools and universities. Finally, because language teaching was not related to a discernible intellectual domain, FL teaching generally has not been regarded as a prestigious activity within the academy.

Multiple Ways of Being "Advanced"

The defining question of our field—namely, what knowing a language means (see also Spolsky 1968)—is answered at the advanced level with a decided nod toward multiplicity: There are multiple ways to "know" and a variety of ways of being an "advanced" language user; their totality represents the richness and complexity of language. These multiple ways of languaging and, therefore, of knowing are embedded in diverse contexts and goals—a fact that is well demonstrated by the contributions in this volume, which highlight the close interdependency between language and content, especially when both are defined and geared to local and immediate needs of specific populations.

If language is a means to deliver specific content, then language proficiency cannot be locked into uniform and systematic ways of producing language. Indeed, language performance is judged not by abstract "native speaker" criteria but by various content- and context-related criteria. There are multiple ways of being advanced, including the use of multiple languages and multimodal resources that vary in time and place and assuredly are not hierarchical.

I have alluded to the powerful connection between language-based notions of the nation-state and certain views of language and language instruction. Hutton (1999) explores that connection in yet another way when he claims that the idea of language boundaries and homogeneous ways of defining and using languages, as promoted by linguists, is based on views of both languages and peoples as "pure" and "correct" in opposition to "different," "impure," and "incorrect." Having adopted notions of language as a finite system, the FL profession—particularly its native teachers—not only taught the language of "the nation" but in some fashion was "ordained" to teach the home language, as evidenced by British Council mandates for teaching English.

A narrow and uniform model for L2 proficiency became especially powerful at the ALP level, when learners are moving toward and approaching the optimal goal of "the native speaker." Thus, to know French meant to know the very standard of France, including ignoring its varieties and disregarding the fact that features such as accent or grammar are socially constructed. Just as there is no single correct way of using language in terms of grammar, lexicon, accent, and all other dimensions of language, there also is no one way to define or to be an ALP user, and certainly no need to perpetuate the aspirations of "imagined" nation states through an "imagined" language.

Ironically, the enormous spread of English around the globe offers particularly instructive examples for a decoupling of language and nation and for the continued evolution of multiplicity. No longer considered as being in the possession of a specific nation or nations, the phenomenon of "global English"—in the form of multiple

Englishes—illustrates the need to part company with the belief that a certain variety of language is the only one that represents the form that ALP can take: ALP implies a variety of ways of knowing, in line with the open nature of languages, and the guideline descriptions of the ACTFL and the CEF are unable to capture these diverse ways of "doing language."

Multilingual Competencies: Languages and Modalities

Traditionally, the construct of ALP, like all other language proficiency levels, has been based on a monolingual construct of language whereby "other" languages, especially the L1 of the learners, had no place and no role to play in the learning of the language; in fact, they constituted an unacceptable, even illegitimate, intrusion by "foreign elements" into learners' and bilinguals' speech. Furthermore, the posited progression and hierarchy assumed that the higher the proficiency level, the less learners engaged the L1 as they reached for the goal of being like "the native speaker."

Recent research, however, shows an important role for L1 in L2 proficiency at all levels. The data presented in figure 12.1, which are taken from a study that examined the academic achievements of Russian immigrants in Israeli schools, point to the significant role of L1 in the performance on tests in mathematics of immigrants who are in the process of acquiring L2 Hebrew. Specifically, they demonstrate how L1 and L2, *together*, complement one another as important resources for solving math problems. Thus, the experimental group that obtained the math test in both Hebrew and Russian showed a significant advantage over a control group that received the test in Hebrew only. The use of a bilingual version of tests for immigrants, often termed "accommodation," contributed significantly to higher achievement over a long period, extending beyond eight years of residence after immigration. Clearly, two languages are better than one, as language learners continue to use their L1 as a meaningful resource over an extended time period.

A similar phenomenon occurs in writing, where students multi-code in two or more languages in the process of transmitting meanings—for example, by using L1 syntax with L2 lexicon. In any case, texts frequently are presented in one language while reactions are expected in another—a common practice in contexts in which the instructional language and the language of public discourse are not the students' home language. In fact, determining the boundaries of "language x" or "language y," often is impossible, as is specifying how the two interact. Clearly, however, the

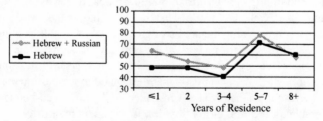

Figure 12.1 Math Grades in Monolingual and Bilingual Tests by L2 Hebrew Students

common view and practice that L1 has no place in the L2 classroom has no basis in observed multilingual contexts or in what we know about human cognitive practices.

In line with such insights, Solano-Flores and Trumbull (2003) argue for a new practice paradigm that incorporates language in context. They note that existing approaches to testing English language learners (ELLs) do not ensure equitable and valid outcomes because they overlook the complex nature of language and its relationship to culture. For that reason, Solano-Flores and Trumbull propose combined use of generalizability theory and research designs in which ELLs would receive the same items in both English and in their native language—an approach that has the potential to reveal more fine-grained understanding of the interactions between L1 and L2 proficiency, student content knowledge, and the linguistic and content demands of test items. Solano-Flores and Trumbull also reject the common practice of using ELL tests to compare score differences between ELLs and mainstream students and decry efforts by test designers to eliminate the effects of non-mainstream language and culture as a way to ensure test validity. In their proposed paradigm, test development efforts are oriented in the opposite direction: "Culture-free tests cannot be constructed because tests are inevitably cultural devices. Therefore, understandings of non-mainstream language and non-mainstream culture must be incorporated as part of the reasoning that guides the entire assessment process." Attending to the contextual factors that shape student performance as part of a new paradigm for language assessment, they call for treating languages as an asset and not as an error: "Assessment is a multidisciplinary endeavor" (Solano-Flores and Trumbull 2003, 9).

Related evidence for the appropriateness of such practices comes from Bialystok (1997, 2001), who has demonstrated repeatedly how first languages, and especially bilingualism, affect cognitive performance even after many years of using L2. Indeed, younger bilinguals and adults perform better than monolinguals in a variety of cognitive tasks. Yet most FL learning contexts continue to deny the existence of L1 and overlook its significant role in contributing to improved performances in terms of communication, interpretations, and production of relevant content. In fact, revisiting the notion that ALP by definition replaces L1 might be especially appropriate for contexts in which learners are challenged to attain unusually high performance in L2, such as academic tasks in higher education. Precisely then should learners be free to use all available resources to make sense of "advanced levels" of texts and content.

Moving from multiple languages to multiple modalities, we can draw on a considerable amount of relevant work. That research has gained wide acceptance, mostly in terms of broadening the notion of proficiency to include nonlinguistic features such as gestures, visuals, images, music, and diverse signs alongside linguistic features (Kress 2003; Kress and van Leeuven 1996). In other words, communicative proficiency is more than using words; it manifests itself in various interdependencies among diverse resources that exist concurrently, with no defined boundaries. Their interaction results in creation of multi-codes, fusions, and hybrids.

Revisiting Interactiveness

An expanded view of language and language proficiency also is necessary on the basis of research in language testing by, among others, Bachman (1990); Bachman and Palmer (1996); Cushing Weigle and Jensen (1997); McNamara (1997); and Chalhoub-Deville (2003), who have argued for the centrality of interaction within the trait of language proficiency. Interaction is central to language proficiency inasmuch as language—a social and interactive tool—occurs between readers and writers, readers and readers, speakers and listeners, and a variety of agents co-constructing meanings in different ways by using dialogical devices (Swain 2001). In contrast with earlier positions, which focused on the learner as an independent and autonomous agent and user, Bachman (1990) discusses interactional ability between the language user, the context, and the discourse.

The dimension of interactiveness is particularly closely related to content-based language learning, which itself is closely related to issues of ALP. Thus, Cushing Weigle and Jensen (1997) promote interactiveness in language assessment along with authenticity—a notion that has long been part of the assessment tradition. They state, "We believe that special consideration should be given to authenticity and interactiveness in CBA [content-based assessment]. The rationale for this emphasis is that the goal of CBI [content-based instruction] is to foster language use through purposeful engagement with content" (Cushing Weigle and Jensen 1997, 206–7).

More recently, Chalhoub-Deville (2003) has called for expanding the notion of interaction by yet another dimension. Criticizing the narrow use of interaction by language testers, she highlights the socially and culturally mediated nature of interaction and argues for a primarily social representation of the construct of proficiency. Describing her own stance, she states, "This position diverges from that advocated by proponents of interactional competence, who view the language use situation primarily as a social event in which ability, language users and context are inextricably meshed. . . . This representation claims that the ability components the language user brings to the situation or context interact with situational facets to change those facets as well as to be changed by them. The facet aspects of the context the language user attends to dynamically influence the ability features activated and vice versa" (Chalhoub-Deville 2003, 372).

Accordingly, Chalhoub-Deville differentiates two approaches to the construct of language. A cognitive approach is based on the ability to use language in context and favors separation of construct and context and an interactional competence that is embedded into a single interacting structure. A social perspective incorporates interactional viewpoints into language testing and recognizes that knowledge is a dynamic process that is both contextual and socially mediated.

The Role of Culture in Language

A focus on language in context inherently foregrounds the central role of culture in any language use, particularly ALP. Although culture has a long history in FL learning, traditionally it has been incorporated in terms of a dichotomy between language and culture. By contrast, Lantolf (2006) supports a unified approach and proposes the term *languaculture* to signal reintroduction of meaning into language study (see also Agar 1994). Among the consequences of such a stance is that meaning would become much more interesting and complex because it entails knowledge of different concepts, encoded in features such as conceptual metaphors, lexical networks, lexicogrammatical structures, and schemas that represent different ways of organizing the world and our experiences in it (for data-based support of these arguments, see chapters 3–5 in this volume). Even very advanced speakers have difficulty moving out of the frame of reference established by one languaculture (e.g., that of L1) into that which is laid down by another (L2). Consequently, to the extent possible, advanced learners require instructional support as they develop the capacity to interpret and generate meanings in terms of the relevant languaculture and the realities it (re)presents.

Whether the National Standards for Foreign Language Education (1996) initiative, with its five Cs (communication, cultures, connections, comparison, and communities), is the best framework for providing that support remains an open question. Kubota (2004), for example, is concerned that the "comparisons" standard expects learners to gain insight into language and culture by comparing the target language and culture with their own—an approach that can essentialize and polarize cultures of the self and the other (Kubota 1999, 26). She fears that teachers and textbook writers might present a polarized view of the two cultures, where the target culture of non-English speakers is rendered as truly "foreign" and American culture is presented as a homogeneous culture of English speakers with a shared set of values and social practices. Aside from ignoring the cultural and linguistic diversity of American culture, such views, according to Kubota, are based on a binary concept of true facts versus false information and fail to recognize the politics and ideologies underlying the ways the culture of the Other is interpreted (Kubota 1999, 26). For that reason, attention must be devoted to political issues that address racism, social injustices, and unequal relations of power, and teaching and learning must go beyond the difference-similarity dualism (Kubota 1999, 28).

Flexible Definitions of Language Quality
I have highlighted the fact that contemporary views of language learning consider the "native speaker" standard inappropriate because there are many ways of attaining ALP, depending on contexts of acquisition and use. Thus, definitions for ALP in one context do not inherently transfer to another, in terms of the status of the language, its purposes, its needs, and desired uses for constructing an identity. Learning Spanish in the United States, for example, is different from learning it in Spain; learning Modern Standard Arabic in Israel among Arabs is not the same as learning Arabic by Jews; and French in Canada is not the same as French in France.

A corollary consideration is that one should expect differences in the length of time learners take to attain ALP levels along different "advanced" variables. In fact, in a study of Israeli schools, Levin, Shohamy, and Spolsky (2003) found that immigrant students in grades 9 and 11 took about seven to eleven years to reach high levels of *academic* proficiency that made them comparable to their native-language peers. These results varied by grade level, age of immigration, subject (e.g.,

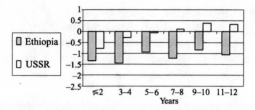

▓ Figure 12.2 9th Grade Math Standard Grades, by Years of Residence

mathematics versus Hebrew), and uses of language. Moreover, academic performance differed between students from the former Soviet Union and those from Ethiopia—supporting the claim that ALP is not a uniform and absolute construct but depends on various factors, including language background.

In sum, ALP is a rich and evolving trait that is being redefined and explored to gain a deeper understanding of the crucial features that characterize it. Although the details of those descriptions remain to be worked out, ALP clearly is broader than either the ACTFL Guidelines or the CEF descriptions suggest. Similarly, although details of the implications of these findings for assessment await specification, broad directions for what would constitute valid forms of assessments already can be discerned.

How to Assess ALP?

In the following subsections I offer some principles that are based on dimensions for ALP that I presented in the first part of this chapter.

Open and Flexible Language, in Line with Dimensions of ALP   Because language is open and flexible, assessment also must have open boundaries and flexible definitions of correctness. For example, ALP often can be multilingual—inherently an attenuation of "native speaker" criteria. Because ALP encompasses different modes of language use and different ways of getting to such forms of language use, one cannot apply uniform criteria of progression: There are different ways of *being* advanced and also different ways of *becoming* advanced. Assessment also calls for reliance on rich corpora of learner language because these corpora reveal the type of language that is acquired and used by learners with different backgrounds, in different contexts, with different uses of language. Finally, to acknowledge multiple competencies, language tests need to draw on learners' L1, address the consequences of multilingualism, provide

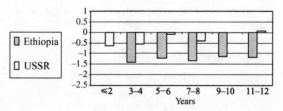

▓ Figure 12.3 11th Grade Math Standard Grades, by Years of Residence

opportunities for multimodal forms of communication, accommodate various backgrounds, and incorporate other test taker/learner knowledge. When we assess these types of traits, we judge learners primarily by "what" they say—focusing on the meanings and content they manage to deliver, using different language and nonlanguage devices—rather than purely on accuracy of language form.

Interactiveness   If tests are to capture the contextual, culturally embedded, and socially mediated nature of language, they must be expanded to accommodate these features. Chalhoub-Deville (2003) argues that evaluation of test takers' performances according to a social interactional perspective offers a serious challenge to language testers in terms of the generalizability of scores. As a potential solution, she suggests keeping some abilities stable across tasks while others vary. When researchers in language testing account for the interplay between the two, they can help explain situated language use. "In language testing research, the challenge is to better understand the associative networks, and to document the connections that language users make in varied situations that help them activate and or/transfer knowledge and skills from relevant experiences" (Chalhoub-Deville 2003, 378).

This approach, Chalhoub-Deville notes, requires a shift in the focus of measurement—from traditional examinations of the construct in terms of response consistency to investigations that systematically explore inconsistent performances across contexts. As a consequence, "social interactional investigations would consider focused hypotheses of the complex interaction of linguistic and nonlinguistic knowledge, cognitive, affective, and conative attributes engaged in particular situations" (Chalhoub-Deville 2003, 380). Examining naturally occurring discourse and social interactions as well as dialogue analysis and verbal report inquiries would be good directions to take. In other words, "the call in the language testing field is to develop local theories that detail the L2 'ability—in language user—in context' interactions. This approach may provide us with more meaningful accounts of the interaction among L2 components in specific language use environments" (Chalhoub-Deville 2003, 380).

Linking interactiveness and authenticity, Cushing Weigle and Jensen (1997) suggest that assessment will be authentic when it simulates as closely as possible the actual language use situations students will encounter outside the language classroom. "Assessment should also be interactive in that it draws on test takers' metacognitive strategies as well as their language knowledge, and thus require test takers to integrate test content with their existing topical knowledge, and take into account test takers' emotional responses to the test tasks" (Cushing Weigle and Jensen 1997, 207). Because test takers can vary in the dimensions of authenticity and interactiveness, the most advantageous tasks are both interactive and authentic. At the same time, the authors note that "these qualities must be balanced with considerations of reliability, construct validity, practicality, and impact for the test to be maximally useful for its intended purpose" (Cushing Weigle and Jensen 1997, 207).

Multiple Approaches to Assessment   Because a broad definition of ALP requires the testing community to acknowledge that no single test can capture its complexity, a variety of alternative modes of assessment have been introduced over the past two decades, including performance assessment, task-based assessment, and portfolios. If ALP draws on a variety of knowledge sources, including other languages and multimodal sources, tests must reflect that reality—for example, by incorporating diverse forms of expression and opportunities for conveying, among other things, nuanced meanings, humor, and symbolic aspects of the culture.

Multiple and diverse ways of knowing refer as well to the various ways of demonstrating such knowledge, using visuals, music, and gestures, as well as two or more languages. In fact, because a variety of ways to perform exist, formal assessment of ALP by means of a test may be unnecessary. Furthermore, if no single test can be comprehensive enough to probe the vastness of possible content, selection of a specific device depends largely on the uses to which assessment will be put—that is, the type of decisions that will rest on it. Methods may include dynamic assessment, performance-based assessment, and content- and task-based assessment.

Following such views, researchers have come to regard *dynamic assessment* as a viable approach, particularly because it affirms the key assessment principle that language must serve as a medium for communication (Lantolf and Poehner 2004). Based on Vygotsky's sociocultural and interactional views, dynamic assessment attempts to erase the separation of testing and learning. At present, testing usually is an isolated event that takes place before learning, as in placement tests, or during or after learning, as with tests for certification or achievement tests. By contrast, dynamic assessment proposes to integrate and connect learning and assessment.

Content   The new focus on meaning has important implications for the design and selection of appropriate testing procedures. For example, Cushing Weigle and Jensen (1997) argue that "a course whose primary goal is language acquisition should not test mainly content knowledge. Beyond this basic premise, however, it is important to consider the interaction of language and content in all three models of CBI and to avoid testing procedures that are biased because of content or language issues" (Cushing Weigle and Jensen 1997, 202). Assessment practices will need to delineate beforehand the relationship between language and content and incorporate that specification into test design: "For a theme-based course where assessment focuses on language rather than content, any content knowledge required by test items must be accessible to test takers either in the test itself or via an open-book format. In sheltered programs, test tasks should be designed to allow students to display their knowledge of the content even if their language skills are limited. In adjunct courses, if it is not feasible to test language and content separately, different scoring criteria can be used for assessing language and content using the same test tasks" (Cushing Weigle and Jensen 1997, 202). Importantly, assessment methods that focus on content should avoid penalizing students whose language abilities prevent them from displaying their full knowledge of content.

Test Accommodations   Strategies for assessing ALP need to consider the importance of various forms of accommodation to enable learners to access the variety of resources that constitute ALP in academic and professional contexts (Abedi 2004). Examples of such accommodations are use of familiar content, familiar genres, multilingual tests, cognitive processing, flexible time, and availability and access to additional materials, such as texts and dictionaries.

Accommodation is not merely a matter of helping ALP learners, however. It also can be regarded as part of the construct, inasmuch as it refers to the multiple devices commonly needed for successful transmission and interpretation of content. Based on the aforementioned example in which immigrant students were accommodated with bilingual (Russian-Hebrew) tests and consequently performed better, we ought to consider whether the use of a bilingual test for these students is simply a fact of regular processing, rather than a case of "accommodation." In that case, students who are not given the opportunity to draw on such multiple resources for interpretation and communication have been placed at a major disadvantage.

Integrating Assessment with Instruction   The kind of dynamic assessment I have advocated treats assessment as an integral part of ALP learning and education programs, along with curriculum and instruction. As Norris states in chapter 11 of this volume, these elements should receive balanced and simultaneous attention as programs are developed, implemented, and improved.

For example, Cushing Weigle and Jensen (1997, 205) recommend, "To promote beneficial washback in CBI, test tasks should require the same authentic, interactive language use promoted in the classroom so that there is a match between what is taught and what is tested. In other words, there is no difference between teaching the curriculum and teaching to the test." Similarly, Byrnes (2002a) reports on the considerable effect on curriculum and pedagogy of integrating assessment and instruction in the German program at Georgetown University.

Judging the Quality of the Language   We know intuitively that assessment is about judging quality. The challenge for assessment of ALP is that all of its procedures, including judgments of quality, need to be as complex as the construct itself. Accordingly, multiple levels of correctness as well as flexible criteria of correctness that reflect the specific context and goals are appropriate. Worded negatively, we could say that rigid "native speaker" correctness criteria no longer apply; worded positively, an explicit focus on content and message intentions is appropriate.

One consequence for assessment is likely to be that emphasis will shift toward diagnostic procedures and relative criteria that are appropriate for specific contexts. In that regard, multilingual assessment will pose particular challenges as testers establish new quality criteria—once more focusing on content and meaning and, perhaps, on use of different language devices and strategies that support effective transmission of messages. Indeed, the entire notion of rubrics and scales may require reconsideration if the various components I have mentioned for ALP are to be incorporated (North and Schneider 1998). If we accept the notion of localization, criteria for quality would arise from local contexts and reflect the immediate needs of the local population.

Such a conceptual move raises important questions regarding the validity and meaning of being "advanced." I have noted that "advancedness" fundamentally is a notion that is relative to context, time, and place. We can see just how far such considerations might go in three contexts. In the first example, a report by the Brazilian government seemingly "lowered" the passing score its foreign diplomats would need to show language ability. Does this change imply that in this day and age, a foreign diplomat needs to know "less" English at a lower level of proficiency than was the case previously? Does the move indicate that different "Englishes," including those that integrate Portuguese and English, have gained in legitimacy, thus making "lower" proficiency levels acceptable even in the diplomatic world? Might this change mean that in the future we will not have a sufficient number of diplomats with high ALP? Or does it simply reflect the realization that different levels of language are needed for different purposes and different periods of time?

Another example of the relative nature of "advancedness" and the need for more contextual ways of judging quality is that immigrants' language levels may be considered "advanced" at the time of their arrival by local populations that are more tolerant of certain "immigrant" varieties and make a special effort to comprehend the newcomers; they would be considered less "advanced" after long periods of residence.

A final example pertains to the widespread use of language tests for citizenship, especially in Europe and in the United States, and as a prerequisite for residence in a new country. My concern is not whether tests are needed or should be used as conditions for residence. It pertains instead to the criteria for deciding what is "advanced" enough to deserve citizenship. As things stand, specific cut-off scores for "being advanced" are made primarily by politicians, often with the aim of preventing immigrants from residing in the new country. Rarely are such decisions made in terms of the amount of language needed in response to questions such as "advanced for what and why and what factors will determine the use of the language?"

Advancedness clearly is a relative term that is context dependent. How we determine the quality of language depends in no small part on whether our expectations of the development of ALP are themselves realistic. As figures 12.2 and 12.3 indicate, for the average immigrant learner nine years of in-country residence may be required before the learner functions academically on a par with native speakers. For some learners this goal may be completely unattainable, thus permanently marginalizing them.

Examining the Consequences of Assessment Practices

I return once more to the influence tests can have on the construct of what is to be tested. Tests can define language knowledge; stipulate criteria of language correctness; perpetuate national, hegemonic languages; establish priorities and hierarchies; and, by using simplified rating scales, trivialize the complexity of language (Cheng, Watanabe, and Curtis 2004; Shohamy 2001). These inherently problematic consequences are heightened in the case of ALP assessment. An area that deserves careful attention is the uses to which tests are put. A particularly egregious mismatch occurs when test results are used to fire teachers whose students do not do well on tests. Another disturbing consequence is that the results of national tests, such as the No Child Left Behind test in the United States, can be used as policy tools that have the effect of suppressing bilingualism (Evans and Hornberger 2005).

The questions go deeper, however. If content is primary, can ALP be a valid categorizing term—all the more so as "advancedness" is politically and socially constructed? Should language performance and language instruction even be categorized by proficiency levels? My own experience suggests that a healthy suspicion with regard to the real reasons for the creation of tests and their actual use is called for as we seek answers. Beyond that, we might adopt an approach that minimizes tests for selection and discipline and enhances their uses as instructional tools (Shohamy 2004). Even more radically, the testing community needs to acknowledge that there are many ways in which one can obtain quality information and that tests should, perhaps, be the solution of last resort rather than the convenient solution of choice. For example, in the case of the No Child Left Behind legislation, states have begun to question the need for additional testing, given that many already conduct extensive testing regimes of their own. True, some state standards fall far below national standards, and those states therefore might benefit from more demanding national standards. It is not entirely clear, however, how a federally mandated testing regime would and could address that disturbing fact in a fashion that ultimately does not reduce students' access to a challenging learning environment—not least because testing is itself a costly endeavor.

A cautious approach is warranted as well with regard to the link between testing and instruction. The fact that a university course traditionally includes a semester-end paper or project is not sufficient justification for the practice, unless one also can specify what instructors and students stand to gain from such test uses and results and can critique their inherent values and beliefs. In particular cases, a democratic approach to assessment, such that learners can choose ways of demonstrating their knowledge through particular methods of assessment that are biased toward their best performance in terms of topics and content, may be appropriate. Greater access to results and the frameworks within which they are interpreted should be among the rights of those who are tested (Shohamy 2004).

On all levels, testers need to adopt interpretations of abilities in terms of patterned behaviors. Nobody knows everything, but the parties involved—testers, test takers, and others—all know something. Valid patterns about abilities can emerge through dialoging, negotiating, and conferencing on an ongoing basis. By attending to these matters, we also might begin to understand how different procedures affect learning; motivation; definitions of language; multilingualism; purity; languages to be taught; and ethicality and social, political, and economic forms of inclusion and exclusion. With regard to the latter, the very act of testing in one language may deliver a powerful message that other languages are not needed, that home languages are not necessary, that previous knowledge is not relevant in the new environment, and that there is only one (correct!) way to use language—usually the native variety.

Connecting Teaching, Research, and Assessment

Amid such cautionary notes, recall that language tests also can be powerful instruments for improving learning, particularly on the level of ALP. Thus, research studies that incorporate assessment data can be used to measure the effectiveness of programs as well as students' learning and can provide significant data on the impact of

L2 learning on overall achievement. Databases can include comparable data obtained from assessment instruments in a variety of schools, districts, and university courses. Such expanded databases also would provide important feedback to the testing community, so that researchers can develop more sophisticated answers about the relation between assessment instruments and strategies and learning. Findings also would inform decisions on program articulation and validate rubrics for rating performance-based assessments in districts and schools. Closer to the classroom, research on how teachers actually are using tests and other assessment procedures on the ALP level—the question posed in a study that currently is being undertaken by the assessment project at CALPER—could lead to more realistic and useful assessment policies, enhance teacher training, and inform more appropriate pedagogies. Case studies, such as that reported by Byrnes (2002a) about a content-oriented and genre-based integrated collegiate program in German that moved to task-based assessment, are likely to be particularly valuable as the field adapts to the new challenges. Byrnes obtained insights not only for assessment practices but also with regard to the relationship between curriculum, instruction, learning goals and outcomes, leading to an expansive interpretation of the notion of task-based assessment.

Conclusions and Outlook

Much of what I have stated about language assessment in general and assessment of ALP in particular implies challenges, mandates, and opportunities for the testing community. Given the effect of tests on language constructs, the current understanding of the complexity and expanded dimensions of ALP requires language testers to work collaboratively with other language professionals to develop assessment approaches that match emerging definitions of ALP rather then fitting language into "testable" units, as is the case with the use of proficiency scales. Not only are there valid concerns about whether current tests represent best knowledge about the construct of ALP; concerns extend even to the fundamentally "made up" nature of the construct of ALP itself—a construct that too often becomes a tool for categorizing people to make decisions about them. Vigilance, close observation, and careful study of developments and new definitions of language acquisition therefore are critical as researchers broaden their understanding about the construct of ALP, including obtaining a more realistic picture on the basis of learner corpora of how languages actually are learned.

Given our present knowledge about the effects of testing on learning and on definitions of knowledge, testers bear great responsibility for capturing the essential qualities of language processing as multilingual and multimodal and of language serving as a tool for creating more complex forms of knowledge and being content-oriented within a social, cultural, and cognitive context. In this day and age, being an ethical tester implies relating to the complexity of all dimensions of language. The challenge is not to develop simplified forms of tests that will be efficient and quick but to expand the repertoire of assessment strategies to accommodate a broad and complex construct for ALP. This understanding may imply developing new and innovative procedures and quality criteria that can capture complexity—a challenge that may demand different types of reliability and validity than those the field has privileged in the past. It also may mean admitting that certain types of knowledge cannot be assessed by any tool that currently is at our disposal. In addition, the results of test development may no longer have the kind of permanence they once did because new findings and thinking about the features that make up ALP will continue to emerge, as will new contexts in which language is learned and used. Finally, valid test development means engaging with classroom teachers and school programs to become informed about existing practices of learning and assessment.

I emphasize this responsibility because in both a beneficial and a potentially harmful way, tests powerfully affect how language knowledge is defined and perceived. Even if SLA researchers present comprehensive descriptions of the features of ALP, interpretation and practice of these features by testers lends status and de facto reality to them. Having accepted their content and their construct as truth, teachers will adjust teaching and learning processes to prepare their learners for the tests by mastering what the tests present as validated.

If investigation of the construct of ALP and suitable tools for assessing it also can convince the language profession that all language use and learning is about meaning, we may be able to tackle one of the most troublesome divides in language education: the distinction between meaning-deprived language classes and language-deprived content classes—a distinction that depends on notions whose validity I have critiqued extensively here (also see Byrnes 2004). In its deepest implications, the conference at which the papers collected in this volume were presented had that vision as its larger goal.   ▓

REFERENCES

Abedi, Jamal. 2004. The No Child Left Behind Act and English language learners: Assessment and accountability issues. *Educational Researcher* 33:4–14.

Agar, Michael. 1994. *Language shock: Understanding the culture of conversation.* New York: William Morrow.

Bachman, Lyle F. 1990. *Fundamental considerations in language testing.* Oxford: Oxford University Press.

Bachman, Lyle F., and Adrian S. Palmer. 1996. *Language testing in practice.* Oxford: Oxford University Press.

Bialystok, Ellen. 1997. Effects of bilingualism and biliteracy on children's emerging concepts of print. *Developmental Psychology* 3:429–40.

———. 2001. *Bilingualism in development.* Cambridge: Cambridge University Press

Byrnes, Heidi. 2002a. The role of task and task-based assessment in a content-oriented collegiate foreign language curriculum. *Language Testing* 19:419–37.

———. 2002b. Toward academic-level foreign language abilities: Reconsidering foundational assumptions, expanding pedagogical options. In *Developing professional-level language proficiency,* ed. Betty L. Leaver and Boris Shekhtman. Cambridge: Cambridge University Press, 34–60.

———. 2004. Advanced L2 literacy: Beyond option or privilege. *ADFL Bulletin* 36:1.52–60.

———. 2005. Content-based foreign language instruction. In *Mind and context in adult second language acquisition: Methods, theory, and practice,* ed. Cristina Sanz. Washington, D.C.: Georgetown University Press, 282–302.

Chalhoub-Deville, Micheline. 1997. Theoretical models, assessment frameworks and test construction. *Language Testing* 14:3–22.

———. 2003. Second language interaction: Current perspectives and future trends. *Language Testing* 20:369–83.

Cheng, Liying, Yoshinori Watanabe, and Andy Curtis, eds., 2004. *Washback in language testing: Research contexts and methods.* Mahwah, N.J.: Erlbaum.

Cushing Weigle, Sara, and Linda Jensen. 1997. Issues in assessment for content-based instruction. In *The Content-based classroom: Perspectives on integrating language and content,* ed. Marguerite A. Snow and Donna Brinton. White Plains, N.Y.: Longman, 201–12.

Evans, Bruce, and Nancy Hornberger. 2005. No Child Left Behind: Repealing and unpeeling federal language education policy in the United States. *Language Policy* 4:87–106.

Fulcher, Glenn. 2004. Deluded by artifices? The Common European Framework and harmonization. *Language Assessment Quarterly* 1:253–66.

Hutton, Christopher M. 1999. *Linguistics and the Third Reich: Mother-tongue fascism, race, and the science of language.* London: Routledge.

Kress, Gunther. 2003. *Literacy in the new media age.* London: Routledge.

Kress, Gunther, and Theo van Leeuwen. 1996. *Reading images—the grammar of visual design.* London: Routledge.

Kubota, Ryuko. 1999. Japanese culture constructed by discourses. Implications for applied linguistics research and English language teaching. *TESOL Quarterly* 33:9–35.

———. 2004. The politics of cultural difference in second language education. *Critical Inquiry in Language Studies: An International Journal* 1:21–40.

Lantolf, James P. 2006. Re(de)fining language proficiency in light of the concept of "languaculture." In *Advanced language learning: The contribution of Halliday and Vygotsky,* ed. Heidi Byrnes. London: Continuum.

Lantolf, James, and Matthew Poehner. 2004. Dynamic assessment: Bringing the past into the future. *Journal of Applied Linguistics* 1:49–74.

Levin, Tamar, Elana Shohamy, and Bernard Spolsky. 2003. Academic achievements of immigrants in schools. Report submitted to Israeli Ministry of Education (in Hebrew).

McNamara, Timothy F. 1997. "Interaction" in second language performance assessment: Whose performance? *Applied Linguistics* 18:446–66.

Morrow, Keith, ed. 2004. *Insights from the Common European Framework.* Oxford: Oxford University Press.

National Standards in Foreign Language Education Project. 1996. *National Standards for Foreign Language Learning: Preparing for the 21st century.* Yonkers, N.Y.: National Standards in Foreign Language Education Project.

North, Brian. 1995. The development of a Common Framework scale of descriptors of language proficiency based on a theory of measurement. *System* 23:445–65.

———. 2000. *The development of a Common Framework Scale of language proficiency.* New York: Peter Lang.

North, Brian, and Gunther Schneider. 1998. Scaling descriptors for language proficiency scales. *Language Testing* 15:217–62.

Shohamy, Elana. 1998a. Evaluation of learning outcomes in second language acquisition: A multiplism perspective. In *Learning foreign and second languages: Perspectives in research and scholarship,* ed. Heidi Byrnes. New York: MLA, 238–61.

———. 1998b. How can language testing and second language acquisition benefit from each other: The case of discourse. In *Interfaces between second language acquisition and language testing research,* ed. Lyle F. Bachman and Andrew D. Cohen. Cambridge: Cambridge University Press, 156–76.

———. 2001. *The power of tests: A critical perspective of the uses of language tests.* New York: Longman.

———. 2004. Assessment in multicultural societies: Applying democratic principles and practices to language testing. In *Critical pedagogies and language learning,* ed. Bonny Norton and Kelleen Toohey. Cambridge: Cambridge University Press, 72–93.

———. 2006. *Language policy: Hidden agenda and new approaches.* London: Routledge.

Solano-Flores, Guillermo, and Elise Trumbull. 2003. Examining language in context: The need for new research and practice paradigms in the testing of English-Language-Learners. *Educational Researcher* 32:2.3–13.

Spolsky, Bernard. 1968. Preliminary studies in the development of techniques for testing overall second language proficiency. *Language Learning* 3:79–101.

Swain, Merrill. 2001. Examining dialogue: Another approach to content specification and to validating inferences drawn from test scores. *Language Testing* 18:275–302.

Printed in the United States
141151LV00002B/122/A